The Smile on My Face

A Journey to
Sexual Authenticity

Cheri Reeder

Reeder.press

The events and conversations in this book have been set down to the best of the author's ability, although some names and details have been changed to protect the privacy of individuals.

ISBN 978-0-9978336-0-7 Paperback

ISBN 978-0-9978336-1-4 Electronic Book Text

Library of Congress Control Number 2019909142

Illustrations by Cutter Hays

Photography by Kondor Imaging

Book Design by Lilly Penhall, Interstellar Graphics

Published by Reeder Press

San Diego, California

CheriReeder.com

Reeder.press

Dedication:

I wrote this book to friends with curious questions about open relationships and polyamory.

I published it for my mother 1940 - 2017 because she could not speak about her sexual shame.

And I dedicate it to all my parents who taught me that family is teamwork, and who provided my childhood dentist visits. As it turns out, my smile is one of my best qualities. I love you.

Mission Statement:

Do books have mission statements? If this one did, it would read: Having responsible, shame-free sex provides a sex-positive example for those you love. As a result, they share more intimacy and create a ripple effect. Awaken your personal power and bliss to promote healing across our sexually repressed planet—spread the love!

Table of Contents:

About the Author:

What if everyone was simply honest with each other, and shared their friendships and lovers? The more honest, open relating in a community, the more real trust. In my ideal world, all the people I hold close would be madly in love with each other, forming an interconnected expanding web to share more love. It may be impractical to share *all* lovers since we each have our unique circle, but I delight in areas of overlap.

It was Christmas Eve, and I was 19 years old when I wrote this poem to you.

ALL I WANT

Wanting to share my Love with everyone I know
Is a feeling from above, but I can't let it grow,
At least not here or now

'Cause Loving the forbidden is discouraged, so
My feelings must be hidden, but someday I will go
To a world where Love survives

It'll be a happy place where Love is freely shared
There'll be smiles on each face; I know I won't be scared
To Love all I want, forever

December 24, 1983

Raised with a shit-ton of shame around sex, I'm passionate about debunking sexual taboos. I like helping others surrender their misinformation about sexuality, and unleash the magic of being a good lover. My goal is to love the whole world, and I can only do it with your help.

My English teacher referenced Alice Walker, saying that she writes like she speaks. It's unclear what Ms. Dietrich meant, but I took the liberty of interpreting it as, write from my soul. My writings are about my life, which doesn't fit into neat, formula driven chapters.

I didn't remember Alice's name or the name of her writings, but with the help of Google and searching all the female authors in my ninth grade English lit' book, I found the last photo was of Alice (Walker being near the end of the alphabet). Then I read, that later she wrote *The Color Purple*, long after I'd studied her story *To Hell with Dying*. Tears welled up as my perception of her shifted profoundly, and simultaneously I felt honored to have been inspired by her writing, long before her fame.

In my late 30's during a Tantra Puja event, I experienced being in right relation with everyone. As I moved around the circle of oddly diverse men, the wise Tantrika with a mesmerizing French accent instructed the women to stand before them one by one, and connect in unique ways with each one. While I was holding the hand of an elderly man, peering into his face and telling him that he's special, I had a twinge of anxiety as I thought I wouldn't be able to say the same thing with sincerity to the next in line because he had an inflamed nose with blue veins spidered across his cheeks. As a nurse, my brain was about to go into problem solving mode. Then the angelic voice instructed the women to move to the next person, turn back to back, link arms, and just listen to his supportive words. So rather than helping him into rehab, I could just be with his soul, and listen to his precious heart eloquently express words of appreciation.

Each time the divinely guided leader said, "Ladies, thank your partner and move to the next man in the circle," there were new examples of being able to drop into the exercise with ease. Even though I couldn't imagine doing the same thing with the next person, each transition worked out perfectly. I knew I could say no to anything I didn't want to do, but my intention was to practice staying present with each one instead of being in fear or judgment. That simple shift in my thinking allowed me to feel connected and see each person's unique beauty. This experience allowed me to be present with most people and let go of unnecessary judgments—a launching pad for seeing myself in everyone and embracing all of it. Later I expanded on this lesson, finding deeper ways to drop in with people in my life and exploring our common areas.

Life is a series of choices. As I notice where I am and the direction I want to go, it becomes easier to see how each decision and action moves me closer to (or further away from) my values and desires. A core purpose for me is being in right relation with everything and making decisions that benefit all. Finding peace within myself is important on my path toward this synergy. I attempt to consider the big picture (as much as I can grasp); consequently, my ideas may conflict with singular thought or excluding beliefs. I like seeing *both* (all) sides of situations and everything in-between. I may be judged as offensive or disrespectful, when I am in fact attempting to respect everything. I live in gratitude to those who strive for oneness and allow me to express openly.

Your accepting eyes and willingness to explore inspire my awe. I embrace my expanding capacity to love myself and others. Our intimacy brings hope—my desires expand as we dive into profound union. Love is the hero that gives my dreams wings, ending the inner battle between wanting an intimate relationship and needing the freedom to explore with others. Dispelling this perceived dichotomy, I can experience real honest connection with multiple beings. This freedom allows me to appreciate the renewed excitement of *choosing* precious time together. I celebrate compassion for myself, for the ones I love, and the ones my loved-ones care about, until our whole world embraces love!

Acknowledgments:

Professor Lynn Pollock has a flair for encouraging my voice. Kamala Devi keeps me accountable with our writing dates. The editors who offered suggestions: Anna Stigen, Ilan Herman, Tracy Jones, and Lilly Penhall. Thank you all for generously sharing your expertise. I appreciate the Beta Readers: Julie Kondor, Allison Manning, Sarah Murray-Novak, Jess Raggio, Iris Thomsen, and Josh Zuchowski; thank you for your supportive feedback. To BodyMindDavid and all the lovers (too many to list), you are my teachers. Gratitude to my gifted muse Brian.

Foreword:

I was not there when she first got her left hip tattooed with a Giant Sunflower, complete with heart shaped leaves. However after the sunset colors faded into her olive skin, I had the honor of holding her hand when she had it touched up. I delighted in watching Cheri Reeder become one with the artist's expert needle as it penetrated her skin.

The symbolic meaning of a sunflower perfectly describes Cheri's way of being in the world, not only because of the irresistible beauty of its sacred geometry, but because the bright and nutritious blossom always turns its face towards the light. One of the gifts within *The Smile on My Face*, is that Cheri continuously looks for the bright side as she draws out valuable life lessons. Her transparent stories are engaging, and provide guiding examples to increase health, happiness, and ease in relationships.

The sunflower is also a symbol of health and happiness, and this book offers many insights into optimizing our physical, mental, and emotional health. Another interesting fact about the sunflower is that it works as a natural purifier. Scientists have planted sunflowers in areas like Fukushima because they pull radioactive contaminants from the soil. Similarly, Cheri seems to have a superpower for skillfully disarming triggers and neutralizing toxic environments, which is essential in polyamorous relationships.

Physically, Cheri has dark eyes that sparkle, and brown hair that always looks wind-blown from driving her convertible, biking, or rollerblading. She is a natural beauty. But it isn't her physical appearance that makes her shine; it's the radiance of her spirit. There's something special about her energy. With an uncanny ability to be present, she observes and listens with care to gather understanding during her pursuit to seek right action. She is a modern goddess who is gifted in the art of love.

I first met Cheri in 2004 on a TV set for a segment about the *Kama Sutra*, produced by the Discovery Channel in Canada. We were destined to fall in love after just that first day of dancing, bathing, partner yoga, and eating aphrodisiacs. We've since done various media appearances together, such as *69 things you need to know about Sex* on Swedish TV, and two seasons of Showtime's *Polyamory: Married & Dating*. Cheri almost moved in with us during the run of the show. In fact, the early version of the sizzle reel that was pitched to Showtime shows her considering moving in with us.

Ultimately, I'm grateful that Cheri didn't get swept up in the spotlight of the show; by keeping her feet on the ground she has remained my deepest and most trusted confidant. Although she is often humble about her wisdom, she embodies the deep feminine mysteries (and masculine too) and is the first person I turn to when I'm having relationship questions, health challenges or an existential crisis. She is a veritable treasure chest of insights and fresh perspectives. *The Smile on My Face* is a collection of anecdotes that fearlessly lean into difficult topics and taboos such as group sex, religion, STD's, bisexuality, jealousy, and more. Reading these intimate stories feels like flipping through Cheri's private diary. How often does a tantric goddess open her life, legs, and her heart to you? Cheri's message not only promises to put a smile on your face, but also to transmit deep tantric truths like intimacy, pleasure, and integrity to assist you in achieving healthy living. She is a master healer, has studied with experts, and is a compelling storyteller, but her true gift is extracting empowering interpretations from her experiences. She models releasing the chains of antiquated conventional ideology, allowing the reader to find their own freedom to create a better than fantasy life. Read this book if you want to witness detailed examples of one woman's journey through uncovering new ways of interpreting the world, and learn how to upgrade your relationships. Explore telling your own life stories with your heart and not just your head!

Cheri Reeder is an exotic breed. She values staying clear so she can remain present to what is true for others. Cheri vividly shares her journey, weaving lessons she's learned and practical applications into riveting true stories. She is usually making love, decorating, gardening, consulting clients, playing guitar, or any number of other temple arts in which she is skilled. With all that Cheri does, it's hard to believe that she found the time to sit in front of her computer for as many hours as it took to write this profound book. When she isn't traveling to Bali, Sedona, Hawaii, Australasia, Tahiti, Fiji, Baja, Europe, or the Caribbean, it's an honor to be her writing buddy. We sit on her flower-covered porch, or in the backyard gardens with our laptops and work side by side on our respective projects, attempting to express experiences and paradigm shifting concepts that are almost impossible to put into words.

This book is filled with real relationships and practical steps to encourage finding the next steps on your journey. Cheri's writings will take you on a heartfelt adventure into her process to assist in the ease of finding your smile.

Liberate your love life,

Kamala Devi

Introduction:

Have you ever been in a room and a topic comes up that makes you uncomfortable? Perhaps you don't know much about the subject, have judgments, or feel left out of the conversation. This book is full of such prickly topics. Humans learn from each other and these pages are a part of my contribution—they reveal my journey of becoming more authentic in order to share intimate details of my life with you. These writings are about loving multiple people and ultimately, loving everyone, which has been a core part of me from my first memories. The topic is second nature to me, but being totally transparent and vulnerable didn't come as easily. My hope is that getting a glimpse into my thoughts, emotions and experiences will allow you to learn more about these subjects, dispel some of your judgments, and feel more included in these conversations. Becoming your authentic self is a process. I invite you to jump into the discussions that will help you discover what that means to you. This book is a conversation starter.

I had a lot to smile about in high school. I was unaware of its impact until years later, when running into old acquaintances they often didn't recognize me—until I smiled. "Cheri!" They'd instantly exclaim. Through the years, former classmates have shared with me that my smile was a memorable part of me. Why was I smiling, and why do I continue to develop smile lines on my face?

I dreamed of getting my college degree in philosophy. Fortunately, it wasn't an option at the university I attended, so I received a more practical BS degree in nursing with a minor in psychology. Science taught me how living organisms mutate and adapt, and brains learn through experiences and from mistakes. This made logical sense, and became a foundation for my understanding that we continue to learn and grow. Before that realization, I simply thought I was created just as I am and my choices were simply good or bad.

These scientific facts inspired my theory that most things evolve, including relationships. The notion of romantic love and finding one mate for life is historically a relatively new idea. Nowadays most humans have all kinds of relationships to meet their basic and intimacy needs. It feels like a transition away from the days of old when two people chose each other out of the slim pickings in their small town to live happily ever after. Now *serial* monogamy seems to be a common choice, but divorce or a string of broken hearts can be a painful lifestyle. Instead of cutting people out, there's a growing need for self-responsibility, improved communication to promote healthy connections, and education about other ways to include more love in all relationships. Living as a responsible adult takes daily commitment to making choices and taking positive actions. Whether single or in relationships, this book will have tools to benefit you.

The vignettes in the following pages are true. My hope in sharing them is that they inspire new ways of responding to challenges or invoke alternative methods of relating with your world. Perhaps they'll stimulate conversations with your significant others, or motivate a spontaneous masturbation session. There, I said the first bawdy word! Warning, these pages are filled with things that may be difficult for some to say out loud, things that might arouse sexual shame.

The premise of this book is releasing sexual shame, and going through the process of expressing authentically to become a whole person. Sex is at the core of human existence. Most people are born from the act of sex, and reproduction drives many of our actions. When there is hidden sexual shame, the love that we *are* is unable to be fully expressed and that shame is unconsciously passed on to others. Humans have as many facets as a diamond in the sunlight. Illuminating all the faces, especially the ones in the shadows, help the brilliance of each one to shine.

This book exemplifies how one person's brain and emotions work. No two people are alike. Chances are you won't agree 100% with the way this book is written. It is rare to find anything this raw and transparent. Each of the stories is true and is told to help demonstrate life lessons. There is much to learn from observing through another person's eyes.

Take a deep breath, and as you exhale remind yourself to enjoy and feel. Take the parts that resonate with you, and stay in the moment as you listen to a unique perspective. The chapters don't go in chronological order. Don't expect everything to make sense to your mind, but know that it makes sense to at least one person and she really wants to help you on your sexual authenticity journey.

The opening scene is the moment I recognize that I've come a long way with feeling confident and transparent about my open lifestyle. I'm able to stay present and express myself without getting suckered into saying any of the outdated thoughts in my head (that you observe) out loud.

Chapter 27 is an interview, and was actually the first thing written before the book began. It is purposefully put at the end so it won't influence the reader to think it's a book of answers. Life is mostly questions.

Embracing your life affirming sexuality may be the healthiest path to a happy existence. My outlook isn't conventional. The stories in this book will demonstrate fresh ways that I react when a curveball flies toward me. Am I wearing a mitt, or am I swinging the bat? I use the tools at hand to catch the ball, or hit it out of the park. Venture through these pages with the curiosity to appreciate detailed thought processes of a fellow human, and hopefully put a smile on your face.

Originally written as a self-help book, these lessons are told through true experiences; therefore it may be considered a memoir. It is written from a sex-positive, open relating, bisexual, post women's liberation, polyamorous, mostly feminine perspective; however, I attempt to avoid labels to keep current and honest. Labels and categories help us understand and identify, but when applied to humans they're problematic. I have found that the more defined a label becomes, the less I can relate. The following are my views on my relationship to: inner thoughts, other humans, the surrounding world, and topics that may be taboo and shameful.

It's difficult for some to comprehend that I've lived a nonconventional lifestyle since I was 14 years old. My relationships don't define me, but honesty in my relationships, and being true to what is real for me is where I start. I've gone days, weeks, and sometimes months without any sex, other times I have multiple lovers, but overall I've learned many life lessons from being in relationship with hundreds of people. These lessons are about self-responsibility, and how to thrive in all kinds of relationships.

Some people choose to numb themselves rather than live fully awake because it's mandatory to feel *everything* present (from fear to love) in order to feel bliss. Life can be messy, and can't be put neatly into a box. Being completely alive is about seeing a bigger picture beyond the obvious. This is a holistic picture of me, and how I've found tools to get through obstacles in life and in relationships to keep me smiling.

Each chapter is a journey into an aspect of life, and was inspired by questions others asked regarding their struggles. My stories are unique, but the themes are universal. Polyamory isn't about giving up your family, or losing meaningful relationships, it's about *adding* more love and being honest in all your intimate connections. The hardest thing about living an unconventional lifestyle is that so many people misunderstand and have unfounded judgments based in fear. Any kind of relationship has its shadow side. This book challenges you to find commonalities and things that are a good fit for your relationship style. This collection of stories is about being human and improving humanity; moving beyond how our parents did things, what we were taught in school, and what has become *normal* for society; deconstructing thoughts and beliefs in order to improve how we react, and the actions we take; and every day finding something to improve, starting now with the situation at hand.

These chapters are written like my life (there was no outline) and they came through faster than I could record them. Some chapters are simple and easy to decipher, some more confrontational, and others are still rather chaotic. There are spiritually oriented ones, playful ones, seriously insightful chapters, and some are simply hedonistic. My intention is to let you find what is personally relevant to help avoid obstacles and achieve the universal goal of finding meaning. It's a daring move to use my life as the example here, but rest easy in knowing I turned out just fine, and you'll make it through, maybe even wanting more.

If you're asking why you feel lonely, or unhappy in relationships, maybe you're taking yourself too seriously! What are you doing to be more attractive? Come, take a pleasure trip with me and free yourself from the thoughts that keep you silent, alone, and hiding under the duvet. Next time you walk into an uncomfortable room, I hope you're able to share some of the intimate details in your life that put the smile on your face.

Chapter 1

Sharing My Smile

"Start where you are. Use what you have. Do what you can."— Arthur Ashe

Still glowing from the week's adventures, and greasy coconut oil in my hair from the massage party last night, I'm a bit disheveled to say the least. Not that this matters because I'm just heading home. Pulling up to a stoplight in my rain-spotted, dusty convertible with my unkempt appearance it's curious to hear a deep, rough voice ask, "Are you from around here?"

Glancing up at the formerly white, dented pickup, I notice two men peering out from the torn interior. Closest to me is the passenger with matted dingy blonde hair under an old, crunched cowboy hat. His plaid shirt is as tattered as the rest of him. He and his scruffy driver are both looking at me. Tilting his head coyly, the cowboy repeats, "Well? Are you from around here?"

He can't possibly be talking to me, I think. Maybe he's in trouble. Should I ignore him? It's a little late for that, as I've already looked up. My mind races through all the times someone's asked me where I'm from. Does he want to know my family of origin? Why's he asking me this? In my next breath I answer, "Yes, I live here."

As a female, attending a strict religious school in the 80's, I was relatively shut down and shy; speaking freely is unfamiliar to me. My turbulent mind is still questioning—Is this too much information? Am I being a smart ass?

He nods, satisfied with my answer and asks, "Can you help us with directions?"

What happens next is a baffling surprise to me—A question pops out of my mouth, "Where are you headed?" I ask. I'm engaging this person. Unlike my previous inhibited social exchanges, now I can speak clearly in a friendly flirt.

"To your house," says his confident, albeit crooked mouth.

I laugh, "Wow, I never heard that one before."

With excited surprise, the cowboy, wearing the used ranch-hand hat (I use the term cowboy lightly, as he may have never ridden a horse or even seen a cow) asks, "Really?"

I'm already amused, and the sincere surprise in the intruder's voice is refreshing. What a harmless little exchange. Then the dreaded question I've heard so many times before, previously evoking such turmoil, sails from his cracked window through my open roof. "Are you married?"

My spinning mind takes off again, but then I hesitate. If I just say yes, it's like kicking a man in the balls, and I hate hurting men. I'm not going to lie and say no; what's the point of that? I can't believe I'm allowing myself to flirt with this strange being. Next to me, in this beat-up pickup these men aren't handsome, and I don't feel sexually attracted to them, but my heart is as happy as it was before these unsavory blokes asked me to dance. Should I stop now, and pretend I didn't hear this rather intrusive question?

"Yes, I am." I reply. For a moment, our eyes are the only thing speaking. I'm aware of this chatter in my head, yet it's in slow motion. With clear intent, I easily speak above it, as if it's in someone else's head. Has my blissful state slowed the chaos down enough for me to choose my words?

Fun interaction I think, assuming that's the end of it. I feel there's been some meaning and purpose—at least I'm practicing my Tantra by embracing all of life. But surely, he's offended by my abruptness, or he's interpreted my calm answers as meaning I'm not *unhappily* married, so bug off!

Holding up my banded-ring finger I think, this will close the door and walk us off the dance floor.

"Would you like an occasional boyfriend?" he asks instead, rising to a new level of car flirting.

I'm pleasantly surprised at his sweet persistence, and shocked at the speed and accuracy of what pops out in return. "I *have* an occasional boyfriend," I say with a big grin that he doesn't see because the light turns green and my Audi starts to roll.

By this time, I think we can go no further, when I hear his clamorous voice over revving engines. "I wish my arm was long enough to give you a high-five, but I can't reach. You're awesome!"

For a brief moment, the rattling pickup is next to me again, and my grin is visible. The Audi accelerates and I glance in the mirror to see which way they're heading. Are they stalking me, or trying to meet me at another light to continue the play? Perhaps they're too stunned by my boldness. I'm not sure where they went, but they disappeared.

Through the next light, still smiling, I realize I'm not desperately single looking for love in all the wrong places, and I'm not stifled in a dying marriage. It's possible to achieve freedom from the pain of that perceived dichotomy. In my blissful freedom, I'm not shy anymore. I acknowledge the fearful thoughts along with my desires to be kind and abundantly share my contagious delight. No longer secluded or separate, I can look anyone in the eye with my windows down and sunglasses off. I just experienced an uninhibited exchange without guilt, and my reservations didn't limit me. I notice how the state of pure bliss I was in prior to the stop light was unaltered by the direct invasion of two ruffians who perhaps had a beer or two and were in no way the type of men I'd choose to direct my energy toward. Yet, I feel elated to have been acknowledged and celebrated through an honest flirt with this part of humanity that I rarely encounter. I'm surprised that even though a few disruptive thoughts crept in, I was able to allow a somewhat intelligent thought stream to flow in those 120 seconds between light changes.

Sharing a blissful state with another person creates much needed connections in our segregated world. Flirting is good for humankind's soul because it helps unite the fragmented parts. If feeling isolated and insignificant, I remind myself that encouraging another to feel included will help me not feel alone. There are many forms of flirting filled with agendas and expectations, but what my red-light cowboy and I experienced was the pure acknowledgment of liking being together (in our separate cars) for that moment. Being open to another person without an agenda, just to connect, can lead to unexpected joy at the unlikeliest of moments. Flirting can be a glance, smile, or any reminder that we're all sharing life together in this moment, on this planet. Just the thought that we can be one, that we *are* one, inspires me to keep smiling, and saying yes to engaging others.

EXPLORATION #1

What are your thoughts on flirting?

_____

_____

_____

I experience flirting as passing the spark of life to others. To flirt is to share life-force energy with others, a key to happiness and spreading the love.

What is your homework on the topic of flirting?

_____

_____

_____

Examples:

Smile at a stranger.

Tell a friend you love them.

Ask someone to dance, or have coffee.

Offer free hugs for an hour.

Chapter 2

Pursuit of Curiosity

"When the student is ready the teacher will appear." — Buddha

It had been a long time coming. I'd never experienced a proper session with a Tantra teacher. For years I'd attended classes about being present and quieting the mind, which interweave many traditions and teachings from eastern philosophy. With many partners I continue to practice yoga and Tantric techniques—being fully present and honoring the one(s) before me. I even have lovers who are Tantra teachers, but the thought of experiencing a professional hands-on Tantra session was arousing. Who will fill those shoes and be the healer I seek? The search went on for years, but the timing wasn't right and the teacher hadn't appeared.

One evening at a local *Tantra Theater* performance, I'm called up on stage to participate in a skit. It's an improv scene about a young nun falling in love with the priest. After a loud laugh, there's an announcement of prizes to be given to a few lucky participants. There are books to give away, a 90-minute massage, and free tickets to the next Tantra Theater show. A private *Tea & a Chat* with Theodor, a Tantric practitioner is the coveted one—the prize of all prizes. He's finishing his first Tantra book, not to mention he makes me weak in the knees every time we kiss, which has been every time he'd seen me for the past year.

My fate is revealed, and I'm awarded the grandest prize of all. We take a few weeks to coordinate schedules while I wonder what to expect in this session. Suspense builds. Will we practice Kama Sutra positions clothed in tank tops and tights, consummate our friendship with passionate sex, or will Theodor pour tea from a steeping pot while we sit in the front room talking about Tantra?

Finally, the anticipated morning arrives. I'm wearing a conservative red and beige dress with a print of large hibiscus flowers. I leave my sandals at the door. Theodor's greeting is professional, no flirtatious kiss like each time previously, although his muscular arms wrap around me. I stand on my toes, as he bends his knees.

"Is that sandalwood I smell on your neck?" I ask.

Theodor smiles. "I always smell like this," he says, and then offers me sweet jasmine tea.

I'm not jumping to conclusions yet, but I wasn't actually expecting tea. The water's already hot. Theodor's the biggest man I've hugged since the football player I dated in college. He has broad shoulders, shiny black hair, and deep-set brown eyes. His full lips and white teeth accent the brightness of his smile.

"Your house is lovely," I say. He leads me by the hand downstairs where we enter a large room furnished with antique desks and chairs, bright Indian tapestries, sumptuous ornate pillows covering a nest-like area on the floor, and silk curtains of varied hue. Crystals and precious stones surround a statue of Shiva and Shakti sitting in Yab-Yum—a seated sex position symbolizing the union of wisdom and compassion. Other treasures include dried sage in a conch shell, a small Tibetan Singing Bowl, and a burning candle illuminating a flower floating in a vase of water.

"My girlfriends share this room," he says, "when they need to use a desk or the computer."

For a moment, I uneasily wonder about the direction of our session, and if Shelly and Valerie will be okay if things go the way I picture it. Valerie and I have been close friends for many years, but I remember the slight frown on his primary partner Shelly's face the first time he kissed me a year ago. The fact that Valerie is his other roommate and has become his lover since then is a good sign that they are comfortable with his work.

Theodor nestles into a pillow on the floor. "What's your background and orientation to Tantra?" he asks. "What type of spiritual path are you walking?"

I sit facing him, fascinated by his questions, hoping to intrigue him with my answers. Is this *strictly business* for him, or is he a bit enchanted with me as well? I'm challenged to put this vast topic into words, but as I begin to speak, my answers flow. "For me, Tantra is the practice of being fully present with what is before me. Sometimes that is nature, or my guitar, or myself, and sometimes it's another person, or group of people. Tantra means listening carefully and reflecting accurately with a clear mind and open heart. My spiritual practice is to love everyone."

Calm pours over me until I feel melted. Theodor seems to have little negative judgment about my answers. Even though we have been to many of the same social events, I know more about him than he knows of me because I've attended some of his gatherings and lectures, but he doesn't know that side of me. I speak openly and honestly about my past, while trying to hide my disappointment that our time is passing and we're still talking. I'm impressed with his intuitive line of questioning. The way he interprets my answers is how I wish everyone would. I feel heard, understood, and seen, which brings tears to my eyes.

"Come lie down next to me," he says.

My mind gets fuzzy with these magic words. I've been naked with him in the past during community camping trips and at group hot springs events, so I don't hesitate to take off a layer to prevent wrinkling my clothes. My dress slips around my ankles, and I step out of it.

"I like your dress," he says, as I set the garment on my chair. I sink into the cushions next to him. "Your strong legs are admirable," he says, "and what pristine breasts."

I feel the familiar immersion into his presence, the way I've melted into his kiss so many times before.

We spend the next three hours in a lover's embrace, moving together like feathers in an ancient ceremonial dance. My ears are met with angelic tones flowing from his soft lips, alternating comforting words with acknowledgments. The smell of amber, frankincense, and sandalwood fuse with our intoxicating pheromones and sex juices. Orgasms blend with the deep red, orange, and blues surrounding our entangled bodies. He doesn't perform any extraordinary moves, but his devoted attention and care allow my complete surrender. Each chakra is sanctioned and kissed, as he makes me feel that my whole being is completely seen. I'm safe, held, my creativity flows, and I have as little to prove as a flower. Laying spread out with my back arched over his belly, one of his hands is on my head and the other's on my sex. Calm and expansion surrounds me as the hand on my head moves down and rests over my heart.

When speech returns, Theodor says, "I see you as a *magnetic magnifier*. Magnetic in that you draw what you desire toward you, and magnifier because you clearly reflect what you see in others back to them showing how to manifest what they desire."

"I feel seen," I say. Fully present, my breath is synchronized with the beloved before me. Our union is the flight between innocence and experience, between falling and choice, infatuation and true love, never and eternity, a still point and infinity. Becoming the ultimate lover in this devoted-cosmic embrace, I seek knowledge, lust, stillness, connection, presence, pleasure, imagination, perfection, and harmonic balance. With this magnetic magnifier perspective, I take chances that other perspectives wouldn't allow me to dream.

My magnetic energy is easily pleased with miraculous

ways of granting wishes. Theodor's power is recognizing and evoking mine. Together we awaken the goddess, inviting her to show us a new rhythm. Theodor's weight pressing down on me is comforting, but as he rolls my body over and up onto his, I feel new life rush into my veins.

I'm in a state of bliss, not thinking about what to do next, and all I want is to give back. My body slowly slides down his torso. My lips kiss his lingam as I inhale his essence deep into my cells. We are one. He enters my watering mouth. My tongue springs into delighted play as the salty sweet taste of my wet amrita penetrates my mouth. In and out, back and forth, round and round, each pass of the tip of his shaft across my tongue heightens my attention. I hold him still in my mouth, allowing the excitement to ease, then slide the condom off and begin again, entranced with the contrast of soft skin and hard shaft against my inspired throat. I feel the pressure build until his skin is so tight against the pulsating, bulging veins that the tension releases. Creamy and warm with a slightly sweet savor, gently swallowing, I'm overwhelmed by this gift—assimilating the essence of his strength, confidence and nurturing love. I pull back, out of his soul to see into his eyes once again. We smile.

I curl into little spoon as his big body embraces mine. Theodor suggests, "Let's use this supercharged, elevated energy and intend for our heightened sensations to bless our dreams. You can start."

"It's time to expand my audience," I say. "I want to share what I've learned from channeling the goddess and her wisdom, beyond answering questions for individuals. It's time for me to write a reference book about my years of experience in sexual freedom and open relationships." I take a deep breath, and on the exhale we both turn over for me to spoon him.

"My vision is to finish my Tantra book, which is dangerously close to being ready to publish," Theodor says. "Self-publishing has become easier, so there's no better time than the present to be heard. My intention is to have my book in-hand before the upcoming convention."

Filled with gratitude, I infuse energy into completing my book, along with Theodor. Sharing similar writing goals heightens the sense of camaraderie created by lovemaking. We've only known one another for a year, yet it feels that we have become deeply bonded as friends. Then he gently tells me that we are out of time. What? Our time is over?

"Okay," I say, but my molecules are whirling around his being. When will I be in his arms again? I think. But then I remember there's an abundance of bliss in my life, and I smile without the turmoil of neediness.

I've yet to realize how this session will set the next chapter of my life into motion. I walk around the block before operating my vehicle; feeling appreciated, respected, understood, and encouraged to take on the challenge of starting my writing. The reluctant Merlin is being coaxed out of the forest.

EXPLORATION #2

What are your thoughts on Tantric healing?

_____

_____

_____

My definition of Tantra is a quality of presence—being one with what is directly in front of me. Tantric healing is what happens when a Tantric practitioner can hold that level of presence with the one before them to facilitate what the receiver needs to feel seen and create space for a shift.

What is your homework on the topic of Tantra?

_____

_____

_____

Examples:

Sit in silence for 15 minutes.

Gaze at an object and notice what you feel.

Hold hands with someone and feel what arises.

Listen to the sounds of nature.

Chapter 3

Finding My Inner Merlin

"Knowing what must be done does away with fear." — Rosa Parks

What's in a name? My Mother's sister died during childbirth before I was born; I only knew her name. As I learned of ancient legends, her name became more significant. Mysteriously, my Aunt's name was Merlin. Stranger yet, my Dad's brother, who died recently, had the same name. Merlin's in my bloodline, but how will that powerful magic express itself through me?

Trying to unveil the Wizard's secrets, I'm aware that the archetypal Merlin has a hermetic intimate connection with nature. I, too, feel this deep connection to nature, but the parallel here is more about the inclination to stay hidden. With my eagerness to express the wisdom brewing in my cauldron, and the momentum of my energy-infused intention, I'm feeling less reluctant. Yet, I'm still hesitant to unleash the goddess energy dancing with the Merlin inside. Am I destined to be a sex educator or poly advocate? I have a professional license, and my clients may not approve of alternative lifestyles or educating outside of the conservative guidelines.

One evening, I experience one of the most awkward sexual scenes of my life. I'm honored to be included in a circle of titillating Tantra teachers and sex-healers. We're a small, intimate group, and the event is being filmed for a television pilot. I'm not shy in volunteering for a kiss demonstration with the mesmerizing teacher, a man I just met. Ayden's lips look like perfect little pillows on his chiseled face, and I'm intrigued by what's been coming out of them all night. I imagine going up and laying one on him, exhibiting my perfected skills in the art of pashing for the world to witness. With a big smile I jump to my feet and walk toward his mouth.

Ayden says, "Lie on your back. I'm going to kiss you."

"Okay," I say. This is unexpected, but not impossible, I think.

"The demo is how to receive a kiss," Ayden announces into the camera.

I'm being asked to do nothing, just allow him to kiss me. My heart plummets. Doing nothing may sound easy, but I don't want to look incompetent. Ashamed of not knowing how to just receive, this feels awkward and embarrassing. I lay motionless as a cold, dead fish.

Ayden is a Tantric healer, trained in the art of helping people release old pain, and with my surge of shame, I'm ripe for the picking. He looks acceptingly into my eyes and places is warm hand deliberately at the nape of my neck. Although he's giving verbal *how to kiss* instructions for the camera to record, his unspoken energy and firm lips on my mouth create a space for healing. I surrender.

After the successful kiss, Ayden talks to the group about being full with your own happiness before engaging with another person. He discussed other Tantric truths like the importance of finding everything we need, including love, inside of the self and then sharing ourselves with others from this whole place.

At the core of my being, I too am a healer, and have

assisted others to relax into a reflective healing state. My role is often to listen caringly, not saying much as they untangle their thoughts. The professional restorative work I do with clients as a nurse is done fully clothed, but the sexual healing that occurs after business hours with lovers is a part of how I contribute to making a healthy community. Many in the group are excitedly discussing an upcoming conference. The invitation is offered, and within an hour I make the decision to join this event for sex educators, sex workers and healers.

My Tantric-initiator Theodor also signed up for the adventure and is available to carpool. I'm excited because we haven't seen one another since our *tea and chat* a few weeks earlier. We travel with ease, as if we've been married for years, or lifetimes. In the idealistic marriage, the Goddess sees her lover with fresh eyes each day. In my daily practice, I strive to see the one before me as the Goddess would, and release any thoughts of unhealthy attachment. After I'm sexual with any lover I practice an ancient ritual called *cord cutting* to consciously let go of agendas and expectations with each connection. Because I did my practice with Theodor, I feel balanced and in right relation with him. This allows us to come together as complete whole individuals, and able to be present with what is real in the moment.

We arrive at the Temple a few days early. The conference will be held at multiple nearby locations, but we're fortunate to be staying at the central location. No place on earth is equal to the stunning red cliffs with water rushing down the canyon lined with cottonwood trees, smelling of sagebrush. Besides the mesmerizing panorama, the main attractions are the mysterious energy vortexes strategically accenting the mountainous terrain. There's an indescribable sacredness of the land present here. Thankful for the extra time, I go to the master's chambers to find the owner of the temple, a dear lover who is resting. Dennis pulls me into a passionate embrace. After a sexy welcome-romp, he whispers in my ear, " I hope you can help my son, Andrew, this weekend. He and Candice are ready to open their relationship, but haven't found the right lover."

I smile, and give him a long hug. I know what he means, but am not sure I'll be the entrusted one. "Andrew is fortunate to have such a generous father," I say.

Excited to be part of creating the energetic container for this event, I unpack my bag and walk the grounds. I stop and take a few minutes at each of the four cardinal directions to admire the rust-colored sandstone and bright blue sky. The property is nestled amongst the trees, and the breeze smells of the Yucca's sweet bloom. I notice the sound of cliff swallows and a creek nearby. There are a few others settling in. I can hear them making love as part of contributing to the foundational energies of the upcoming affair. My intentions are aligned with them as we invoke the open-minded, open-hearted Goddess. This Goddess creates sacred space, allowing authentic connection so the magic can unfold.

That evening, Theodor and I go to bed after an early dinner. As we lay our naked bodies together the alchemy comes alive. Theodor says, "My intentions for this weekend are being fully present and radiate love on everyone at this event."

I agree, and add, "Mine are to remain congruent with what's real, and be of service when needed this weekend." Then I say, "I've been looking forward to this embrace." There's just enough light to make out Theodor's silhouette and facial features.

He pushes me back just enough to gaze into my longing eyes for a moment. "Let me see into you. I'm completely yours," he says, "and delighted we have this meaningful time together."

At Theodor's seasoned touch, my skin again sends waves of ecstasy coursing through my cells. I feel myself drifting in and out of time continuums, from the ancient past to the future as a magical, loving unity weaves around us. I'm completely focused with the one before me in the magical energies of this land, opening into an invisible layer within our universe of timeless space.

I practice *sex magic* by using orgasmic energy to infuse my intentions, but it's about to be redefined for me. The bedroom's suffused with a luminescent glow as twilight lingers through the sheer curtains. Each time my gaze meets my Tantric lover's eyes, reality slips into another realm. I desire to be met where I feel whole, that place inside that includes all aspects of my being. I enter a transcendent journey into the unknown as his strong hands guide my hips into a gentle rocking. I can't contain my excitement to be lying with him again, and as the wetness between my legs touches his hand I feel his erection nudge against me. As if for the first time, he leans away to witness my glowing body then pulls me close. His fingers slip into my mouth, as I reach down and one-handedly bestow the skin-thin sheath over his willing lingam. As he pulls me closer, his hard body enters me. We undulate in a comfortably unfamiliar rhythm.

In the midst of our penetrative sex I feel the light yet powerful presence of another man enter the room where we're making love. By the door, I see Ayden's form with my inner eye. I know he's not really standing there, but the vision is real enough to recognize. Inclusion is the theme of the conference and we're creating the esoteric platform, so I energetically welcome him in. As he comes before us, I watch as Theodor's physical body envelops and includes Ayden. My eyes widen; continuing to make love, I see both men before me. We continue making love as one by one all the lovers, from ancient to the future, enter our union. They all morph into the God in my arms. As my clarity returns I see this is Shiva, the God of wisdom.

Speechless, I allow my vision to settle in before attempting to share this vision with the treasured man in my arms. How do I put this into words? I'm making love with Shiva, who has become all men! I feel large, like my body's expanded past the walls of our room out into the gardens. Beyond the red rocks, to the oceans on all sides, I feel large enough to take all that Shiva is inside me. Perhaps I'm embodying a portion of the Goddess. Morning light is clearing the room; I gently begin to find my words.

"I'm experiencing difficulty focusing on your face, because Shiva is still before me," I pause, "I mean, you're still

Shiva."

"Do explain," Theodor says. "I'm Shiva?"

At first it's awkward, then the anecdote begins to flow from my lips. "I have my own ideas about the ancient Hindu deity. If he attained enlightenment through transcending and including all the earthly pleasures, then he is the god of inclusion and understanding humans. He represents the broad scope of every person," I say. I go on to describe the details of my inner journey. The significance of my vision is revealed, and it's an honor to realize the depth and breadth of the grid we established, sealing it in with our lovemaking.

Every cell of my body is pulsing, and as I finish my explanation I feel relief. There is a quiet release as I acknowledge my insights and I feel my uterus begin to flow. I reach down to touch my life giving organs, and hold up blood on my fingers. Surprised I say, "My period is almost 2 weeks early! This has only happened to me one other time—in Los Angeles I went with a friend to hear an Indian guru speak. When he entered the back of the room I felt him and my menstruation spontaneously began to flow."

As the weekend commences, my blissfully high state continues to burgeon. It's improbable that it can get any better. I'm grateful that the conference is a drug and alcohol free space. This allows everyone to keep going higher without hangovers or needing recovery time. Finally, the attendees begin arriving from all over the world. I'm ecstatic to see openly loving, sex positive, spiritual beings. We're all working together with the same familiar intention I've practiced for years: to live and share new ways of relating. I feel as if I'm in love with 100 beloveds simultaneously. I'm free to express my sexuality as a celebration of life. The essence of God/Goddess is flowing through our unity like a serpent, representing both a masculine phallic and a feminine creature with her belly coiled on Mother Earth like a yoni around her eggs.

I'm filled with wonder and curiosity about what I'll learn here. With the symbology of Shiva present, he may bring to light some old beliefs that are ready to be destroyed. His path to enlightenment was through parties and dancing; I'm probably in for a good time. I feel a wave of uneasiness as I prepare myself to keep the beginner's mind willing to learn. I've been a teacher, leader, older sister, and pioneer for most of my life. It's a familiar prayer to keep my heart and mind open. Finding a cool spot in the shade of a large Mulberry tree, with only the sound of hummingbirds sipping the running water from a bubbling fountain, I sit to empty my thoughts.

The next night, lying on giant pillows in the mostly empty front room, exhausted from all of the activity, I notice a young man who flirted with me earlier. I'm pleasantly surprised when Leo walks toward me. "May I massage your back?" he asks.

"You're an angel," I say, "that's exactly what I need." I lie in complete surrender, hardly even noticing that others are gathering in the room after their very late night class. My back is revived and I feel vitality returning to my body. Leo rolls me over and sprawls his body on top of mine. Provocatively, his lips press against mine, as I catch a wave of ecstasy splashing over every inch of me. My lips exhale into his ear, "Do you feel that?" This is the exact feeling I crave, as a tear wells up and runs toward my ear.

Lifting his head up enough to look into my face, I look away, a bit embarrassed.

"Look at me," he says, "that feeling is you."

I know he's right. Everything I want from the outside is already inside me, but I feel it in a new way as this barely-legal young man shares this ancient wisdom with my contrastingly older bones.

Leo's inner Merlin is communicating with mine— coaxing my shy Merlin out of the secluded forest to unite with my powerful inner Goddess. When these seemingly opposite inner aspects come together, I can express in the world as a whole being. These ancient mythical archetypes of Shiva and Merlin merge, showing me the oneness of all humans. Shiva is an eternally young god, attaining enlightenment through experiencing all things including wild partying and destruction, and Merlin is a reclusive old human wizard. Both symbolize wisdom, but from different storybooks. I find it fascinating, that one situation can evoke the Shiva, another Merlin and yet another Krishna. Ah, but Krishna is another story.

The next morning, completely nude, heading out to the sunny poolside, I round a corner and almost collide into my young Merlin mirror. Smiling, Leo catches me in his arms, and asks, "Wow, how do you stay in such good shape?"

"*A good body lasts a long time,*" I say. Pleased to use my favorite line from my namesake movie, I quote Michelle Pfeiffer when she responds to her young lover. When I'm in bliss, with my life force turned on and flowing through my body, I actually look and feel physically youthful.

Leo skips along to a house meeting because he lives here and is part of the staff for the event. I spend the next few hours communing with the sun, water, gentle breeze, and resting belly-down on the magnificent red rocks.

During the course of the weekend, the wizardly Leo reveals to me one explanation of why I've attracted so many lovers half my age these past few months. Seeing my critical self-thoughts of who I was at their age is part of what these young lovers are giving to me. As I love them unconditionally, I'm able to let go of the judgments I had on myself at that age. Realizing I was doing the best I could all along, I forgive my 20-year old self for rushing the natural flow of things and not understanding how to trust in myself. I forgive that part of myself for wanting answers, but not always listening to what was offered. I allow my younger self a newfound compassion, a new appreciation for inexperience and innocence. I've been so hard on myself, but I'm grateful that everything worked out better than planned.

I also recognize that I've played the role of initiator since I was young. I enjoy being a guide into new experiences for all ages. I embody youthful energy, while paying attention to my wise spirit guides. While receiving my Reiki Master initiation years ago, one of these ancient guides appeared in front of me, and her translucent, aged body transformed into that of a young woman before my eyes. She was always both. When I look at the world through non-dualistic eyes it's easier to experience wholeness. Opposites are different views of the same thing.

The breakthroughs continue into the next evening as I release awkward feelings and confront self-sabotaging social patterns—such as playing ignorant, or worse, a know-it-all talking *at* people. It's been a long day of experienced teachers showing me there's more to learn. Emotions surface and I vacillate between emotional indulgence and stoic austerity, as I try to process new ideas. Dinner is over, and the eclectic assembly is gathering in the central room at the main house with a live DJ and ambient lighting. The assignment is to boogie and let go. Theodor's busy on his phone, having challenges with the rest of his triad at home—apparently Valerie's cat is fighting with Shelly's dog. Leo's out directing incoming cars, as more guests arrive for the evening event. I revert back to a perplexing shyness. I'm probably not the only one having this experience, but that doesn't help. Stepping outside, I settle onto a large bench-swing. An alluring stranger stops to sit and chat. I say hello, but am in no mood to respond to his subtle summons. I look up and my oldest lover (the moon) catches my eye. I'm hurled back to my pre-adolescent custom, when contemplating feelings, staring at her hypnotic reflection.

Eventually, a bowing tree branch obscures my commune with her mesmerizing glow, suggesting I've been out much longer than I realize. I return to the party in an attempt to connect, or at least have some fun. Surprisingly, the dance floor is still only scantily populated. Everyone out on the floor looks intimidatingly attractive to me, and the sinking feeling returns. Scanning the room, I spot a familiar face. My friend Katie from home is sitting on the sidelines. A spark of hope returns as we make eye contact. I swoop her up into my arms, and with her feet on top of mine we mix it up by awkwardly dramatizing the Frankenstein dance. Giggling and dancing, our ruckus soon becomes irresistible. The room begins awakening, and others venture out to join us. My previous feelings of inhibition and separation are disappearing. The ridiculously sexy people are now joining in and playing with us. They're still as attractive, but the difference is we're now equally as attractive. We got our party started.

It's the last night of the conference, and I find *my Shiva* doing some work in our room. "Hi Theodor, tonight I won't be staying here." I say, "If only I could be in multiple places simultaneously."

"Thanks for letting me know. Who's the lucky one tonight?" Theodor asks.

"Andrew and Candice," I say. "I'm honored and excited to be a trusted person for them to practice opening up their relationship."

"Blessings, and have fun," Theodor says with a big smile. As a Tantra teacher, he understands the significance of the exploration upon which I'm about to embark.

The DJ is now playing soft, quiet music, after the cops came out to the house a second time to tone it down. Only a few people are still awake, soaking in the hot tub. Andrew, Candice and I slow dance the last song together. Playing together at the party led us to this moment, and into this dance. As the song ends, they each take one of my hands and lead me to their door.

Entering their room, the fresh scents of lavender and rose greet my senses. Dim lighting and slow-burning candles enhance the atmosphere. Their careful preparation enchants me. Sitting close enough to stay touching as we discuss safer sex and boundaries, creating safety to explore in. We're all Aquarians, and quickly discover a number of things in common besides our birthdays. Time seems to warp while in this connection vortex, and I feel a lifetime of affinity in this one single night. Starting with a three-way massage then rotating into multiple positions, I focus attention on each of their bodies, and graciously receive from them, while maintaining our connected touch. There's so much love running through my body.

Then jealousy enters the room. I feel everything slow to an immeasurable pace. It's a shock to my system, but not entirely unexpected because many people feel the feelings of jealous overwhelm when they see their partner having sex with someone else, even when it's planned in advance. Because this is a completely consensual experiment and the intention that it's a practice session is clear, it's a safe place to listen to the greater wisdom that's present. In this moment, it's not about orgasms and pleasure, although that heightened, creative state remains present. These overwhelming feelings are welcome, because we're exploring myriads of possible outcomes tonight. Andrew and I listen to Candice's thoughts and fears, while reassuring her with complete focused attention and acceptance. Acknowledging that the cohesive unit is gliding over a speed bump, I express gratitude for that awareness, and the fleeting fear and jealousy dissipates into laughter. It's okay to not take things so seriously when simply exploring this natural part of life. We lean in for a three-way kiss, and resume our sexual play. Not a moment for sleep. It feels like I've become one with the infinite void where magic resides, yet I can't find any extra hours.

Morning light comes too soon. After Andrew shares his experience with his father, we gather with the others to say our goodbyes. In this precious moment, I witness Dennis observing his son's ability to manifest the honest, open relationship he wants. This proud father hugs me close and says, "I'm thrilled that one of my own lovers participated in my son's wish to sexually include others in his relationship with his partner."

"My healing is feeling the ecstasy of openly experiencing both a father and a son, and with both of your blessings," I say. In my past these attractions were socially taboo. I was cowardice under the negative judgments and hadn't openly loved all that I wanted. Embracing my desire for both the father and the son allows me freedom from the shame of thinking that these natural feelings are wrong.

It's time to leave the temple, and the day seems to be passing in half an hour. Merlin's warping the magical concept of time, by making a minute seem like an hour, or an hour pass in a minute. This feels familiar, like the years I dedicated to guiding people through meditative-healing trance; I often had to show them a clock to prove the real time after a session. I feel homogenized into the temple, having a hard time pulling away and differentiating my physical body from the others still remaining. Merlin represents the older wise masculine archetype, and holds his course through the misty veils between the perceived realities.

Leaving all the love from the conference is hard, but at least most of the people are also departing. It's excruciating when Dennis, Andrew, Candice, and Leo ask me to stay another night, or week. I'm torn, but grateful that Theodor has his chariot waiting to escort me home. For the last few days I've experienced a transcendent phenomenon with layers of symbology and valuable lessons. I'm about to return to an equally magical place, but I'll need to bring the quilt of connectedness back to weave it in with my former reality. I hold on tight as Theodor cracks the whip to drive our asses home.

We were first to arrive, and we're the last non-residents to leave. My Gatekeeper perspective is actively present during ceremonies, monitoring what energies enter and leave the designated area. I'd participated in creating sacred space for a community experience, and as the last to leave we're closing that vortex. I take responsibility for integrating the wisdom I witnessed. For me, Merlin represents the Gatekeeper between realities, and lover of the Goddess. In my past I learned of ceremony and sacred space through the teachings of my ancestors: the Shamanic Native Americans, Zen Buddhism, ancient Celtic culture, and Greco-Roman mythology. Remembering these prior studies, I add Shakti, Shiva and the Tantric Hindu Goddess into the mix, and they all fuse into one *Great Spirit* in the mist between the worlds. I find my inner Merlin entwined with his beloved Goddess.

EXPLORATION #3

What are your thoughts on sacred sexuality?

_____

_____

_____

I experience spirituality in many forms. Sex and intimacy allows me to be fully present with another spiritual being and ignite creativity.

What is your homework on the topic of sacred sexuality?

_____

_____

_____

Examples:

Take a candlelight bath with essential oils and relax into the creative flow.

Use your imagination to visualize, and see what you create.

Put one hand on your partner's heart, and the other on your sex organ (at the base of your spine) have your partner to do the same with your heart and their sex organ, and then feel the connection.

Sit in Yab-Yum, align all your chakras, and breathe together for five minutes.

Chapter 4

Slowing Down

"No matter where you go, there you are." — Earl Mac Rauch

Theodor and I head for home with Margo, a fellow attendee who missed her flight and hitched a ride with us. I'm grateful for the reintegration time as we travel across the desert. With a third, unfamiliar party present in the car, I become keenly aware of my communication because I don't want to break confidentiality or gossip. Theodor holds steady, as a tumbleweed the size of the car, nearly misses the back bumper. Saguaro Cactus stand tall between piles of reddish-black lava stone, while inside on the plush leather seats we share lessons learned, highlights and disappointments from the weekend. I listen intently to the things they gleaned, unveiling additional insights.

Over the next few days, I'm aware of many different emotions and perspectives simultaneously. I feel deep longing for my new lovers; I miss their physical presence. I also feel gratitude for being trusted in Andrew and Candice's opening of their previously monogamous relationship. Sadness is felt for being far away from the now dispersed conference group. I feel loved as I appreciate Dennis and Theodor's wisdom, and Leo's feedback. I feel peaceful, scattered, and centered all at the same time. My new capacity to feel many different emotions, while observing how multiple perspectives might react is a novel experience. The depth is intense, but the way I'm experiencing without reacting to any of them is a new level of awareness that I want to practice going forward in my life.

Back to my daily life of consulting clients about their health, and starting the new writing project while still expanded from learning and feeling so much, I experience an all-time high. This transcendent state is higher than I can imagine, and the only way to go is down. Or is it? I come crashing down, slowly, as if on a cloud, floating in a light breeze, but down. It's amazing to be at peace with this letdown process, and open enough to feel more of life than ever before. From this broad vantage, I find it impossible to get caught in just one of the various emotions. Then I land at the ground floor. How could I forget I'm held in Grace? Strangely, what comes next is pure joy.

Exhausted and alone, I slow my thinking down and settle into bed. My mind wants to stop at lonely, sabotaging thoughts. Those thoughts can easily trigger tears, but because everything is in slow motion I become aware of the space between each thought. A comforting feeling arises when I remember that crying releases hormones that make the body feel better. Just noticing that I'm on the verge of tears makes me feel a slight rush, like a good sneeze. I stop before the tears come, but I feel a sense of relief as if I cried. The discovery of this excites me, and makes me think.

I notice shame for crying in the past. Does crying make those around me uncomfortable? It makes my eyes puffy, which fuels the thought that I look old or unattractive, which can become a *pity party* if not interrupted. How do I stop the downward spiral of negative thoughts without closing off to joy and the uplifting feelings too? I know the feeling of shutting down because I used that technique to get back at my mother (and life) during my teenage years. The problem is that it's not fun to miss out on the good feelings as well. I don't like being shut down, obstructing my free and happy tendencies by distracting with loud music, or constant activities to avoiding feeling sad or angry. I also tried the tough-guy approach to stop these thoughts, but it seemed hardened, and too similar to being shut down. I may have just found a preferred way to stop my reactions to what I judge as negative before the drama of cascading emotions spiral out of control.

Lying in bed with my thoughts still in slow motion, I realize that I found a key to dispel these indulgent, self-pitying patterns. I can use my brain to imagine and feel the self-comforting (like crying) behavior to release endorphins and shift my attitude. Then, as if on a psychoanalyst's couch, I remember vivid moments from childhood: one when I chose to continue crying after being finished, to prove I had a good reason for crying, and another when I chose not to cry, and felt worse and worse. I also recall a span of time when I didn't have any tears, until I was confronted by this block when I heard about it during a college grief psychology class, and then released the pent-up tears. This flood of thoughts brings to mind a somber memory from a few years ago, when I suffered through the dark night of the soul, crying for months with only short breaks in between. In this slow state I'm able to unwind this string of associated moments related to crying, freeing me from the fear of hitting the rocky bottom. All of this was simply included in the sea of thoughts and emotions I'd been swimming in. I wasn't drowning; this is pure bliss, I just need a rest.

Pulling up the covers my body begins to relax, and my brain winds down before drifting into deep, dreamless sleep. The key is to slow down. As I take time to grasp the significance, I notice the space between these thoughts. I distinguish thoughts from feelings as they pass through my body and brain so I can choose a desired outcome. Through all of this chaos, the part of me that's always observing becomes my eyes, so other parts of my psyche are free from getting hooked into the emotions associated with those thoughts.

I think of Shiva, often pictured in a seated meditative

pose. I've never been good at sitting still for a long period of time, but now I understand. When living life to the fullest, and open to simultaneous emotions and points of view, it's important to *sit* and notice how life fits together.

This night I'll sleep in my heart shrine—an imaginary place I've gone to meditate for years. Only this key can let me in. My heart shrine's a cozy room, located in the center of my chest, with red, velvety walls. Inhaling deeply allows this sacred space to widen, and invite me in. The lighting's peaceful, with a golden hue. Beyond the chiffon curtain, near the back, there's a round bed filled with majestic purple pillows. When I sink into the familiar comfort, I enter into a blissful sleep.

EXPLORATION #4

What are your thoughts on slowing down?

_____

_____

_____

I experience meditation and slowing my thoughts as an exciting exploration of space—the space between the thoughts. It's a way to experience all the emotions associated with each thought without having to react to any of them.

What is your homework on the topic of slowing down?

_____

_____

_____

Examples:

Set an alarm for 1:45PM each day for one week. When the alarm goes off stop what you're doing and take two minutes to listen to all the sounds you can hear.

For two weeks practice noticing your thoughts and feelings when you first wake up in the morning.

Put your thoughts on paper, no matter if it makes sense. Write for ten minutes. Then read between the lines.

Sit quietly for 15 minutes, or take a 30-minute walk without talking.

Chapter 5

Girl on Girl

"Don't cry because it's over, smile because it happened." — Dr. Seuss

How do I present myself to the world? These days, there are many ways to identify. Before the information age, people adhered to rigid dichotomies of the basic male or female, black or white, animal or fungi, Yankee or Confederate, etc. The human brain tends to geek out on this stuff, which has lead to a wealth of knowledge about diversity. Thanks to people like Alfred Kinsey in sexology, Carl Linnaeus in taxonomy, and Eric Wolf in anthropology, we have more defined labels, categories, and a better understanding of our postmodern world. With all the detailed study, life has become less black and white. Science has discovered that, in perfect lighting conditions, the human eye is able to see 100 shades of grey.

For most of my teenage and young adult years, I identified as weird, or at best, different. I didn't fit into any category. I had a female body, but mostly felt and acted masculine. My skin was neither black nor white. I learned I was part of the animal kingdom, but as the mushroom joke goes, I'm also a fun guy! I discovered my dislike for politics, or choosing sides because I can usually see the pros and cons of each side. I usually feel most at home somewhere in the middle of two extremes. I'm not far from weird now, except now I know it isn't all that I am, and that *weird* equals a good thing.

Looking back, I see many reasons why I felt different. Most of the kids in my school lived with their birth parents. My parents lived in separate states, with different partners and parenting styles creating diverse home environments for my siblings and me. One benefit of this, however, was that by the age of ten I realized there was more than one perspective, more than one way to do things, and more than one answer to most questions. As an adult, it also helped me to appreciate feedback from a variety of people, and sparked an exploration of my relationships with sexuality, philosophy, psychology, shamanism, business and Tantra.

Observing my parents' separation spurred my interest in relationship dynamics, which led to deep contemplation of the self, and a fascination with how people influence one another. I desire that my masculine and feminine unite as my inner lovers. The intention is not to disrupt their dynamic play, which could lead to stagnation or boredom, but to delve into the full spectrum of the masculine and feminine duality until it bleeds into one. I acknowledge all aspects of their polarity and similarities, and engage the erotic energy between them. It's a delight to allow my inner lovers to open so much that it inspires others to do the same. As I understand the wholeness of my sexuality, I'm drawn to connect with other people. I move with the energies within an individual, discovering together how the flow of our essence coalesces—unite like the God/Goddess becoming one, where the dance is both solo and simultaneously connected with all.

I awaken early morning in this finite body, identifying as such; I wake to the feeling of suffering. Not aware of the blissful sense of oneness, I feel disconnected from everything. My head is a battleground of thoughts. I flash back to a powerful woman I'd recently met, and my upset mind reflects on the fact that Dossie Easton, co-author of *The Ethical Slut,* didn't have a straight man as a companion by her side. I notice anger and feeling sorry for myself as I consider my judgment on men, and the masculine energies within me. Why are there still so many men looking for the perfect monogamous relationship, an unspoiled flower to keep all to themselves, to possess and control 'til death? Invariably, they'll also search for the nasty bawdy one to play with, and have unattached, erotic sex on the side. It sickens me that they can't see that I'm capable of both. Then, in less than 30 seconds, I gratefully count the men I know who love and want to go deep with sexy, open minded, loving, amorous sluts. In these wee hours, I'm feeling the disconnection in our culture, and want to understand how I can help improve the way humans relate with each other. I begin to understand that the basis of my suffering is forgetting that I'm part of everything and identifying as only an individual, or attaching to any one of the ever-flowing thoughts passing through my brain.

The way humans relate is not directed at me, but I feel a responsibility to understand human nature. My exploration of other humans is an exploration of myself, and I realize we're experimenting with new ways to live together. If only people could feel loved, regardless of whether they're single, married, have a menagerie of lovers or practice celibacy. If we could freely embrace our own individuality, let go of conditioning and judgments around how men and women are supposed to act, we could communicate freely and explore all of ourselves. If each of us spent more time in gratitude for our relationships, we might discover a deeper appreciation for the people in our lives.

I sit well into the afternoon, tangled in emotions and thoughts about loving and being loved, when my girlfriend Autumn calls, caught in a similar frame of mind herself. She begins to unload her suffering and questions. We laugh about feeling alone together, how strange that we magnetically find each other today to share our parallel pain.

"What is your experience processing attachment?" Autumn asks.

"We know there are different attachment styles, or levels

of attachment necessary to feel comfortable in a relationship," I say. "Being aware of my partners' styles, and knowing my own, makes for better understanding and ease of relating. Recently, I was asked the mirror question of how I feel when someone becomes attached to who they think I am. It feels confining. Also, if I become the sole object of someone's obsession, I'm no longer a living, dynamic person to them."

Autumn sighs. "Yes, I don't like unhealthy attachment, but what do you mean by no longer a living person to them?"

"Maybe they're imagining what they'd like in the future, or wanting our interaction to be the same as it was in the past, but either way, our connection isn't based in the moment. If how I'm seen isn't based in reality, I feel objectified." I smile. "Don't get me wrong, identifying as just this body and having another objectify my body can be sexy, hot fun when I'm aware that I'm playing that role." We laugh.

This brings me back to the thought that started my day— identifying as an object can equal suffering. "I've told those obsessed with what they think I am, that I'm an illusion. I'm in this physical body that is *real* and does exist, but the thoughts of who they think I am, are only partially real."

"Isn't that pushing others away?" she asks.

"Not sure," I say. "Maybe, a more honest thing to say is that I want to experience true love."

"That sounds more like it," Autumn says.

"I agree," I say, "When I listen to my heart, I feel that freedom is an act of true love. The more I love with non-attachment, the more love there is in return, freely returning to me without attachment. I want to be free, and I want to be loved."

We decide to meet for tea to continue our conversation, and agree that poolside at my house is the perfect location. Autumn and I have been friends for years, and tried being lovers. She hasn't found her relationship style but her go-to is the traditional Waltz. I prefer Hip-hop but that hasn't dampened our love for each other, it only makes our sexual relationship sporadic at best.

Autumn arrives, her sculpted body in a bright green sundress. The red highlights in her short, wavy hair catch the sunlight. We greet each other with big smiles and a long hug.

It's been a rocky process cultivating mature, healthy attachments, but I now have a solid understanding. When reality is clear of muddying thoughts and emotions, then I can trust the natural flow of life, releasing my need to attach to the outcome. Like right now. I gaze into her deep hazel eyes, releasing breath and feeling totally okay. Nothing else matters in this moment. I don't need an agenda like possessing Autumn as a lover; life is unfolding naturally and I feel content. We smile and giggle. I hold the term 'attachment' loosely in my hands, with gratitude in my heart, the concept of free choice around each finger.

Exploring one's motivation for becoming attached to another can be frustrating and overwhelming. Part of me loves pouring my heart out to someone, feeling seen, accepted and treasured by that being. I don't want that feeling to end. Being attached to another can hook me in, and I struggle to admit to Autumn how my process of detaching enough to truly love is sometimes a painful dilemma. I'm grateful that Autumn wants to chat about this because I know responsible communication is finding a consenting listener, and sometimes a friend is helpful to sort out emotions.

Another topic Autumn and I discuss is how it feels if a friend doesn't return a communication attempt. "My lover didn't call back last night and I can't understand what I did," Autumn says.

"If I take it personally, I assign unfounded meanings that they must not like me in the way I like them, or that I'm being obsessive. That could very well be true, but there's little evidence, only an unanswered call," I say. "Thoughts can mislead if I believe it's real," I reason with her, "I remind myself not to identify with a thought, or take myself too seriously."

"I really like that," she says. "The other part of it is I

have difficulty talking with him about things."

"Do you want my thoughts?" I say.

Laughing, she says, "Yes please. That's why I called you."

"Here's the secret: if you're afraid to talk with them, they're probably not the one for you. But, if you let them go and they come back, communication will be easier because you went though that fear of losing them," I say.

I practice keeping an open mind by considering as many points of view as I can see. This is difficult if I get stuck on the perspective that always views situations through a lens of grief and causes me to feel sorry for myself, or if a sneaky point of view judges another and pulls the wool over the observer's eyes. The outcast perspective is disowned and becomes a disliked, unwanted aspect of the self.

A tool that keeps me focused in the present moment is exercising—breathing and moving my body so that thoughts (and perspectives) don't get stuck, and I can move through each emotion faster. Sex can be extremely conducive to releasing and re-grounding if that's the intention.

As I speak with my sexy girlfriend, I notice I'm not allowing the addict perspective, or the one that thinks obsession is necessary for an exciting relationship. I realize those perspectives are being judged and therefore disowned. My mind races to the distant future—what happens when the *new love* feeling wears off?

I can really go in circles with all of this. Keeping relationships fresh and exciting comes back to being fully in the moment and loving what is, thus allowing the other person to choose whether to love me in their way. I can be pleasantly surprised when I let go of attachment and expectation.

Late afternoon is approaching, stirring the cool ocean breeze. One of the green silk straps has slipped off Autumn's shoulder, drawing my attention to her erect nipples. We walk toward the house. I open the door and kiss her rosy cheek as her body slips past mine. Am I the man, or the woman, does it matter? I feel surprisingly calm and relaxed about that familiar angst. Autumn and I had struggled to understand how to initiate our sexual play. It's a unique blend of hormones, chemistry and personality that make our individual sexuality.

Complexities arise if I judge the masculine energies as male and feminine as female. Before English was created in medieval times, many ancient cultures and languages assigned masculine and feminine qualities to objects. The difficulty was that the blending cultures didn't necessarily agree on which gender went with what object because it had to do with the gender of the invisible spirit that was protecting that object. Logically, the feminine is receptive energy, and the masculine is a doing, giving energy. If we consider everything besides the genitals, human beings possess both. Regardless of gender identification, both men and women have the capacity to give and receive.

Today beside the pool, I feel balanced. I'm not expecting a sexual encounter, but Autumn's feminine energy has been flirting with my masculine all afternoon, twirling the hem of her skirt and resting her hand on my leg. My feminine side is at peace, enjoying hers as we talk, listen and explore our emotions together. Meanwhile, I sense that her masculine energy is quietly present and relaxed.

I decide to bring up the subject and share how my masculine side had recently shifted—no longer the young boy still afraid to explore, or the teenager wanting to tackle anything with a heartbeat, or the young man trying to find someone to possess, or an immature, *dirty-old man*. I feel my masculine side desires to take her, if there's mutual consent. "Have you experienced your masculine and feminine energies dancing inside?" I ask.

"I typically experience my feminine side, but I know the masculine is in me too," she says.

"I enjoy practicing this dance with partners. I've learned that my masculine energy can be strong, even forceful as long as it's consciously present and shares the space with my receptive feminine energy," I say. I wonder if her masculine side is willing to engage with me, or if I'm to be the one to initiate a sexual connection tonight.

Snuggled on the sofa, watching the sun dip behind the hill, my stomach rumbles and we realize it's time for dinner. Autumn's hand strokes my hair. Mine are lost in the sensation of the soft skin on her neck and cheek. I pull the curve of her strong jaw toward my face, as her hand tightens its grip on my hair. Our lips smoosh together, like a perfect ass lowering onto a velvet couch, into a deep passionate kiss. Slow at first, rotating around to feel each angle of the lips, our mouths open and our tongues touch. I advance. She slinks back. She presses forward. I retreat, until we come together and I enter her mouth. It's the kind of kiss to get lost in. Time fades for awhile, and as we surface I notice the hunger pangs have passed.

"The man I'm trying not to be attached to is okay with me kissing another woman, but I don't want to push him away entirely. We haven't been together long enough to make official agreements, though he knows you and I have been lovers. Maybe we should stop for tonight," says Autumn.

"Negotiating dating is a process, and it sounds like you're still uncertain about your connection with him," I say. "Can I cuddle with you for a few more minutes? That was a super sexy kiss and my body got juicy for you!"

"Yes, I'm turned on too, I'd love to wind down gracefully," she says.

She holds me tight, we take a few breaths together, and then walk down to the corner for sushi.

I'm up early the next morning, making it to the gym in time to take an intense cycling class. I have a sickening feeling, like the Indian summer is over and leaves are starting to fall. I allow myself to bawl my eyes out in the middle of class, during an Eminem song about the pain of addiction. This music comes on during the steepest climb of the ride, as my sweat drips, muscles burn. I can relate to the pain of attachment. I feel addicted, as if I want to be loved in a particular way, and conflicted because I know I prefer attention that's given unconditionally and unsolicited. I feel like throwing up.

Addiction's easier to spot when it's obvious—drinking too much or gambling. Other addictions like attachment, drama, or comparing myself to others, are harder to recognize. Once identified, addiction becomes a choice, and the key is to repeatedly make a healthier choice until the new habit is the preferred one. I embrace the addictive thoughts haunting my psyche. My tears release the emotions and thoughts from my conversation with Autumn, as well as disappointment from my unrequited sexual desires. The feeling that remains, under the angst, is serene calm, knowing I'm at choice, and how good it feels to have someone choose to be with me because they want to be with me. I smile with the memory of last night.

Are these passionate desires—to attach *and* to be free—at the core of human instincts? Maybe they help keep my body alive and moving forward? What if this variety of obsessive love keeps my heart open and my feelings deep?

I feel open, alive and free, without an object to crave. Even then, there's still the idea of having that perfect relationship, a primary partner who loves only me. Do these obsessive thoughts lead to crazy thinking? Allowing illusionary thoughts doesn't mean I need to act on them. I'm less likely to act without choice if I allow all perspectives to be noticed and considered. That way I can choose the highest action based on the big picture. Ideally, I can be free *and* have deep relationships with people who are committed to integrity and open-hearted loving.

If I go deeper, this passion and desire to connect from the core of my being is what motivates connection with the Divine, or to be *one with all*. I know this finite body can't connect with ALL, and my limited psyche is challenged by so much of the ALL, but I can connect with all of myself, with all the perspectives in me. Perhaps it comes down to being whole within me—integrating all aspects of myself so I can connect with the one before me without attaching goals or agendas to them. To achieve this, it's helpful to let go of beliefs and remember that I don't know some things I thought I knew. Together we can ponder whether the phenomenal world is isolated by the space between each proton and electron, or stays connected through invisible communication.

My external process is a simple dance. My heart desires to learn the creatively graceful moves between my inner masculine and feminine energies. Heaven and earth come together in marital bliss, uniting through the hearts of mankind. From this vantage point, all beings have their unique way of channeling Father Sky and Mother Earth, allowing them to make love in their hearts. I'm available to love more when I feel positive and negative emotions simultaneously.

Part of my life's purpose is to be one within myself and learn more about relationships as they continue to evolve. I permit these thoughts to pass through my mind in order to find a path of less suffering. Being able to accept my lovers where they are, with the freedom to connect with me when and how they desire, allows me to enjoy a full life in loving union with the Divine. The more I experience, feel, allow and move through, the more I can accept, heal, love, and allow all of me—which includes all of you. I love you! I love all of you! Not just the sexy one that I adore by the pool, or the ones who give me what I think I want in an illusionary moment. The ability to observe the mind, body, and emotions is valuable, but what an absolute pleasure it is to share these experiences together.

EXPLORATION #5

What are your thoughts on being in right relation?

_____

_____

_____

I experience being in right relation with others as paying attention to what is in the highest good for everyone involved. I may have a crush on someone, but if they have other relationships then I consider what is best for all of us before taking action.

What is your homework on the topic of being in right relation?

_____

_____

_____

Examples:

Join a dating service for one month. Set up coffee dates with five people and ask each of them about all their relationships, and how a new person would fit into their lives.

Invite a group of family or friends on a play-date. Ask each of them if they would prefer to invite other people, and then include them.

Join a band and listen to each instrument to see how you fit into the music.

Next time your best friend wants to spend time with another person, notice all the feelings that arise and be okay with being second best friend for the day.

Chapter 6

First Threesome

"Normality is a paved road, comfortable to walk but no flowers grow." — Vincent van Gogh

This is my second time in a Catholic church.

The first time was many years earlier in Ireland visiting a friend's family. There was a funeral that day, included in the service that was conducted entirely in Latin. My conscious mind was clueless about what they were saying, but my body experienced everything. We sat much too close to the front, and were being asked to stand and sit, then stand again. Each time I stood up a pressure mounted on my shoulders, heavier, and heavier, until I could barely get up. I felt a strong urge to run out. As I turned, the church had filled behind us, and the embarrassment and obligation to stay became greater than the overwhelming need for escape.

After mass, Morgan, Sal and I visited a neighboring farm. There were layers of history on a single parcel of land, where each of five generations had built a new structure, using an existing wall of their father's farmhouse. The little houses from each generation had varying degrees of deterioration, as they spanned over a few hundred years. We witnessed a newborn foal, only hours old, nursing from its mother in the pasture. A magnificent roan mare had delivered this life while I was kneeling on the hard ground at a funeral.

Today, in California, I'm in a Catholic church again. It's not as gothic as the first one but it's still Latinate and imposing enough. I'm here for John and Brenda's wedding. He's a statuesque carpenter, towering over his stunning bride. I've never seen such a colossal bridal party fanned around the couple. Nine bridesmaids wearing identical violet dresses with lavender flowers in their ostentatious hairdos, stand opposite the men in black tuxedos with lavender cummerbunds to match. It comes as no surprise, based on my last experience in a cathedral, that the ceremony drones on past the point of enjoyment. Vincent and I drove many hours to celebrate with our playmates, who'd recently turned traditional. They decided to "do it right" and get married before having a baby. I'm unable to fathom choosing just one in this generous sea of love, with each potential mate offering their personal version of heaven and hell. I'm still working on staying present without projecting my vision of the perfect partner onto those swimming in my pool.

The priest instructs John and Brenda to each take a lit candle and use it to light a larger candle that symbolizes their union. I notice an uneasy feeling in my gut when he then instructs them to blow out their individual candles. I'm alright with people consciously choosing to join together if both want to be exclusive, even though I prefer collaboration, but it feels unrealistic to blow out the light of individual sovereignty in doing so. How do we expect to be self-responsible, not take what our partner does and says personally, or allow the other to express themselves, if we commit to this level of uniting with another person. Is this any different from my esoteric thoughts of being one with everyone? It's hard enough to identify your own individual reactions and feelings, without the added pressure of this unspoken agreement to be responsible for the actions and feelings of your partner too. It feels like the makings of a codependent mess. It's uncomfortable to identify the cause of my upset, but now that I see it clearly, I can bless my friends with the highest intention, and commit to carefully selecting symbology for my wedding if I ever decide to publicly choose one above all others.

There's dancing and cake, laughing and wine. Vinny isn't good at dancing, but he has other mad skills, and tonight I don't have a clue what he has up his sleeve. Because I don't expect to find all the qualities I like in one person, it's easier for me to appreciate his unique gifts. We've embarked on an adventure and, because it's an early wedding, we plan to make a road trip out of it before returning home.

The reception's over, so we get on the road. To my surprise, we pull into a nice hotel, not far from the church. When traveling overnight, we typically stay in his revamped conversion van, right out of the 70's with a comfy built-in bed and a sink. This is a rare treat. A breeze gently flutters one side of my flowing skirt as we walk to our room. Did Vinny prearrange this? He already has the key. He opens the door and says, "Go on in."

Walking into a sweet, familiar scent, I can't believe my eyes. Flowers, not just any flowers but crimson roses with petals everywhere. "Wow," I say, practically speechless.

In high school, my sister received dozens of red roses from a guy I had a crush on. He worked in a flower shop and would make deliveries to our house, usually on a Friday after school, but always to my sister.

Intrigued, I slip off my shoes while my gaze is drawn into the mirror, where I see a reflection of the bed. The white spread has velvety petals in the shape of a huge heart. I'm finally the one getting exquisite roses, and on someone else's wedding day. I notice a bucket filled with ice and New York Seltzer Raspberry Sodas. I ask, "How, when?" I have no idea that the events to follow will leave a lasting impression, and change the way I am wired, forever. "What have I done to deserve this?" I ask.

Vincent smiles, and takes my hand. "There's a special guest joining us," he announces.

As if on cue, I hear a knock on the door. To my amazement, a mysterious young man saunters in, and elegantly sets his keys and cap on the table by the door.

"Happy Beltane," says the stranger.

The two men embrace, and then pull me into their hug. Vincent introduces Blake from his second family, the Native American Antelope tribe. Years ago they endured a sun dance together, bonding them like brothers. They've prepared to spend the next 24 hours telling me stories of the Beltane, initiating me as the May Queen, and tying me to the glorious, mythical Maypole.

Blake lights candles around the bed to signify the purifying Beltane fires, when winter leaves and the warmth of the sun resurrects all life. Slowly, they undress me, christening my body with soft petals. We visually inspect one another's perfectly unique bodies, then they lay mine down like a sacrificial lamb over our cushioned alter. This is our own version of a Beltane celebration, and I'm a willing offering to please the gods, to feed the village. I melt into Blake's soft features and wavy, sandy-blond hair. "May I massage your legs and feet?" he asks.

"Yes please," I say, "you can touch me anywhere."

Blake's warm hands pour love into me. Sitting behind me, Vinny gently massages my shoulders and arms, with his strong legs wrapped around my hips. Feeling the thrumming of his heartbeat under my head as it rests on his chest. The sun's setting while the dancing candlelight, reflecting off our naked bodies onto the walls, creates an artful décor, and a shadowy depth.

I slip into a blissful trance state. Unable to track which hand's sending which sensation to what part of my body, I feel every inch of my skin. My mind fades into the serenity of being completely worshipped. Between the waves of silence, my mind drifts from images of dancing gowns, champagne and cake, to the Celtic green hills with maidens skipping around the Beltane fire, and in and out of the romantic, sensual hotel room. Every inch of my body and mind surrenders, as I melt into their arms. All sense of time escapes me. There's no worry about when this rapture will end. Feeling more freedom than I've imagined. Can it ever be any better than this moment, right now?

In the midst of ecstasy, my body becomes a conduit for the two men. I'm aware of their energies making love through me. Intrigued with the sensations in my body, I reach as far as possible until my imagination can't follow any further and my mind springs back like a stretchy band at its max returning to its natural state. There's no sense of anticipation, yet I'm aware of the swelling waves of our collective energy currents.

Like magic the three of us simultaneously crest a wave. I hear the quiet tear of a condom wrap. We enter into blissful communion as Blake penetrates the slit between my plump vulva with his wand of light, and I take sweet Vinny into my mouth from above. *As above, so below*—the union of heaven and earth imprints upon my heart. Our wedded bodies become one pure and open channel, allowing a current of endless, orgasmic waves to flow through, lighting up every creative cell.

We voyage further than our 300-mile road-trip. Our journey opens my heart and mind to incredible possibilities, rewiring circuitry in my body as I let go of societal and religious sexual shame, and dogma that conditioned me to close myself. I don't need to choose between the two loving, caring, generous, sexy men before me; it's okay to love them both. My controversial struggle before this adventure was attempting to find *the one*, and trying to shut off my connections to everyone else. A heavy weight lifts from my shoulders as I acknowledge, for the first time, that I'm OK, and free to love more than one person at a time. In fact, it's my natural state to be in love with everyone; after all, we are one.

We received blessings by being fully honest and open about our experience together. It's not *the norm* for three people to share intimacy, and have each person aware of it, or present for it. Before this, I had witnessed and participated in lying and sneaking around about dating multiple people. What a freeing experience to openly connect sexually, then talk about it, and remain loving around it. The ecstasy from that affair stayed with me, and the truthful relationships I've encountered since that Beltane ceremony continue to put a smile on my face.

This initiation is worthy of being called a first. I hadn't experienced conscious group sex with intention and open communication like this, and it was my first threesome with Vinny. I had played around in college with a group of boyfriends, but that was more like group sex experimentation, besides, it was a foursome. Also, shortly after college, a girlfriend and I often shared our boyfriends in the same bed together, but I was clueless about how to weave a multi-person connection, and oblivious of her bisexual crush on me, which I joyfully became aware of much later.

After our excursion, Vinny and I enjoy many more open sexual experiences with friends who are also figuring out what kind of relationships work for them. Releasing shame and guilt around veering from convention, we encourage each other to find our own authentic sexual expression. There isn't a name for our kind of relationship, but we know what we have feels healthy and sustainable. One of the principles that keep the drama out of our inner circle is encouraging our lovers to maintain honesty with their partners, and include them as much as possible. We create a safe place for those we love to examine outdated ideas of needing to find one perfect person to enact an often unrealistic fantasy. Sadly, the idea of venturing out sexually is too intimidating for some of our friends, usually because they don't want to risk chasing away a partner, or family member with rigid beliefs about relationships.

I begin to see how society's *norm* is fear based. If we don't solidify a chosen mate, we may become social outcasts, die alone, or be excommunicated and shamed. 'A good person can only love one individual at a time,' and 'it's immoral to have sex with anyone unless you're wed,' are a couple of the outdated romantic relationship beliefs that create deeper shame when one has normal human feelings of attraction for others. These conventional beliefs promote lies and distrust in these relationships, creating pressure to do what's considered normal, rather than risk losing the social standing conferred by marriage or the emotional security that even the unhealthiest of romantic attachments provides.

I see how fear plays into the race to find and cling to one person. There's the looming anxiety that if we don't find a life partner while we're attractive and young, then we'll die alone, a spinster or bachelor. Detrimental thoughts say 'there aren't enough potential partners available,' and 'there's only one magical mate to find.' If we act on our desires, or follow our bliss, we'll be punished. When banned from pursuing sexual wants, people tend to choose their first connection, remaining together even when the relationship drains happiness, stifles creativity, or prevents them from experiencing spiritual depth in life.

These limiting beliefs usually lead to thoughts like: sexual attraction is age related, or those with a partner are superior to single, *unchosen* people. This can lead to discrimination, and labeling people. These outdated beliefs can also cause someone to feel like a failure when the *perfect* relationship cracks.

As I explore open relating, I find others who want to understand alternative lifestyles, asking how to navigate jealousy, honesty, and possessiveness. As I mature in my *weird* lifestyle, my answers become more refined. Dating multiple people evolves into honest, open relationships. We encourage verbal communication and relationship agreements with everyone involved. Relationships are conversations.

I start with the one in front of me. If they're too afraid to be truthful, it's better to know now than to risk creating a painful mess to clean up later. I strive to be a non-judgmental, safe person for others. It's good practice to be transparent, which will magnetically attract those who have honest relationships. At first this may feel like a lone effort, but the more success with communication and finding others who want to engage in honesty, the easier it is to enjoy the freedom to love openly. I like to allow the one who initiates the idea of a sexual experience to take lead, but they don't always know what to do. Often I'm asked to create the space for a successful first experience with multiple partners or same sex partners.

Kris, a lover of fifteen years, who I haven't seen much in the past five years, called me for a threesome. His new girlfriend, Rosa, has never experienced being with a woman, and Kris trusts me with the initiation. I feel the sincerity in his voice and agree to a date. We briefly catch up on our sexual health, and I assure him I'll create a comfortable environment for the three of us, to go over all of the important safer sex details together.

They arrive at my door with a elegant bundle of purple irises and golden orange sunflowers. We enjoy casual conversation and a light meal I prepared. After dinner, we proceed to the warmly lit living room. I gently direct the conversation. I begin with questions, and then use my personal history and preferences as an example template for them to follow. I share the date of my last sexual health exam, the tests included, and my results. I explain that my sexual agreements with my lovers are simple, and are designed to keep us healthy. They include using condoms and having this conversation with any new lovers. Finally, I give an example of a sexual thing I like and don't like.

"How about you?" I ask, turning to Rosa.

Sitting with her hands folded in her lap, Rosa communicates the details of when she was last tested, which tests, and her results. "The only agreements we have are to use condoms and to be together during sexual play with others. I like being undressed slowly, and I don't like my nipples touched before I'm turned on," she says.

"Do you have any agreements with anyone else?" I ask.

"No, I'm only dating Kris right now," Rosa says. She pauses, then says, "I don't like all the talking. Doesn't it spoil the mood? It's just sex." Her fingers twitch.

"I understand that talking can be uncomfortable," I say. "I have these conversations with each potential new lover. It tells me a lot about their health, and how honest they are in their relationships. If we hadn't had this conversation I wouldn't have known that you don't like your nipples touched until you are warmed up, and that you and Kris have agreed to be in the same room during sexual play with others. Speaking into these questions before diving into sexual play prevents potential disruptions from crossing unknown boundaries. It ensures that each of us are aware of how best to play together."

"That sounds like a good thing. I guess I've never linked common sense with sex before. Thank you for sharing. This is new for me and I do appreciate all the details," Rosa says.

"How about you?" she asks, turning to Kris.

Kris follows the process, inserting his details. Then feeling more comfortable, we share fantasies and ideas of how we imagine the night unfolding. We begin to picture the scene.

"I want to watch the two of you, and feel the connection between us," Kris says.

"I like being watched," I say.

"I want Cheri to show me what she likes by doing it to me first," Rosa says.

"That sounds fun," I say.

Rosa stretches her arms out in front then rests one in her lap with the other on Kris' leg. She exhales and leans back into the cushions. Kris smiles, puts his hand on my knee, and leans over to kiss her shoulder. Rosa beams, scooching her leg closer so it's touching Kris, and places her hand next to his on my leg.

I'm confident that we've created a container of trust and will be able to speak any needs that may arise. I take their hands and lead them into my cozy bedroom. The dim colored lights shimmering on the textile-covered walls create a mystical effect. My eyes track her reflection in the full mirror, giving the illusion that we stepped through into an otherworldly existence. Before my hands reach for the first button on her blouse, my eyes scan her face for any missed clues. I'm drawn to her eyes, and my gaze is met with hers. She smiles as we both reach to pull Kris closer. Then I initiate a playful three-way kiss, which starts off Rosa's evening of firsts. Each time I look into her eyes, I see her heart opening wider, and all I see is pure beauty. What's shared between the three of us is sacred, exciting, and unexpected.

I gaze upon flowing silky hair, smooth lustrous skin, his shapely muscles, and her slender curves. I see the essence of perfection in male and female form. Through our eyes, touch, and energy exchange, I'm making love with the archetypal Krishna and Radha, simultaneously. While our naked bodies are sliding across one another, I pause. This interlude allows us all to slow down, and make sure we're all present to enjoy every nuance. I pleasure her for hours with wave after wave of glorious climax. We sense Kris' eyes exploring our bodies, and his mounting desire as he feels our surges.

Then Rosa explores my body with her soft touch. Her curiosity budded for years but then withered. Now it's not only rebudded but it's emerged into iridescent blooms. We experience orgasms, tears and gratitude. After Kris goes through a few condoms, making love with both of us, I watch their graceful bodies as she straddles across riding his writhing pelvis. I'm in complete bliss, my every sense heightened. Their silky skin, brown and white, glistens with sweat, coconut oil, candles and moonlight.

In the morning there's a warm, relaxed feeling while we devour a hearty breakfast. When it's time to say goodbye, the glowing, evolved woman looks deep into my eyes and says, "I'm so grateful for the superlative introduction into this new world."

"I'm delighted to experience such an exquisite transformation," I say. "The way you express love so freely with me is precious." I take one of each of their hands, and continue,

"I'm pleasantly surprised by how juicy, and effortlessly we all explore together."

Kris looks at our radiant faces and says, "Witnessing the two of you was truly my second favorite part."

Rosa and I laugh. His presence was cherished, and we agreed that it felt like heaven when all of our bodies finally united.

Participating in threesomes, foursomes, and moresomes is a sensational part of my active sex life, and has proven to be a successful way to introduce a new way of relating to those in my world. As I learn and share with others, my reward is the radiant smiles on all their faces.

EXPLORATION #6

What are your thoughts on choosing partners?

_____

_____

_____

I have always found it difficult to choose just one partner when each person is so unique and each has amazing qualities as well as dreadful ones. I love the romantic notion of finding the one and only, but in my reality adding to that story and having multiple partners is much more realistic.

What is your homework on the topic of choosing partners?

_____

_____

_____

Examples:

Ask a friend to explore this thought experiment with you: What if I desired two (or more) primary relationships instead of one?

Make a list of all the qualities you want in a partner. Do you possess all of those qualities? Can you imagine that one person could embody all of those qualities?

Make a list of all the things you want to do in your lifetime. Do you want one person to participate with you in those things? Can you imagine more than one person or different people for some of the projects?

Invite six people to participate in building a farm table to use for Thanksgiving dinner. Observe how everyone works together. Did you all have fun? Did the end result turn out the way you imagined? What were the downsides and advantages of working together?

Chapter 7

Who's Going to Heaven?

"The greatest thing you'll ever learn is just to love and be loved in return."
— Eden Ahbez

Excitement is in the air. I purchased a used 325i convertible, spruced it up, and made it my shiny new toy. Eagerly, I dart down the coast to a summer birthday party for my old friend Ruth, and her twin, Rebecca. Their invite list is always eclectic—Ruth's friends, hubby's friends, sis's friends. Each has vastly different careers and social connections. Guests are from different cultures, religions, and socio-economic backgrounds. There's a live jazz band, and the smell of fresh handmade tortillas with carne asada on the grill.

I rock up in my smart pinstripe pants, fedora, and a short, faux fur jacket. Ruth's eyes light up as she catches me walking up the path toward Rebecca's new Tuscan house. We hug, and she parades me around the manor, introducing her friends with an irresistible enthusiasm. As we walk across the sprawling deck, overlooking the Pacific, we're greeted by an awestruck audience, still buzzing from the glorious display of a sunset. For the past hour, I too had been captivatingly entertained as the sky pranced through various light formations. Crepuscular rays beamed down through the blushing clouds, sparkling on the ocean's surface, the sky slowly infused with hues until the colors completely took over the show.

I eventually make my way to the bar, where a kid I've known since his birth, and his college roommate are mixing double shot drinks to liven things up. I sip my gin and tonic while heading out to the large grassy backyard, where a cook in her toque and chef's whites is grilling carnitas for tacos with authentic Mexican fixin's. A woman next to me doesn't want the chicken taco on her plate, because the fresh corn tortilla was warmed on the grill with the pork. I gallantly volunteer to rescue her from this plight, taking her pork-tainted taco onto my plate.

Ruth's husband Roni motions for me to sit with him. I ease up onto the soft leather bar stool at a gigantic marble island (the size of my kitchen) embellished with bouquets of blue iris, sunflowers, and rare orchids. Our saga began 20 years ago, when I spotted his curly black hair from across a dusty campsite, and instantly knew he was the one who would marry my friend. Because of our knotty history, our conversation is lively and we quickly dive into the juicy stuff. Roni asks about my love life, including my marriage and our lovers. We discuss a recent Quodoushka workshop that he attended, and explain to an inquiring woman as she washed her cup in the sink, that it's a sexual workshop to transform insecurities and rejuvenate relationships using our orgasmic vitality.

We aren't quiet, and the content soon attracts attention. Roni's friend Bill pulls up a stool and sits next to us. Bill brings up the subject heaviest on his mind—his three teenage daughters. It's a normal parental dilemma—he wants them to be happy, but doesn't want his daughters to become sluts. The word slut is my invitation to share the realizations I discovered just two nights before.

"I'm a slut," I say. This shoots out of my mouth, uncensored and louder than the previous volume. I'm shocked at my outburst, but I continue, "I feel it's a lifestyle choice, rooted in honesty." A few more heads turn my way as I continue. "I choose to be honest about my natural attractions rather than detaching from my real feelings or lying about affairs." I say, "I don't like to play games and pretend I'm a *lady*. I'd rather be honest in my relationships about what I like and need."

"Can you give an example of playing games?" Bill asks.

"The other night," I explain, "a friend demanded all the attention from the men in the room by repeatedly saying no to their advances. Unaware that she was taunting them by smiling and playing with her hair. She appeared to be in a battle with herself between enjoying the focused attention, and being uncomfortable with the content. She continued to say no, but didn't change the subject. They seemed to be attracted to her naivety, and by her helpless vibe."

"How did that affect you?" Bill asked.

"I sat observing from the sofa, felt left out, and questioned why I'm unable to play games with men," I said. "I felt similar emotions in high school, when I questioned being too honest with boys. Being honest about liking prohibited sex was a risky move in a conservative school. It was in private intimate moments, when they confided in me and I held their precious truth, that I knew our connections were valued."

"I remember my first sexual experience in school," Bill said.

"Adolescent sex is a valuable initiation for some, and a place to explore emotion, desire, and express budding passion," I say. "Between my adolescent legs my schoolmates could explore the forbidden, release fears, and experience a new form of intimacy."

"You're not a game player," Roni says. "So, what happened the other night?"

"In my silent stillness, I found real clarity—I'd rather attract men who appreciate my honesty, rather than try to fit into superficial games," I answer. "I recommitted to being a slut and being honest about that reality." Laughing, along with most of the faces I can see in my periphery, I say, "Guess I've always liked sex, variety, and deep connections with multiple people." That's a little more info than some are willing to hear, but fortunately the room is loud and laughter drowns out most of it.

My focus hones in on the one before me, as everyone else in the room fades to distant background chatter. Bill broadens his inquiry, asking, "Do you have girlfriends to share with?"

"Back then, no way. Being a slut wasn't okay. I went to a religious school where sexual expression wasn't allowed, but now I not only have girlfriends, I also have a husband, family, and boyfriends I can share honestly about anything in my life." I smile, and say, "What a sense of freedom and feeling loved. I even have friends like me, who call themselves sluts without any shameful or degrading connotations."

"That-a-girl," Roni says, as Bill looks somewhat puzzled.

Savoring the last few sips of my first G&T pour from nearly three hours earlier, I head back to the college guys. On my way to the makeshift bar in the far corner of the living room, a fiery redhead peering over the balcony distracts me. Stopping next to her, we view the handful of twinkling streetlights down the hill between the dimly lit porch beneath us and the black ocean. Quietly she turns and flashes a worried smile. Our exchange of casual compliments digresses. "May I tell you something?" she asks, nervously fidgeting with the chain around her neck.

"Sure. What's on your mind?" I ask.

"I lost the gold cross necklace my husband bought for my birthday," she explains. "It took me weeks of searching on the Internet to find a replacement. The worst part was paying $1,500 and shipping it to a friend's house, so he'd never know how careless I'd been."

"That sounds stressful," I say. She'd gotten away with the deception, but it still seemed heavy on her mind. Looking down at my nearly empty glass, she recommends the champagne, and I go on my way to see if there's any left.

Unimpressed with the rate at which I'm consuming, the

bartenders, Ethan and Zac, find me a proper champagne glass and put a splash in it. "This'll take me about 45 minutes to drink," I kid, trying to hold a straight face.

They laugh, and Ethan says, "That was good." Standing in their little corner sipping, I ask the barkeeps how they met. An endearing story of their high school friendship emerges, continuing with how they discovered they're going to the same college, and decided to be roommates. In a matter of fact tone, the tall, dark, and handsome Zac says, "We love each other." Then the awkward laughter begins, as if stumbling between the boyish childhood meaning, and the world they now find themselves thrown into, where it may be inappropriate to say such things aloud.

In that moment a Rabbi walks up to the bar. "Love, or in love?" he asks.

"What's the difference?" I titter. "I am love, and I just share what I am." The words fly out of my mouth with a big smile.

The Rabbi nods, gesturing for me to down my champagne like a shot, inducing a roaring applause from *devotees* that have gathered around him. I graciously decline his temptation, but pick up the pace on my sipping; after all, it's champagne. I think he just changed the subject. Perhaps he doesn't want to directly answer my outspoken question. Maybe I'm being overprotective of my buddies' potentially fragile emotions. I can see he's interested in a conversation, but perhaps we can conspire to be diplomatic to avoid upsetting the young men.

"I've been writing a paper about love," says the Rabbi.

"I too am in the process of writing about love," I say. We discover more commonalities, like our years of experience helping improve communication in relationships and marriage. We both have similar values of integrity, honesty, and considering the highest good for everyone involved in relationship decisions.

"I'm not your typical Rabbi," he says, "I consider myself open-minded."

"My lifestyle involves open relationships," I say.

"How's it working for you?" the Rabbi asks. He seems non-judgmental and genuinely interested.

"I feel free and loved, and it's great to include more love, rather than be exclusive or possessive of lovers," I say.

"More love sounds good," he agrees. "How's it possible to keep your loved one, but add another person?"

"I don't own, and I'm not owned by, any of my partners," I explain. "We freely choose to be together, and continue to make that choice even when more people are involved. Our relationships are strengthened by the knowledge that each individual connection is unique and not threatened by others. The ideal is that no one will be tossed out or abandoned if a new person enters our dynamic. It's about adding to, not taking away from, each relationship."

Then the Rabbi asks, "What's the most important thing that makes it work?"

"Self-responsibility, and being in right relation with each person," I say. "Everyone has freedom of choice, and I choose to be love, even when relationships transition and change. Any relationship requires active negotiation of which parts are working, and which parts need refinement."

The Rabbi nods slightly. "I understand, but loving more than one sounds like an overly idealistic view of what's possible in a relationship. Is it practical?" he asks.

"In my ideal world, everyone is a free individual, can connect with who they choose, and experience the abundance of love. It'd be heaven if each person *followed their bliss* (as Joseph Campbell says) and was encouraged to pursue natural attractions without being chastised." I add, "and those who claim to own their spouse could freely choose consensual slavery."

The Rabbi's good at listening, allowing me safety to express my unorthodox ideas. We touch on the topic of patriarchy, and the consequential suppression of the fact that females are equally human. We venture into the thought experiment of how a dualistic paradigm interferes with a full expression of love. "If a person identifies as straight or gay they're more than just that identity," I say. "A person may also *identify* as either masculine or feminine, both, or neither one." This is heading down a rabbit hole, then I ask, "What if humans are love at the core, and we share that love with one another, in order to fully develop and learn how to express it, without holding too tightly to how a person identifies?"

"Yes, love is what we are," the Rabbi says.

The discussion comes back around to making sure these boys aren't mistaken for fags if they said *in love* instead of *love*. As if God wants to forbid anyone from being in love. I may never know what the Rabbi meant by the inquiry around differentiating between love and in love, or what the boys meant by saying they love each other. We did agree that, love is a good thing, and more love is better. "I'm in love as often as possible, and include as many people as I can," I say.

"This is a new way of thinking," the Rabbi says as he turns toward a man waving from across the room.

My hope is that this Rabbi is inspired to incorporate some of these ideas about love and relationships in his article. I'm including his inspiring attitude and love in this book. I'm pleased to see the similarities of our thoughts on love. Many religions teach that their paradigms are the only way, and everyone else's idea of God is wrong. What if God is love and everyone is part of that love?

The band starts up again, distracting me with their fresh, clean sound. The jazz ensemble lost a few members, and transforms into dueling guitars. The lead first catches my eye while singing Van Morrison's *Brown Eyed Girl*. I blush. He's the music teacher of Ruth's son, and he's wearing a ring. I join the birthday girl on the couch, a front row seat to the live concert. Ruth whispers in my ear, "The sexy singer is a LDS."

"What does that mean?" I ask.

"Mormon," she says.

We chuckle as she hints about polygamy. Then Ruth says, "I admire how masterful he is at inspiring my boys with their music."

We marvel at his artistry, then talk about the great deal I got on my car.

Later, as I'm walking through the moonlit flower gardens behind the house, the previous slut conversation brings Bill, the married father of three, back for more questions. "I only dated sluts when I was young," he admits. "My wife had sex with me before our marriage, so technically she's a slut. I married this slut, and had children with her, but I don't want our daughter to be as free and easy as we were back then."

"You have the dilemma of wanting your daughter to be fulfilled, but you don't want her to be a prude," I reply.

"I didn't date the prudes because they were unavailable for the kinds of adventures I wanted. The sluts were much more fun, transparent and able to have intimate connections," he recalls. "Now as a father, I'm in a predicament, feeling like I'm pretending to raise my children in a proper way, but they may rebel if being proper doesn't bring them happiness. What do you advise?"

"All I can share is my experience," I say.

He agrees, so I begin to recount aspects of my life as a promiscuous, adventurous, successful woman. I start with the present. "My partner Jacy, and I have a deep spiritual love, and openly have additional sexual partners. After 5 years together, Jacy and I have transitioned to no longer being sexual partners, but we're still connected and share the love."

"I'm doubtful one can live an open, sexually free lifestyle, and be married with a family at the same time," he says.

"I have successful relationships, and personally know hundreds of families with children, happily living a sexually open lifestyle. Many of the lovers in my life are parents, or raise children in their open relationships," I say.

Bill's curiosity is peaking, and his questions are coming

faster. "How did you arrive here? When did you realized it was ok to be who you are, and how does it work for you now?"

I sigh. "Life's a process. I've had mentors and heroes along the way, helping me realize I'm not just one thing; I have all perspectives in me. I can choose which perspective to express in any moment. I have the prude perspective inside me as well, but she doesn't get out much, due to her extreme shyness."

We laugh. Bill and I go inside and sit on the abandoned sofa. "I respect the women who came before me," I say, "they showed the world that women are equally free, smart, sexual beings." Then I sit up tall and say, "I'm inspired to tell you how meeting Madonna made me feel that my exploration of sexual equality and free love was sanctioned."

It was a warm fall afternoon in Los Angeles. I drop off my friend Franco at a local coffee shop to get in line, while I circle the block to find a place to park. I turn the corner approaching the perfect spot, just across from the crowded café. A polished black car pulls up to the curb ahead of me. I mysteriously know Madonna's in that car. My heart speeds up, and my eyes widen as I pull into the spot that my parking fairies reserved, directly behind the car. Frozen with astonishment, I stare at a large, muscular man stepping out from the back seat. Avoiding blinking, I'm filled with awe as a small woman, in simple clothes follows him out of the car. I still can't see her face, but I know it's her. They walk across the street and down the sidewalk, past at least 50 people. Her energy is held so close to her body not one person notices her.

As they round the corner, I jump out of my car and run to Franco. Throwing my arm around his shoulder and leaning in close, I say, "Madonna just walked right past you!" I motion in the direction she went. Fumbling my words, I'm thrilled just to share about knowing who was in the car without any external clues; I try to convey all that happened. Franco's next move pushes my edges of spontaneity and propriety.

He snatches my hand and pulls me in the direction I had

pointed. Sitting back on my haunches like a pitbull playing tug of war, I try to resist. With a momentary glance, eye-to-eye, he convinces me to run with him around the corner. We see the couple at the back entrance of an old theater. We stop. The woman turns, looks right at me, and smiles. I can see Madonna's face for the first time. For a brief moment, our eyes meet. A download of feminine wisdom pours into me, about controlling personal input and output of energy. Madonna cloaks herself simply by pulling her energy inward, the opposite of performing on stage. I look into her and smile.

My story of meeting Madonna is a little off track, but what she represents in my life is exactly what I want to convey to this struggling father. Madonna's a shining example of a powerful, brave woman. Exposing her soul on stage, she influences an audience of young girls who want to be free. My psychic connection with her was an experience of being one with this eternal icon.

"Speaking openly about women's desires and sexual expression, is vital for peace on earth," I say.

"I can see what you mean," Bill says. "Give an example of your interpretation of that experience."

I answer, "This spontaneous, energetic transfer with Madonna took years to decipher. It started with activating deep peace inside me, awakening every woman's soul, eventually spreading to peace between man and woman, and continuing to spread the equality of all humans worldwide. To me it felt like that moment was a vital thread in the web of mankind's evolution. This experience changed my life, encouraging me to be real and express my true self."

Bill prompts, "How'd it change your life?"

"It was empowering to have a clear example of my accurate intuition, providing a reference of what's possible. Each time I trust my intuition it's easier to recognize in the future," I say, adding, "Madonna's stealthy-energy control was superhuman, showing me how to use life force energy, and that it can be directed outward, or held in. I'm grateful for the women who expose themselves to the world, demonstrating it's okay to be every aspect of woman from the sacred to the profane."

Next I share with Bill, my earlier conversation with the Rabbi, discussing how my relationships aren't traditional. It's strange to be at an event, where the religious leader of the community is engaging in what others might consider "sinning." I haven't experienced a preacher or minister drinking and dancing with members of his congregation. The Rabbi doesn't know me, but he knows I'm friends with the birthday girls, and encouraged me to drink and talk freely about my open relationships and thoughts on love.

The curious father of the potential sluts begins to open up, saying, "I wish I could live honestly, and playout my desires to have true attractions, and flirt."

"What would change?" I ask.

Bill confesses, "I've been married for over ten years to my second wife, and I don't think she's open to these ideas."

"You might want to let her speak for herself, you may be pleasantly surprised. Perhaps it's easier not to keep her in the box of who you thinks she is." I suggest. "A little trick is to practice what it might feel like to get an answer you don't want, then it's easier for you to be ok with any answer she gives. This makes it safer to tell you her truth because she can feel if you have anxiety when you ask, and to her that might be interpreted as pressure to say what you want to hear."

Bill agrees, "It feels better when I'm allowed to be myself, and am seen with fresh eyes."

"Have you seen the movie 'Kinsey'?" I ask.

Bill's head tilts to the side and eyebrows furrow, then as I mention the continuum on the scale between more conservative and more alternative, his eyes widen and he says, "Yes, I've seen it, but it's vague."

I remind him, "Detailed research, with thousands of

subjects, shows gender specific choices aren't as society tells us. In fact, it's pretty balanced with both men and women on the more conservative end, as well as women and men on the more alternative end of the continuum."

He nods with recollection.

I continue, "In the past, women like myself, who aren't traditionally proper, felt alone, weird, and different. It's empowering to see Kinsey's work, normalizing human sexuality."

Bill then reveals a deep insight he holds, and is unprepared to change at this stage in his life. "Monogamy is not natural," he says. He sounds so innocent, yet so certain. My heart goes out to him. I can sense his relationship frustrations.

The party is winding down, and most of the guests are disappearing into the night. The chef dismantles her outdoor kitchen, packing up the last of the limes, carrots and radishes. The only entertainment left playing is a Ray LaMontagne music video on a huge wall-mounted monitor. The bar is out of juice. Ethan and Zac are getting restless, and announce they're continuing the party down the hill. I hear Rachel attempt to push Ruth into a guilt trap. "You should be a good mother and take your young kids home," Rachel says.

Roni's willing to take that task and let the birthday girl continue playing, but Ruth and a few of the lingering adults, say they'll catch up soon. Ruth says, "Send a text with your whereabouts and we'll meet you after the kids are tucked in."

Ethan says, "Okay. The after party's about to begin."

With new excitement in the air, Ethan grabs my hand and whisks me through the cluster-fuck at the door. We have the task of finding a lively spot down the hill. Ethan, Zac, and I hitch a ride with one of the departing guests, landing in a bar filled with *20-somethings*. The boys, entertaining themselves and others while trapped behind the bar for most of the evening, are finally free. They arrange for six of their former high school buddies to join us.

At first I feel like a fly on the wall, hanging there watching. Soon, the fact that all eight men are nearly half my age completely disappears. I'm a part of the conversation and playfulness in our little assembly. I've never felt generously included by a group of men before. One of the brave ones convinces me to help solicit a group of pretty girls to join us. Unfortunately, the girls are meeting to plan a bachelorette party, and decline.

While hanging with these young men, I have a realization that could've changed my life if I'd seen it as an adolescent. They walk with surprising confidence and tell intelligent jokes, yet sound confused about what classes to take and talk about being unsure how to do laundry and how they'll miss home cooking. Boys aren't the way I previously imagined. I thought they were tough, and could handle anything, but they're just like I was— enjoying my newfound independence while confused about how to do new things and managing my overwhelm of discovering the world's immensity.

After we settle in, Ethan texts the birthday girls, and a few of the others who expressed interest in joining us. The messages are answered with, "I'm heading to bed" and "I've got to get the kids to sleep" and a few other lame excuses. Here I am, alone with these young men. That feels a bit awkward for about a second, until I notice my excitement. Laughing on the inside, I feel 21 again. Soon we're bumping elbows and the pop-punk music increases a few notches. Without obligation to wait, the nine of us mosey out of the joint, down a few blocks to a less lively place with a pool table. The wristband I managed to score at the first bar is handy, because I left my ID back at the house.

It's glorious being with these guys, each flirting with me in his unique way. They're friends without rivalry or competition, and we're really having fun. Taking turns holding my hands, one shares a drag on his cig with me, and Zac offers the gentlemanly gesture of opening the door as we leave the second bar. One playful chap steals my hat; it looks great on him so he keeps it until Ethan and Zac are ready to go home. Our original trio bid the others adieu, linking arms as we trek up the long, steep road.

We laugh, and kid around, as we wind our way back to the now silent house on the hill.

They each told me that they've only dated a couple of girls and are fascinated by the concept of loving more than one person. Our arms release when loose change is spotted on the curb ahead. We all run to the glitter, gathering coins like kids after a piñata busts. They give me the spoils as a gift, and Zac announces, "It's over 25 lucky pennies, make your wishes."

Continuing up the hill, I wonder what to wish for, and then as if reading my mind, Ethan turns to me and says, "You're in charge of the rest of the night."

"Oh, I like the sound of that," I say. Are they ready for the exploration that comes to mind?

Quietly, we enter the dark house, not wanting to wake Mom in her end of the house, or Dad in his. Finding leftovers from the party we devour a midnight snack. Zac fumbles a fork and catches it just before it lands in the sink. I smother a laugh as we attempt to move stealthily toward the only room where we can safely relax. As the door opens I see the bed, and hesitate. I've been enjoying the thrilling sensations up my arms and down my spine when one of their hands contacts my skin. Now they consented to turning the rest of the night over to my direction, and I want to keep a slow, steady pace to allow each of us to feel as much as possible. After flirting for so many hours, I'm horny and could easily dive right on top of these two sexy creatures, but I want to maintain my focused attention equally with both. This bedroom's the only place the three of us can lounge and continue touching. Even behind closed doors we remind ourselves to lower the volume; it's late and everything's so funny.

Heating up the room with desires, my anticipation continues to build. I lead by example—slowing my breath and softening my voice. Still holding hands, legs entwined, I feel a deep ache stirring at the base of my body, like the primal urge to create tingling up my spine. I'm pleased that they were also moderate with the alcohol earlier tonight, so we all can be fully present right now.

"Come out to the living room with me," Zac asks. He squeezes my hand.

It catches me by surprise! That's not what I have in mind. "Let's all have fun together," I suggest.

There's a second of uncertainty as they realize they're in unfamiliar territory. Then, with the next breath, a shift occurs. Smiles return, but our faces are brighter, calmer, and more present—as if we entered a room lined in red velvet pillows and perfect light.

Excited expectation bubbling up again, and Ethan hushes our snickering. Then Zac repeats his offer. I put my hand on his face and ask, "Can you explain why you want to leave?"

"I want you to come with me," Zac says.

"Let's all stay right here," I insist. "I really want to understand."

Zac then becomes forceful in his tone, pulling my arm. At this point I sit up, look him in the eye and ask, "Do you mean to tell me, if I offer to give you both a blowjob you'll still want to leave?"

Zac pauses, looks at Ethan on the other side of me, smiles and says, "She really knows the way to a man's heart." Then he adds, "Okay, but I go first."

I understand learning to share can be tricky, and this is all new to him, so I give him a break on that greedy request. Reaching up, I dim the lights, and begin a deliberate disrobing, to the striptease music in my head. Just when I think the smile on their faces can't get any bigger; I slink catlike across the bed. My right hand on Zac's leg, and my left on Ethan's; I slide up slowly. Warm skin, pulsing veins, and hard muscles all the way up. I unclasp each of their belts simultaneously. Moving one hand up each of their bodies, resting at the heart, I use just enough pressure for them to feel my intent, and then lower my breasts onto their chests. I deepen my breath and the three of us exhale slowly together. I press my weight down onto their bodies, pushing off and arching back, then dragging my hands back down to the jeans. I kiss each of them as they undress. I receive soft, deep kisses from Zac, then a little lip bite from Ethan.

Before I start with the promised first BJ, I turn all my focus on Ethan. I notice his penis is much smaller than his mate's, and I want to be careful not to show any favoritism, or make him second place all night. Straddling his left leg, and slowly lowering myself against his right ear, I whisper in a firm voice, "You can be as rough as you want, I like it." I feel his energy rise under my body; he runs his hand up against my scalp and gives a snug hair pull.

I keep my promise, and keep my energy on both of the beloveds before me, behind me, beside me, under me, and yes, on top of me. I forget how excitable and rechargeable bodies can be. Circulating energy through my body and sensing theirs, I feel Zac moving toward climax. I say, "We don't want to be done yet."

"There are plenty of orgasms to come, I won't need to stop just yet," Zac assures.

I smile.

Completely blissed out, each of them has cum three times with an endless energy much like a woman's multiple orgasmic state. Eventually, Zac's strong, soft lips kiss me again, this time with added confidence and care. He announces, "I'm going to get some sleep on the sofa in the other room."

"Goodnight bro," Ethan says.

"Sleep well love," I say. We embrace, and our entwined bodies untangle slowly. Quieting our voices again before Zac opens the door.

The fiery one is not ready for sleep yet. Ethan's staying power inspires me. As the door shuts, he takes me down to the floor so we don't wake anyone. Ethan knows how to keep me engaged with his clear and direct intention. "I'm not kidding," I whisper, "I really like you being rough."

He reaches his hand up, cupping my mouth, and takes

his turn at dominance. We continue our frolic for as long as the night gives us. Finally, we lay spooning as I softly speak my appreciation.

"I love the way you connect and are present with me," I say. "The way you move your energy while feeling mine is divine."

"I don't believe you," Ethan says. I can tell by his reactions that he doesn't realize how unique and amazing he is.

"Not all men understand these things, you're developing important skills," I say. "Thank you for the way you included me all evening. Being with you feels good." Just before he drifts off to sleep, I kiss him tenderly on the lips, put my clothes on, and carry my shoes out.

As I pass the sleeping man on the couch I whisper, "Goodnight." Zac raises his arm, reaching towards me. I take his hand saying, "Goodnight sweet man."

He asks if I'm okay to drive this late. His hands are warm, and I feel his kind and thoughtful spirit.

"I'm good," I say, as our fingers slip apart. I feel harmony as we part. I gently close the door.

The golden morning sunlight adorns the rolling hills. Driving home, I can still feel Zac's soft lips on mine. Should I have told him I appreciate how he was able to shift his mind from a complete "No", to a wonderfully inclusive "Yes"? I didn't verbally acknowledge how he helped create our exquisite experience. He was, however, amply rewarded for his choice.

Affairs like this remind me I'm in the right place. I'm grateful to share my creative life energy with the people at the party, regardless of their chosen beliefs. Who's going to heaven? I don't think I'm going anywhere. Heaven and hell seems like a dualistic concept and maybe there are more options within that continuum. Maybe heaven is right here if I choose to be positive. I'll admit sometimes I experience hell, when things don't go my way, but usually life's a mixed blessing of getting exactly what I need.

Later that morning, I wake in my own bed. My family of lovers is curious about the party they missed. I start with the glorious sunset, and details of the evening, but when I get to the juicy parts they bombard me with excited questions. Jacy wants to hear everything, and each one's personal fascinations pull the conversation in a different direction. Each has a twist of how they think the night unfolded but in the end, as I reveal the last scene, Jacy says, "You-go-girl."

Allowing myself to venture into uncharted explorations increases my capacity to feel. With this expansion comes reflection on how I use my body, ideas, words and entire psyche. A few days later while watering the garden, as part of my routine walking meditation, my ecstatic state fell from grace into a hell of self-judgment. Allowing freedom triggered an opening into layers of fear, shame and guilt. I don't want to disappoint, be judged, thought of as ugly, wrong, or less than desirable. The mainstream definition of slut is loud in my head—a promiscuous floozy, or a dirty tramp. This is a spiral that reaches into darkness. I lay my belly onto the ground to help me energetically release the physical tightness and nausea related to these thoughts. They reach a depth that can't go any lower, yet the positive thoughts and feelings are all still here, right next to the ones I judge as negative. In feeling the continuum of emotions, there is a calm. I feel the cool grass cushion the weight of my body, as the fresh scent of wet rosemary and jasmine flood my senses.

From this place of stillness I feel sad for the suffering I witnessed at the party. Why did the Christian woman lie to her husband about the necklace? Why did the Rabbi question being *in love*? Why did the father of three want to oppress his daughters, and not trust his wife to be open to the idea of loving more than one person? Why is it such a stretch for best friends to share a sexual experience together? Accepting suffering is my key to returning to bliss.

Once I exhaust my thoughts in that direction, I roll over and look up at the blue sky. I feel the ground supporting my back, and close my eyes. Moving my physical body helps shift my perspective. The woman had practiced telling the truth about the necklace with me, the Rabbi was a great debate starter, and able to provoke a loving conversation, the father was open to seeing the females in his family in a less judgmental way, and the young men negotiated a situation that worked for everyone involved so that we all could enjoy connecting. Each *had* opened up in one way or another.

I rise to a seated position. My plants will get watered soon, but I need a different kind of meditation today. I pray to be non-reactive when I feel challenged, and choose not to suffer over the suffering. I want to be part of creating heaven on earth by being a conduit of an inclusive, peaceful bliss state. I have faith that there's a good punchline ready to be birthed as I think of the Rabbi at the bar, but maybe it's okay just to notice when the joke's on me, and get back to smiling.

EXPLORATION #7

What are your thoughts on judgment?

_____

_____

_____

I experience judgment as the thoughts on the continuum that keep me aware of all possibility. What I judge isn't good or evil, it just is part of the whole picture.

What is your homework on the topic of judging?

_____

_____

_____

Examples:

Have a conversation with a stranger. Are your judgments negative, positive, or just what is possible about this unknown person?

Go on an adventure with two of more friends. Notice all the judgments and remember these are only part of the whole picture. Create a heavenly experience.

Identify one helpful judgment that keeps you out of danger, but may also cause limits that form a cage. Then identify a positive judgment.

Sit and notice five negative judgments. Then stand up and observe the positive aspects of the same five judgments.

Chapter 8

Believe, or Make Believe?

"Did I dream this belief or did I believe this dream?" — Peter Gabriel

Someone once asked me if I believe in reincarnation. My response was lengthy. The short answer is, I don't *believe* in anything. Holding a firm belief on any one thing seems outdated and limiting. I want to remain fluid, able to adapt to the rapid changes in perception, and keep up with the continued evolution of human development. I think I understand some things, until I learn more about them, and there are other things I don't know anything about, yet. I can only hope that if I really need to know something, the understanding will come to me through an experience, teacher, or the miracle of awareness and contemplative thought.

The stubbornness of a mule was once thought to be about fighting moving forward. But after communicating with horses most of my life and observing donkeys and mules at the Grand Canyon, I don't think they're obstinate, it's more about fear and self-preservation. That cliff is real and pain or death could occur if the next step slips. Those smart little furry creatures freeze when they get scared. Stubbornly holding on is often out of fear of the unknown.

Releasing my grasp on a belief is easier said than done. I know how this may sound to anyone raised in a dogmatic religion. Even the most strict conservatives might agree that we'd all just be puppets if we didn't let go of the obsolete parts of the agreed upon rules. I try to keep an open, flexible mind.

With most things in life, there are different points of view that allow us to understand them more completely. My friend Ned said, "If you don't like something, change it. If you can't change it, then change the way you think about it."

"That's a great example of managing the way we react to things. It sounds a bit like the serenity prayer," I say.

Then my, broader thinking friend Ted says, "What about beliefs like women have rights? If I saw someone trying to take that away again, I wouldn't want to just change the way I think about it!"

"Well, that's a strong point," I say. "I want to clarify; I do have a few fundamental *morals*. Human rights are a basic principle of right conduct. I strive to let go of outdated beliefs that no longer serve the higher good. Conversations like these help upgrade our thinking."

If there was a possibility of reincarnation, I probably was a prostitute a few lifetimes. Perhaps a courtesan or concubine, or more recently a hooker, slut, or nymphomaniac. Not just because I love sex, and don't judge having multiple lovers, but because I have a strong sense of how human connection is vital for our survival. In this world where the natural sexual urge is restricted, I can understand how this ancient profession is needed.

Why has sex gotten such a bad rap? Historically there's a logical progression, and somewhere down the line it became important for men to know which children were theirs, so they made rules against adultery. Now with DNA testing that's not our reality anymore, yet sex is still a shame-filled, forbidden act if engaged in outside of the law. Some children are taught to not have sex until marriage because it's a sin, or wrong unless wed. This may have been thought to prepare children for the laws of marriage, too. There were practical reasons like avoiding teenage pregnancy and spreading diseases, but now it seems that sex education would prove to have better compliance. A new way to view our changing world is to respect children by giving them age-appropriate truth, and teaching them how to make educated decisions about their health and the health of their friends. This may be a productive solution to the rebellion against outdated rules.

I don't think it matters if I lived in a past life or not. I just want to live my life as if the consequences of my actions matter now. Maybe I'll be reborn, or go to heaven, get caught up in the rapture, be abducted, or just turn to dust; no one knows these things for sure. I just try not to hold beliefs too firm, because as we gain wisdom and knowledge, I want to be able to change with newly discovered facts.

I examine what's viewed as truth, and often find falsehoods. In school, I learned that some birds were monogamous, but now scientists have studied Aves' mating patterns and found that penguins for example may stay together during a season, but rarely for more than that. With topics such as the origin of consciousness, it was believed that spacetime and objects were the nature of reality—what we perceived with our eyes and senses was actually real. Now scientists have discovered that the brain doesn't cause our perceptions or behaviors, and reality hides the complexity of the world and guides adaptive behavior. Our interpretation of reality is more like intuitive survival instincts that guide us toward procreation of our species.

The process of science rules out what isn't true and points out that there's more to be discovered. We only have speculation and make-believe about these deeper questions. We know there are layers of things happening at the same time—more than what the eye can see. On the surface we can see that a tomato plant grows and produces fruit, but what we don't see is that these plants are utilizing water and specific nutrients from the soil, air, and sun.

When I was three years old I had a vivid dream of flying, about two feet off the ground, around my bed and my sister's bed next to mine. My parents and grandparents were talking down the hall, but they didn't see me. I really believed I flew that night. As I got older I thought there's no way humans can fly, but maybe it was some kind of psychic travel like the clairvoyance that Shirley Maclaine talks about. Perhaps in the future we'll discover that consciousness is the combination of all human brains, animals, insects, plants, even the earth and stones—the total of everything creates our cause and effect. Communication and our ability to take what we understand and add another perspective to the interpretation is part of evolution. Science and technology continues to show that reality's more complicated than our brains can comprehend.

Are some beliefs in the predominant paradigm blindly followed to maintain a false security of the past, in order to avoid the fear of an unknown future? I've heard that people change their beliefs, not release them, but this implies a change to another belief. Perhaps the key to staying fully present (and smiling) is *releasing* past beliefs, admitting I don't know all the answers, and being willing to have a standoff with the fear of the impending future.

Even good things run their course. Feminism was extremely important in the second half of the 20th century. Women were judged as second-class citizens, but now men and women need to focus on optimizing our communication and work together as equals. This movement needs to adapt. Marriages will end. Some will last until one partner dies, but that doesn't mean life's over for the other one. If good things can't adapt with change they become destructive, but when they do adapt they continue to improve life.

With any path, there are brilliant blessings and cruel consequences. The fine edge between dangerous chaos and controlled order is difficult to walk unless you discipline yourself to step confidently like a sure-footed mule. If I take one step at a time and stay alert, then it's possible to go to the bottom of the canyons and the top of the mountain. There's joy in staying present through the pit of the bad experiences, so I don't miss the peak of the good ones, as I develop the skills to navigate the center of my path. In the unfamiliar there's new possibilities. Everything changes, but in the unknown I find hope because we evolve and grow.

EXPLORATION #8

What are your thoughts on beliefs?

_____

_____

_____

I experience beliefs as rigid ideas that tell us how things are. In most cases the world isn't that easy to define. There are multiple ways of viewing most situations.

What is your homework on the topic of beliefs?

_____

_____

_____

Examples:

Recall a belief that someone taught to you. Notice if there are any new ways of looking at that idea now.

Have ten people write two definitions to the same idea. Read them all and count how many different ideas in total.

List three beliefs that have changed for you over the years.

Interview six strangers to give their definition of the same three ideas.

Chapter 9

The Unlearning

"The Earth delights to feel your bare feet, and the winds long to play with your hair." — Khalil Gibran

Saturn return, turning thirty, life seems complicated. It's time to weed out the lies, discover what living in truth means, and unearth the misleading stories I've been told that just don't serve me any longer. Fairy tales, television, movies, plays, billboards, radio, music lyrics, gospel songs, advertising, books, church, school, parents, teachers, friends, peers, new job orientation, language, old sayings, clichés, rules, laws, and societal mores all contain messages about how we're supposed to live and what we're supposed to want. These are some of the information pathways that need updating.

Before now I hadn't questioned clichés, and popular jingles rattling around in my head. Misleading, *backward* sayings distort the truth, and I've been allowing them to influence my naive ignorance. I dive deep to see what's influencing my thoughts and obstructing bliss; I'm both shocked and amused. I quiet my mind to sort through the noise.

I start with the most obvious, and stop watching television. Then I turn off the radio because it influences my mood, and instead choose music based on my desires. Gardening, watering plants, and mindless chores give me space to contemplate. Exercise, as well as helping others through Reflexology, Reiki, and teaching yoga serves as meditation to calm my mind. I reflect on my travels in various countries, studying customs and languages, pursuing a lifelong interest in the origin of words.

I find a dysfunctional cliché, passed on without consideration of meaning or truth—*ignorance is bliss*, and *love is blind*. I'm surprised at the incongruous way they're mixed up. Ignorance has no clue what bliss is, and love sees all. The meaning of ignorant is uninformed; therefore, if one hasn't seen the answer yet then truly ignorance is blind. Likewise, those who experience the state of everything in perfect order know that love is bliss. I must remove my blinders and be in a state of love, to bring sight to my ignorance. Then I can see what's keeping me from bliss. Trying to define love is an endless debate, but in this contemplation, love is the very thing I'm made of, and bliss is the state of knowing this love. Following this train, to love another is simply being love and allowing the other to be love—sharing who I am, and allowing the other to be who they are, together.

I didn't question when I was told—*it doesn't matter what people think of you*. That might sound comforting in the moment if people are judging something stupid I've done, or if someone's just being mean. The more I thought about it, the more it does matter how others perceive me. After talking with hundreds of clients, I realized I'm not alone in taking into consideration the feedback from other people in determining who I am and learning to self-correct. If enough people treat me like I'm not intelligent I may start believing them. Likewise, I discovered that if I *hold my chin up high*, I might be able to convince others and therefore myself that I have worth. Confidence is attractive, and as long as I continue in the direction of proving that worth, the momentum toward success is in my favor. This is why I think it's important to smile, often.

How about—*smile and the world smiles with you, cry and you cry alone?* What a depressing worldview, one badly in need of an attitude shift. I agree that when I see a smile, it frequently triggers a smile on my face. Crying alone, however, is a choice. Next time I feel overwhelmed by a need to cry, I'll try letting it flow with Valerie or Ruth, or call one of my sisters. I've experienced empathy from dear friends when they witness my sadness. I've also been deeply touched by the tears of others.

One cherished memory was not so long ago, at my house with an intimate group of friends. We're all in the mood for fun. The fire is blazing, adding to the ambiance of candlelight. Because of our familiarity, the opening circle check-in, and safer sex updates are brief, leading into three-way kissing and getting naked.

My senses are titillated as I feel the room ebb and flow with waves of orgasms and laughter. Until tonight I was unable to get to the depth of my grief over losing Drake, a cherished lover who'd left us all to be with one person. I've been sad most of the week, but tonight I'm having no problem holding my shit together; in fact, I'm effortlessly enjoying myself. Sex toys are introduced, and I volunteer for an experiment involving a giant silicone penis attached to a Sawzall. My orgasm is epic. This isn't my first dildo-induced orgasm, but I haven't been penetrated that deep since I was last with Drake. As a rush of hormones flood my body, I burst into inconsolable, lamented wailing. I can't use my words, but I want to get it out, so I continue. Without a word, Rona curls her body in front of me, like a little spoon. She falls asleep in my arms, tears wetting her hair, until I empty all the pain out of my heart.

Here's one that's caused generations of damage—*men improve with age, and women age.* I remember my Aunt saying, *Grandpa has become more handsome,* and *men look distinguished with grey hair.*

My young mind interpreted that as: men improve with age, while women just become frumpy. I realize now, from women like Diane Keaton, Meryl Streep, and my own Mother, it's possible to age with grace, beauty and sexuality. They're uniquely gorgeous, and naturally attractive from the inside out. Perhaps there was a time when women weren't allowed to let their inner light shine, and only the physical, aging body was seen. In that old paradigm, only the young, childbearing women were attractive. Men are able to father a child well into their senior years and express their creative energy much more freely than the subservient woman of old. Society labeled the distinguished man and the young woman as most attractive. Now there's more to create on this planet than babies, and we can see creative, life-force energy flow through all people at any age. I'm grateful for the women who came before me making their voices heard, and educating society. Because of them I can express my creative life giving energy in unique and sexy ways.

Another haunting phrase—*a woman's period is the curse*. In actuality, it's a vital ingredient for creativity and magic. During that most blessed time of the month when my awareness is heightened, I've learned about vulnerability, and my connection to nature's cycles. Ancient societies used sacred menstrual blood in ritual, empowering men before battle. There are rites of passage and earth blessings that encourage bleeding on the ground as a symbol of life, health, and strength. I've attended traditional moon lodges, in honor of the women who bleed. They were held at night so we could expose our naked, bleeding bodies to the earth and moonlight. The only curse is the shame directed toward young girls making them feel dirty and unlovable for a week out of every month. My hope is that people become aware of the benefits, and bless the gift of this sacred blood. I celebrate a woman's period as a time of more sensitivity, and heightened sexual arousal.

In an effort to discard outdated information, I acquired a new term. I often find, when I've examined things that I took for granted I become available for new information. Like cleaning out my closet and then happening onto a sale at Nordstrom Rack. I first heard of Ecosexuality from Beth Stephens and Annie Sprinkle. There's a quote from their Ecosex Manifesto in the

Urban Dictionary website that defines ecosexual as, *"Being in love with Earth and giving and receiving pleasure with nature. Exploring the erotic sensuality/sexuality of nature."*

How can nature be sexy? She's definitely chaotic and angry at times. I think of grass and how in late summer the tiny seeds fall into every crack for miles around. If birds, animals and humans didn't keep it eaten, trampled, and cut, this prolific organism could take over the planet. After seeing a few examples, I realize I was born loving nature. I became aware of my life force energy while playing in nature. At first the energy flowing through my body was chaotically unidentified, but by the time I was eleven years old, I discovered sexuality at its origin.

One warm spring morning in my fourteenth year, I flirt with my boyfriend over the back fence. After a few minutes he goes back to his chores and I sit by the swimming pool to write a story for English class. Mom scolds, "Don't talk over the fence with Adam."

"Yes, Mom," I shrug. Finally everyone's inside, and I'm alone. Being told not to flirt is a confusing and frustrating request. I began to explore my voracious sexual appetite. I've been flirting since before I could put complete sentences together. Even more infuriating, is being told not to experiment with my newfound intense energy that grows with excitement when I flirt. Directing all my sexual curiosity and frustration into my writing assignment, to my surprise, I complete it in record time. No need to announce I'm finished with my homework just yet, I take advantage of my little piece of freedom.

I lay my belly on the smooth pebble deck, and begin to feel my skin. Chilled hard stone pressing into my thighs, hipbones and nipples, while the back of my body is tingling beneath the prickly, pinching heat of the sun beating down. As I focus on the bursting sensations, I become more aroused. Reaching my hand down between my legs, my finger dips into wet. Pulling my hand back, a droplet stains the tiny stones. A new scent, it's different from previously smelling my first experience of sex, mixed with Adam's fluids. Unadulterated, my essence is sweeter and salty like butter. My attention is drawn again to the feeling of the sun on my back. Ever so gently, the warmth begins to pierce my skin as if entering into the core of my being. As the intensity of the penetrating sun deepens, my senses climax into a rolling orgasm.

Having a physical orgasm just from the warmth of the sun on my body, allowing myself to feel it from the inside, was one of the landmarks of my sexual relationship with nature. My very first kiss was in nature while riding a horse, I first touched a penis sitting under the stars, and making love in the wilderness has long been my favorite.

I once had an orgasm while sitting in bathwater. Turning the faucet to the right, the water warmed at my feet, and rose up my legs. When the hot water reached the top of my thighs I became breathless, and soon ecstatic orgasmic energy pulsed through my whole body.

A few years later, driving up the coast to visit a friend at the Esalen Institute in Big Sur, for a juicy weekend of adventure, I experienced a stimulating sight. In the distance, a huge water fountain is spraying thirty feet in the air. As I get closer, the great force shooting upward gives me a rush of energy, exciting me sexually. I feel my body wanting to orgasm just from seeing the phallus coming out of the ground and penetrating the sky.

There have been other times when I lay my belly on the ground and give to the earth, releasing my energy into her, while simultaneously feeling her support and cool, vast substance. In my experience, just knowing I'm intimately connected to nature is vital for my human psyche and emotional health. After all, this earth sustains me. I eat from her garden, drink from her rivers, and make shelter from her mud, plants and rocks. Beauty and diversity in every direction is satisfying my endless desire for variety.

In my twenties, I lived in Los Angeles and had a core pod of friends. Before I allowed myself to entertain the notion of being sexually intimate with women, I wrote this poem–inspired by a flirtatious moment when Gaia (one of the pod) stood, straddling over my torso. I didn't stop my gaze from scanning every inch of her naked body. I'd never seen a woman's vagina from that angle, not even my own. That night under the shower, my feelings hiding in a metaphor, I made love to nature rather than the woman herself. Attraction to the same sex was taboo; consequently, shame disguised my fantasy into these cryptic words. Unlike any other poem this one preoccupied me. This poem expresses elements of the unseen threads connecting our world. Nature and spirit feel familiar, like they've always been part of me.

GIFT AT THE WATERFALL

I desire
To describe water touching skin
Yet deeper
Falling through the sky from earth
To earth
Her heart opens
Invites me into her warmth
I smile
She offers a crystal from her depths
Joyful thanks
Celebrate her gift I hold in my hand
But wait
There's more
I feel her touch deep in my soul
I'm home
Life blows with the breeze across my cheek
I breathe in Father Sky
He rushes into the depths of my being
As he enters my body, she licks me
So wet
In the moment I feel their kiss
Ecstasy in my bones
They make love through me
Thank you Great Spirit for the magick
Of life

Gratitude is one of my favorite choices, keeping me in my preferred state of bliss. The shift between what puts a smile on my face, and what drags it off, can be such a slow process that I don't notice I've stopped smiling. I declare bliss my *normal* state, and relax, allowing life to flow with ease. This makes it easier to notice when I'm not smiling. Sometimes I feel miserable. *Misery loves company*—a saying that at first glance seems true, and doesn't belong in this chapter. A peak experience can often shift me back into bliss, but as I inquire into misery I discover old, subconscious patterns running under the surface, pulling me down into that sticky place where my mind loops in the thought—I am the miserable part of humanity. I identify that old thought, name it, and remember it's a part of me, but not all of me. It becomes clear that I'm choosing this pattern, and I simply observe the negative energy as it flows through me.

Feeling miserable may be due to seeing a friend's perplexing film on the big screen, or perhaps observing Drake discover a new lover without me. Having one of my favorite people tell me he's allocating more time to other people in his life, and being torn because of wanting to go with Jacy and his girlfriend on a trip that I already said no to, are all possible excuses for my misery. Overwhelmed, I fight with myself trying to get my head straight. That night, a strange dream reminds me of the pure, unrestrained bliss in my heart. Waves of orgasmic energy run through my chest as I wake with a gasping start. I write to the person in the dream, as a way to bring that energy to life, and in the morning awake with a new clarity. I'm not in misery, or searching for something external that's causing me to be miserable. I'm simply not seeing all the possibilities, and am stuck in identifying as the miserable one. Instantly I'm free, and choose to look deeper, untangling my upset emotion.

I start with my most dominant thought. The *searching perspective*, also known as the *seeker* is closely related to *the one who wants to be attached to another*. This perspective searches for a beloved to attach to, get satisfaction, and feel complete. Yet, for me this doesn't lead to bliss. *Misery loves company?* The searching, unsatisfied, needy, stuck, attached, miserable perspectives want to have another to connect with. The attached perspective, wants the object of attachment to also be attached in return. That's the *loves company* part. If the object of the attachment is not suffering along with the one wanting to attach, then it feels unloved. I use the word *it* because it's a perspective, making up only part of the whole, therefore it's not I, or you! The one who wants to feel love from another is not I, it's a perspective that I've unwittingly, wholly identified with. Feeling unloved is an impossible thing because I am love, and can never get it from anything outside of myself. I can only share what I am with another, and allow them to share the love they are with me, or with anything they choose.

I'm not in bliss when I cling to one point of view. I forget my thoughts aren't all of me, get caught in this illusion, and consequently feel unloved. Here's where it gets a little Zen, or my rendition of Zen, where everything seems to be contradicting everything else. From the perspective of the observer, I clearly see that what I identify with isn't who I am. This permits me to release the identification of thinking I'm only the seeking one. I allow all those thoughts and triggered emotions, to flow through me like a river, wind, or a *wild* fire. Then I see all the perspectives streaming through me all the time; I am the seeking one, an unloved, unsatisfied, needy, stuck, attached, miserable person. But then I'm also the observer, an empowered choice-maker.

The realization is, I'm none of these thoughts, perspectives, emotions, and yet all of them are part of me, flowing through me. Not blocking unwanted thoughts or feelings is just as important as opening up to wanted thoughts and emotions. Humans have done things, felt things, and interpreted stories for so many years, and this conditioning can imprint in our feeling bodies. They seem so *normal* that we think we *are* the feeling, thought or perspective. True freedom is when I embrace the feeling, identify the thought, and see the perspective as a choice.

When I notice that I'm choosing to identify with one particular thought, I tap into and allow the associated feelings. Then, I look for the opposing perspectives to that thought. The more perspectives I can see, including their opposing counterparts, the faster everything shifts. No more pain, suffering, misery, or the insatiable feeling of endlessly searching for something to attach to. The one that feels left out will always be there, but that isn't what defines me. All negative thoughts flow alongside the empowered, happy and brilliant ones, and are available for me to choose which one gets the tongue, when I want to speak. As soon as all the viewpoints are present, it becomes a simple choice—peaceful bliss. The edges of my mouth relax upward, and I feel the smile on my face. A deep breath enters my lungs. For the first time in days, all the elements are flowing with ease in my body, creating a state of health and happiness.

The word *empowered* reminds me of the saying—*power corrupts; absolute power corrupts absolutely*. When a person is handed a position of power, or wins the lottery and with it the power that money can buy, they may not be psychologically equipped for the change in circumstances. If they don't have a broad understanding of the world or themselves, and aren't able to see all of the perspectives, then the accelerated experiences that power affords can lead to their corruption. On the contrary, if they are capable of compassion, understanding multiple points of view, and knowing how to make decisions for the highest good, then it's possible to have a benevolent person with power.

What if compassion is the opposite of corruption? If a compassionate person knew the good, the bad, and the ugly, they'd see how it's all part of the whole. A compassionate being, with a developed ability to predict consequences, could empathize with those affected by their power. This wise person would be aware of both the corrupt side, and the evolved positive aspects of things. Compassionate power expands in all directions at a strong, rapid rate, and becomes inclusive. If those in power are capable of generosity and moderation along with their greed and gluttony, then there's hope that they'll make wise choices.

There are layers to unlearning, and untangling beliefs. After resting in bliss for a while, I noticed I'm still feeling uneasy from viewing a friend's feature length movie in a popular theater downtown. I may simply be in a letdown state after the big high of seeing friends on the silver screen. Before the movie premier started, one of the stars led the audience in a sex magic exercise. Moving life force energy through my body, and envisioning what I intend to create in my life, was magnified by doing it along with a packed theater. I felt on top of the world experiencing this creative energy that I cherish.

I feel triggered about the final cut of the movie. Uninformed audiences could easily misinterpret the unorthodox ideas; it's a complicated message. It takes until the next day for me to get clarity. The main thread in the film is a man wanting to be in a primary relationship with a woman named Maya, undoubtedly named after the Hindu goddess of illusion. It's an illusion to think it's possible to own anyone, or think anyone can take away another's freedom of choice. In my thirty plus years of experience, the most obvious benefit of open relationships is that each person has freedom to choose whom they want to be with. Having choice keeps relating fresh and real, instead of people staying together out of obligation or complacency.

In the film, the editors create a storyline that made the hero/protagonist appear to use sex magic to try and sway this elusive lover to come back to him. I didn't like the potential of audiences getting confused about the purpose of sex magic. He was also discovering his own healed masculine/feminine within. His own masculine side was calling his feminine into harmony. I could relate to his tortured process because when I discovered my inner marriage of masculine and feminine I explored outside of myself, projecting the lover that I am onto others and then lamenting if I was rejected.

The movie demonstrates that the deep, inner wound of sexual shame, self-judgment, and antiquated beliefs can be upgraded. It reveals brave and willing healing practitioners helping others, and providing examples of how an individual acts when the masculine and feminine within them has been examined and allowed to mature. I remember my shame of being vulnerable and imperfect. It's human nature to compare ourselves to someone who is better than us or has already learned a difficult lesson. I was humbled by the character's journey in this real movie. Seeing him sob with grief conjured my guilt of wanting to control a lover. I was stirred up, and I slipped into the trap of identifying with the controller inside of me.

How do I catch myself when I'm not smiling from the inside out, and the outside in? When I set my standard to have a true smile that's congruent from my face to my cells, and from my healthy cells to my lips, then all I need to do is check in with my face. I release any attachment to a single point of view, so I can follow inspiration on my personal path of bliss. Once I affirm what direction I'm heading, I need momentum. I remind myself to start with a small win. My favorite example is when faced with the daunting chore of housekeeping, I start with the bathroom (the smallest room). With a sense of accomplishment I feel happier and gain more energy to move forward. Next I may clean the second bathroom because then I've got 2 out of the 9 rooms in my house completed—well on my way to accomplishing the bigger goal.

These little steps forward are the foundation to a fulfilled life. *It's the little things in life that make us happy.* As do the bigger things, but I won't know how to handle success if I haven't learned how to appreciate the little wins that got me there. This is a glimpse at my process, and how I keep my feet on the Earth, untangle the complexities of reality, and remain smiling.

EXPLORATION #9

What are your thoughts on sexual shame?

_____

_____

_____

I experience sexual shame as a core wounding as humans in physical bodies. We are taught sex is wrong, but because we have masculine and feminine energies within, we take on the shame of our inner nature. We are also born from this shameful act. If we have shame around our sexual core it affects every aspect of being.

What is your homework on the topic of sexual shame?

_____

_____

_____

Examples:

Recall six feminine and six masculine qualities. Do you feel more shame around the feminine or the masculine qualities?

Ask five people if they can identify what sexual shame feels like. How does it feel to talk about sexual shame with others?

Write about a time that an adult reacted automatically toward a young person and passed on their shame.

Identify three times you have felt shame, and tell a partner.

Chapter 10

Learning to Play Chess

"Whether you think you can, or you think you can't, you're right."
— Henry Ford

The most fundamental lesson I learned started in Ireland many years ago. It's at the foundational bottom layer of a pyramid. The mystery I sensed on that island was similar to the way I felt when I was 12 years old, the first time I climbed to the top of the 98-foot pyramid in Chichén Itzá, Mexico. The layers of information and unanswered questions were stacked up beneath my feet, and revealed as I watched and listened. Climbing that great structure was like walking from one goalpost to the other on a football field, only straight up 91 gigantic steps. After returning to the grassy floor, my papa pointed out the serpent's head, and I realized we had been climbing on a cleverly disguised, coiled snake. I also did the math, and the number of stairs on all four sides totaled 364, plus when the top platform was added there was one step for each day of the year. Two ton stones were quarried, transported and placed to build these temples with only chisels, logs and people power.

Whether talking about a physical structure or

Maslow's hierarchy of needs as steps to self-actualization and transcendence, the base is the valuable ingredient needed before proceeding upward to the next layer of development. Lessons return again and again, disguised in new scenarios to be replayed, until they're integrated and solidified. Only after a step has been properly constructed can the next step be built.

Lessons are often more complicated than at first glance, there are multiple layers. Imagine a checkerboard with little round pieces on the surface, some black, and some red. Look down and notice that you're round and red. Where are you going? You can jump, and learn that the purpose is to become two stacked pieces, together as one, on the other side of the board. Reach that goal and say *King me*, you're still here, but with more abilities. Try it a few times as red, and then try it as black, but all you do is go back and forth across the board.

One night you go to sleep and wake up as a pawn. It's the same familiar checkered board, but all the pieces have come to life in a new way. This game is more complex. The round pieces showed that taller is better, and black or red is a choice; so now you choose to be the castle. Learn how to slide and guard. As soon as you master the moves, choose a different one. The knight is fun, on such an agile horse. The intimidating Queen is so free and important. One day, quite by accident, you awake as the Queen. It's thrilling. You can do whatever you want, and that's the same day you realize the importance of the pawns.

Eventually you choose to hop along as a pawn. By this time you know the value that the other pieces possess, and figure out how to choose which one to be. Without each of them there'd be no game. From the pawn's point of view you study interacting, and moving toward the goal. Soon recognizing your importance—if you reach the other side, you too can be Queen. What about the King? If we're energetically connected to everything then the king is always a part of you.

It's Drake's birthday weekend. He and I've played chess, without sitting at a board, for two years. We make our moves, with glances, texts, and role-playing during sex. If an issue is triggered in one, the other steps up to be a sounding board, providing feedback and clarity to find balance. We've been one another's muses since our first glance.

That auspicious first meeting was exactly two years ago today. It was Drake's birthday then as well. I walk across the patio wearing only my towel, drop it at the poolside, and step into the steaming Palm Desert Hot Springs. As the towel slips from my fingers, I glance around at all the eyes that have turned to the newcomer, smiling and greeting each of them. I lower into the water; coming full circle around the pool, suddenly I freeze. It's undetectable to those in the pool, because my body continues to lower into the water. Everything inside me instantly stops, and reloads as I glimpse into Drake's eyes. It's only a split second. Covered in water to his neck, mostly hidden by the young woman sitting on his lap, but when I see his eyes, I can't look away fast enough. Danger I think, what am I seeing? How can there be an attraction when I can't see him, smell him, or hear his voice? All I see is a little grey hair, pale white skin, and blue. I'm shocked at how much detail the brain records in a split second, with so many other thoughts going on at the same time.

My heart's racing; maybe it's the hot water. Not good timing as Jacy and I were fighting on the drive up, and the platonic friends we're vacationing with aren't involved in our open lifestyle. It's an inopportune time to meet new lovers, or is it? Jacy and I've been together for a couple of years, and the only other lovers in our lives are my previous lovers of many years. Afraid, curious, cautious, but my excitement is harnessed with the intention of seeking the highest good for all.

Not wanting to act on selfish motives, I decide not to pursue this obvious attraction, feeling that it's not appropriate at this time. Then Jacy says, "I'm attracted to one of the guests at the resort."

My heart jumps with the thought that it might be Felina, the woman sitting on Mr. Blue Eyes. Indeed it is. The stars are aligning faster than I can imagine.

I ask the alluring couple, "Will you join us for an after-hours soak?"

"We were hoping you'd ask," Felina says.

The conversations reveal that Drake is a health professional, and has much in common with Jacy and me. Our shared values intrigue me. The four of us are in the warm tub, exchanging stories like excited school kids. Then it happens; below the surface of the water, Drake's hand brushes past my leg. It's like an electric current ran through my entire body, shooting up and out the top of my head, stimulating every inch along the way. As we continue to talk, I begin to sense how much we're clicking, and I feel we're resonating together. Drake's knowledge of the human body, overall honesty and intelligence captivates me. I like how he helps others, and who he is in the world delights me.

Jacy and Felina are engaged and focused on the temperature of the water, and the stars. I look at my pruned hands, just as Drake asks, "Do you all want to come to our room, where it's dry and we can stay warm?"

Jacy, Felina and I answer with a synchronistic, "Yes."

Soon, all four are snuggle in a warm bed. We agree that sex would be fun to explore, and complete our safer sex conversations. The forces between Drake and I are unstoppable. Desire is ignited, and the room is barely big enough to contain our passion. His deep blue eyes engage mine, and we slowly initiate with a gentle firm touch. Our bodies are eager and ready. I feel my sex spill out onto my inner thigh as I intently roll a condom up his long shaft. As Drake slides his magical wand into my eager body, he completely fills me. Time has no relevance, only pure pleasure. With superhuman strength he lifts me with ease, and slams me up against the wall as we continue wildly fucking.

Viewing with eyes of wonder from the other side of the bed, our lovers, Jacy and Felina, continue at their much slower and graceful pace. Sweetly talking, kissing and caressing, they delight in discovering one another's bodies with their own momentum. I enjoy the unique expressions of passion and romance. Investigating the myriad of ways to connect with another is divine.

Exploring late into the night, until we lay spooning, smiling and exhausted. What creates such strong attractions? Am I paying attention with multiple parts of my brain? My visual cortex likes what I see. The kinesthetic part is lit up; the way Drake feels is exhilarating, familiar and desirable. I'm turned on by his stories, and understand what he's saying, so the auditory parts of my brain are engaged. But I didn't have any of that information at the moment of our instant attraction. Does the way our body shapes fit together confirm some unknown visual communication from our initial glance? Is it an esoteric phenomenon of our frequencies energetically matching up? Or simply that a fantasy of what I thought I wanted was erected from the deep, spilling out into the waking life?

More than one love seems natural; I can't remember a time in my life when I only loved one person. Each person shows me new parts of myself to help me grow and evolve. Each relationship dynamic is unique, and some people who love more than one person express it differently than me. Loving more than one person deeply isn't a standard lifestyle choice. I tried the cookie cutter or normal lifestyle choice once, and came dangerously close to death.

The strong erotic and intellectual connection with Drake and Felina turns us into fast friends. It's a small, half-empty resort. We have plenty of time to discover each other over the next few days. Getting to know Drake and Felina, we trek through an oasis in the desert. Jacy and Drake talk about their similar professions, while Felina and I marvel at the towering palm trees shading tiny animal prints in the sand. There's a sparkle on the trickling water, whistling wind brushing my skin, and the fragrant blooming sage wafts through the air. Loving a new person doesn't take away from my love for the other intimate partners in my life. Instead, each partner makes me more aware of my whole self, and juices my enthusiasm for exploring life in a unique way with each one. When new partners are added, there's increased opportunity for everyone to evolve, leapfrog information, and learn from the others. Jacy and I want to see more of our new friends, soon. We did; now, two years later, I've planned a special birthday celebration for one of my closest friends.

Creating a weekend getaway provides the chance to relax, and prepare for his new year. I chauffeur Drake down the coast to our chosen play destination. My intuition is right, getting away from his responsibilities, and everyday life is the best gift I can give him. Well, almost. Hours of relaxing with his guitar reignite his musical creativity. Drake's grateful for this opportunity, and I'm happy to listen to this talented and accomplished musician. We hike through elegantly carved sandstone hills overlooking the ocean, relax under a huge Banyan tree in the park, and eat home-cooked food, with hours of lovemaking dispersed throughout each day.

Our sexual connection is probably the only one I've experienced that doesn't improve every time we come together; it was that good from the start! Each divergent mating encounter is unique, depending on how we synchronize. Diving deep into the twisted psyche of mankind, and emerging on the other side with a renewed appreciation of what it takes to be whole. With a passionate ability to relate through our sexual expression we fall into each other's eyes as the submerged stories surface to be played out. Uncensored, unedited, the dark and the light, terrifying at times, but so good to have terror mirrored back in a safe way. This is real.

This birthday weekend is about giving Drake a deep level of care, so that he may discover desires for his new year. Ritual is a cherished tool I use to usher one through the gateway, into the next step on life's path. Traditions and routine can be a part of ritual, but it has an extraordinary element of mystique. Birthdays

136

are my favorite occasion, because of the obvious opportunity to give focused attention to the one entering the gate into their new year. There are many ways to do ritual, but the main ingredient is intention.

The timing works perfectly, and I introduce Drake to Katie. The night is progressing charmingly. What an exquisite scene; her naked body, his overflowing joy, my excitement and love for both of them. Feeling everything he's feeling, ecstatic new energy entwining with ours. She and I honor and celebrate his birth, and life with a three-way kiss. Our kisses cover the entirety of his body, as he watches and caresses each of us.

What an example of being the King. He's full of gratitude for the opportunity to let go. We're both overflowing by the time we head back to his place, and it'd be impossible to mask our smiles, but thankfully we don't have to. It's good to live a life where we don't need to sneak around or lie to other partners.

Getting back in my car to return home I feel abundant love, along with the letdown of leaving my close companion. It's a long drive, but I still need more reintegration time before returning home. I drive to my favorite hideaway, where I go when I need a break from my existence. I escape to the big screen, and go into the Chronicles of Narnia. Strangely, I identify most with little Lucy, who in Narnia is the Queen. She's brave, facing her fears of wanting to be her older sister. Realizing she's in the right place even when she doesn't know why, or how she got there. Her intuitive gift is listening, and she gracefully accepts her destined role. They won't return to Narnia after they become adults.

This brings up questions in my mind—is Narnia a symbol of innocence? Maybe it's like the receptive state of mind called the beginner's mind. This reminds me of being like a little child to enter the kingdom of heaven. Can't anyone, at any age, access any dimension that's outside the ordinary? Then I shift gears, and question whether my takeaway is about the narcissistic child inside, always wanting things their way. It's so easy to get upset when I don't get what I want, even though I know not to set up expectation, I still react when things don't go my way. Maybe the expectations come from my childhood when I made choices of how the world should be, before I was cognizant of creating hidden meanings. No wonder disappointment can sneak up on me even when I think I'm being diligent.

I've been denying my inner narcissistic child. She's worthy of love and acceptance. She wants to be special and the truth is she's always special. Nothing on the outside can make me special. I'm relieved to know that I unconsciously created how I see the world based on the way my five-year-old self saw it. I had gone into this movie to avoid my world, and now I can't wait to embrace it. I want to see my world as my little self saw it, and share my adult wisdom with her self-centered mindset with the intention of growing up.

Just yesterday, I faced a similar fear when I shared my beloved girlfriend with Drake. What if Katie's better than me? What if Drake chooses her? Vulnerable, in the state of not knowing what's next, I realized that I can't control every possible outcome. The fear's fleeting as I breathe into feeling all the emotions present inside. Slowing down my thoughts until I can see the bigger picture. The reality is Drake can choose both of us! Katie isn't better than me; we just play different roles. Each of us has unique talents that can't be replaced. My mind stays open to the possibility of loving and living in an innocent, more inclusive way. Not closing off to fit into some concocted idea of adulthood, irrelevant to the reality of what's actually happening in the moment.

Knowing that what I offer may be exactly what's needed in any moment calms my mind. I can't control the roles played by the people around me, but I appreciate the choices that move each piece on the chessboard, making the game possible. Staying present and being my best is enough.

Ireland is where I realized I wasn't playing checkers anymore. I wake up as a pawn on Tara, the hill where Kings had been initiated for centuries. The morning of our venture, up this mystical hilltop, our small group is met with resistance. Sal, Morgan, Shain and I get a late start after a night of singing folk music in a local pub. We aren't accustomed to such quantities of thick, black, easy-to-swallow beer. Finally, all buckled in, and starting to roll, we notice our car has a flat tire. It's tempting to go back to bed, but I've had a strong pull to be on that little mount since I arrived on the island. It's a Holiday and the shops are closed. Shain waves down a Peace Officer, passing by on his beat. His buddy owns a nearby mechanic shop, brought us a tire, and soon we're on the road.

It's an Irish summer with long northern days, and my sense of time is askew. A few days earlier we'd been driving in the country at dusk when we pulled into a small town for dinner, to find everything was closed because it was 10PM! Lack of sleep is a plus when communing with fairies, elves, and gnomes, but less helpful for the more mundane like eating.

We drive for hours, stopping along the way at an ancient castle for food and chocolate. Morgan and I walk into a wooded area with soft moss-like grass and dainty flowers next to the parking area. "Shhh, look!" I point at a rustling shrub as a creature about a foot tall illusively vanishes.

"I thought I saw Pixie just over here!" Morgan whispers as she points in the opposite direction.

I wonder how much the chocolate and Genius Stout contributed to opening the veils between our known world and the magical world of Avalon? Finally, we arrive at Tara.

Walking across the grass to buy our admission passes, we hear the announcement on the loudspeaker, "We're closing for the evening."

Disappointment crosses our faces, but before we can respond the curator says, "You can join the last tour." The tour consists of an elderly woman and her eight-year-old granddaughter. We must skip the historical movie, and tour of the artifacts inside, but with smiles we run to catch up with our group on the bright-green hill. Bard, our guide says, "From the top, the entire island can be viewed."

I exclaim, "I see the ocean to the south!"

Smiling at my enthusiasm Bard continues, "Imagine an ancient chessboard, where the kings strategize their moves." Then he asks, "Where are you from?"

"California," Sal replies.

When Bart discovers we're Americans, he says, "A Native American woman performed a ceremony on the land beneath our feet a few hours ago."

My eyes light up, "Wow."

"I'm fascinated with the similarities between the Celtic and American natives," Bart says.

"Me too," I say. This sparks an exchange that's excited and enthusiastic like schoolmates sharing what we did on summer break. "I'm reading about Celtic traditions right now, and have studied Shamanism from my Native American ancestors," I say.

"My education's in my ancestral Celtic culture. Today, the ceremony I witnessed was from another land but was similar to ours," Bard says.

We make our way to the large phallic stone implanted in the ground like a pillar, and Bard instructs the women to walk around it. The grass is trodden down to dirt around the stone. Morgan remarks, "The four women in our march represent the stages of womanhood."

Looking down the hill, I see a father with three young girls, reminding me of my Dad and sisters. I'm no longer that little girl. I graduated from a virgin maiden years ago, though the eight-year-old in our group fits that description. I'm not yet a mother, not sure where the queen fits in, but I've many years before becoming the wise crone. I've heard that middle stage referred to as the goddess, queen or warrior woman. That's me, I'm the queen.

The virgin maiden, wearing a Nirvana cap, is out of her mind with excitement to learn I'd met Kurt Cobain before she was born. Touching the end of my (queen's scepter) extended finger, she hoots and jigs around like a leprechaun.

Our little tour walks down to the standing stones, erected for the choosing and initiation of the king. Bard says, "The knights raced their horses between these extremely narrow stone gates, and the last one remaining on their horse was crowned king. This is also the place where the old kings were buried."

"Layers of history, culture, and other worldly events, all compress together under our feet," Sal comments. No one says anything, only the wind rippling the tall green grass behind us.

That night I slip into a multi-dimensional dream; I see my present life, and simultaneously an ancient life. In the past one, I'm a virgin girl, blindfolded and taken to a cave by the elder women. The cave's pitch dark, warm, and smells of peat moss and fresh cut branches. They disrobe me and lay my body on a bed of soft leaves, then abandon me. I wait anxiously, with a sense of honor and wonder, as I've been chosen for the initiation ceremony. This yearly event is an integral part of our tribe's prosperity and evolution. It's a symbolic ritual uniting us, igniting each soul's purpose, giving a fresh start, and inspiring each member to give wholeheartedly in the following year.

In the distance there's a faint drumbeat, cheering and an occasional scream. I hear the crackle of a fire just outside the cave. Lying still, I begin to hallucinate. Was the water, or soup I was given earlier, laced with a psychedelic sacrament? They would have prepared me for such a journey. It didn't taste or feel anything out of the ordinary. My dreaming mind agrees this doesn't feel drug induced. I've experienced this type of seeing before.

At first the visions are sporadic—animals, places, and faces I recognize from both worlds. Suddenly, all is clear. As if I'm a hawk, I soar out of the cave, down the hill, just beyond a group of drummers. Brown skinned men dancing around a raging fire with white clay painted all over their bodies. Ghost dancers. How did I know that? What are they doing here? Then my focus turns to a group of young men with their bellies on the cool grass in the center of my clan. I can't see their faces.

A feeling pulls strongly on my heart and loins. He's coming. The chosen one is blindfolded, further disguising his identity, and is escorted by the elders up the path toward the cave. Maybe he's one of my childhood friends, who was taken away for training and initiation years ago with all the boys his age, but which one? Had they returned as men on their strong horses? Will I be able to feel who he is when he's here next to me? What if I'm wrong, and he's from a different land? Why can't I see his face? My body begins to shake with waves of fear, each surge becoming more intense. Suddenly, they approach the entrance. I freeze. They enter the cave in silence, and I strain to hear his robe fall to the ground.

The powerful anticipation almost wakes me from the dream, but I slow my breath and go back under. Led to the edge of the nest where I lie, he is left standing. The drumming is closer now, and the beat slows my racing heart. Finally, he reaches down, touches my thigh, and begins gently exploring with his hand over my skin. Neither of us have any idea who the other is. After what seems like hours of exciting exploration, he lowers his body down onto mine. His smell is not foreign, his energy's familiar, and his kiss brings the recognition of my friend's long awaited return. As we consummate our reunion, shifting from childhood mates into the adult world, we infuse vital enthusiasm into humanity, sparking a renewal of life once again. We make love until the sun comes up.

As I open my eyes, I'm alone in a little bed, in a cottage with a grass roof, peat smoldering in the fireplace, a changed woman. I've undergone an initiation, and can see how I'm an integral part of a bigger plan—not just living my life for me, but it's clear that how I live influences others around me. I'm still aware of my humble insignificance, but I also see my virtue. No longer a little round piece, I've moved from checkers to chess, and have begun my education of the different pieces, learning to identify with each of them.

The weekend in Palm Desert, meeting my muse with my dear beloved, opened my eyes to playing chess with Masters. The Masters who experience being different chess pieces, and who play each one well. Again I'm reminded of my father who was a well-loved doctor. He also loved my stepmother, and she often shared age-appropriate stories of how fun and romantic he was as a husband. He was a tenor in a quartet and played the trombone. He was also a good farmer, growing our food, and a rancher with many animals and horses. He was not only proficient at many things, he was also a patient teacher and helped many medical students as well as his six children to gain from his wisdom. I'm humbled by the caliber of people with whom I experience life. These mentors and lovers are my trusted friends. Who am I in the lives of those closest to me? Do I affect you in the way these Masters influence me?

In order to master the game, I acknowledge that I have all the pieces inside, choose which one to play at any given time, and do my best in each role. I keep my eye on the board and make eloquent moves. Life has ups and downs, but as I play along I gain experiential wisdom. I listen intently to the part of me wanting to express, so it can be heard and allowed.

Watching and staying open without clutching onto one perspective takes practice. I remain vigilant to keep a strong point of view from igniting the opposite reaction that may have repeatedly played out between warring perspectives for generations. Being present to all perspectives can be a balancing act, allowing each one to be heard while not getting caught up in any single point of view. Knowing when and how to express a point of view is sometimes the greatest challenge.

The fundamental lessons are about being love, staying present, holding space for those around me to feel free, and making choices that contribute to the highest good of everyone involved. Each individual is a vital piece in the evolution of all the players on the board. There are extreme opinions on opposing sides of any topic, as well as many points in between. If I communicate with kindness, and learn to see the opposing points of view, there'll be less separation. It may be more courageous to find common connections than ignore people's extreme opposing opinions. When my values align with those around me, there's harmony. This synergy is fruitful. It's fun working and creating with those who're willing to see beyond the obvious differences.

Life's much more intricate than the game of chess. There are multiple parts of reality happening simultaneously, similar to the layers of history that I saw on the land in Ireland—five generations of homes were built in a row, each one using a standing wall from the family before them. Hundreds of years from crumbled stones to an occupied standing home, and every stage of decay in-between.

By sharing my ideas I assist those around me. I choose wisely because each choice creates my next move. I'm responsible for knowing what role I'm playing, and how to play impeccably so that those closest to me can be stronger, see further, and make the moves that will influence the players closest to them. Not only am I the King, I'm also the opposing King, and the Queen and the pawns, knights, castles, etc. the whole time. I'm every perspective, and at exactly the same time I'm not any one of them. When I die I may realize I'm also the chessboard.

EXPLORATION #10

What are your thoughts on your identity and perspectives?

_____

_____

_____

I experience myself as capable of holding multiple perspectives and identifying with many roles.

What is your homework on the topic of identity and perspectives?

_____

_____

_____

Examples:

Look in a mirror and ask yourself, what do I see?

Ask five people how they would describe you.

How many different hats do you wear in any given week?

Pick a topic then give three different explanations of that thing or topic.

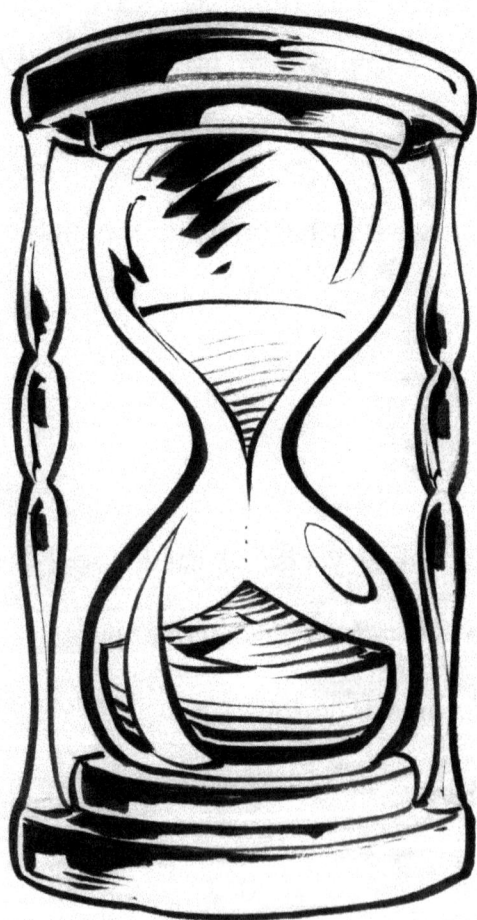

Chapter 11

Healing with Time

"Carpe diem! Rejoice while you are alive; live life to the fullest; make the most of what you have. It is later than you think." — Horace

Some people say time is speeding up. When contemplating the vastness of time, I look to the past. I'm not certain about much, but I know that 40 years ago, I heard my Grandfather say that time is accelerating, and that clocks used to have only an hour hand. As a child—looking forward to turning 16 and driving a car, or waiting for playmates to arrive—time moved slowly. As an adult, I prefer time not pass so quickly. Sometimes I wish for earlier times. I move slower now, so time appears to move faster. Perceptions depend on what's between me and where I'm looking.

Sometimes it feels like time is just an illusion, but it appears to be recordable using basic mathematical science. I love using the camera to play with time and document moments, changes and growth—capturing something as elusive as a memory.

Time, relative to earthly events can be a mind trip. I was

25 and my father was 50, half his age already. I felt old. Then before I knew it, feeling half-of-a-century stress, I realize time and how I feel about it, is all perspective. A few hours before the stroke of midnight, ending the year before my 50th birthday, I wrote this essay and poem:

50 is The New 21

I can still see the silky brunette with sparkling blue eyes and a bright smile entering the room filled with guests celebrating her 50th birthday. Mother still dyed her hair black. She had just happily married for the 3rd time.

Last year I purposefully had a big 49th party, and was planning to skip this one, but Mom wouldn't let it go. She hadn't fussed over my birthday in 33 years. Why now?

I was fine as long as I didn't think about my age, or the idea of announcing it to everyone. Still I felt a twinge of guilt for leaving my first "husband" when he was 49, which was just unfortunate timing. Avoiding is what I did with him, but I'm not avoiding anymore. So now why all the angst over a silly number?

Two weeks later, still pissed with Mom for making me face my predicament, I sat intoxicated on red wine by a raging fire with one of my closest friends. He empathized with my lament of feeling old, and mirrored back my skewed perception of turning 50. I felt completely heard.

Within a few days I smile, noticing how vibrant I feel, almost eager to reach this new right of passage. Forty was cool, but this is indescribable. I wanna do stuff, be better, and somehow learn to love more extravagantly. I want to surrender completely to a lover, and learn how to melt the strongest man into submission. I want my girl to swoon when I kiss her luscious lips, learn how to command the molecules in a room when I play guitar and sing, and speak in a way that inspires others. I want to go places, learn and create.

This morning in the shower, as I rinse away the sleep and sex juices, these words come to me: *50 is the new 21*. There's a new flavor of elixir of life to fill my belly. I'll be the drunken lover of life, taking it in and flowing it out like there's no tomorrow. I still feel 28, but with more insight and much calmer. So much more to give back, so much joy to create, ecstasy to share, Love to be.

Happy to be where I am. Happy Birthday to me!

50, THE NEW 21

50, the new 21
Anticipation
Drink the elixir

Rite of Passage
Sweet 16 no more
Vibrant, yet calm

Rinse away avoidance
Not even close to done
Listen, Sing, Inspire
Freedom

Time captures my attention. I continue to be curious how others relate with me in time. There's a natural pace of doing things. When someone's pace is similar to mine, it's part of how we synchronize. As a young person, I often felt out of sync with time. I didn't fit in. I now realize there's validity to learning how the world works, while balancing it with my own creative interpretation. Learning to interact with others and communicate in inclusive and inspiring ways became a valued focus. There are times I'm out of integrity, trying to act how I'm expected to, but things are not aligned. There are times I'm not proud of. Out of sync, unable to align with others, over the years I've begun to understand how to heal the incongruences. It's now a top priority to align with the people in my life, and be at ease with where I am in time and space.

There are many aspects of time to explore as it relates

to the physical reality of this planet. Once while daydreaming, I wonder if I'd been somewhere before I journeyed there, like a time traveler. Sometimes when meeting for the first time, a stranger can feel like an old friend. I don't necessarily identify with a beginning or an ending in relationships. Most intimate relationships are in present time, in my heart. I have a sense that I'll always know you, even after we're dead. Pinpointing when we first met is tricky as well, like when I see a movie and fall in love with actors, then realize I'd seen them in movies before, but just hadn't discovered them yet. There have been times when a person amazes me the first time we meet. It isn't clear why—maybe it's as simple as my fantasy of what I think I need aligns with that person on that particular day. Or perhaps, when I'm paying attention with all my brain, and someone lights up my visual cortex with the way they move or look, and the kinesthetic part of my brain adores the way they feel even from across the room, and if what they're saying is easy to listen to and makes logical sense to me, all at the same time, then I am wowed. I desire to explore a deeper connection with that person. The day I meet such a person is remembered like the first time I saw fireworks on the 4th of July.

I'm learning how to be responsible with how much time I have left, and where I choose to spend it. I had an awakening experience with the concept of time many years ago. I was practicing Standing Tai Chi with two beloveds—my partner Jacy, who's also my teacher, and live-in lover Tracy. The three of us stood in a circle on the grass, by a tall eucalyptus, arms outstretched in a hug-like position above our heads. Starting to shake, the second hand ticking 690, 691, 692… Burning muscles, arms slowly inching downward, emotions surfacing, and there it was: complete awareness that I'm choosing this moment—no place I'd rather be than standing, fully present, with two lovers.

One day, I agree to assist with a woman's circle in the high desert. It's my first time with this group, but I've known the organizer Shawna for years. I'm drawn to deepening our friendship, perhaps with more physical intimacy. I also plan to visit our mutual lover Timmy while in their town for the weekend.

I arrive early. "Can I clean and arrange seating? It's an honor to help create sacred space for the circle," I say.

"Thank you," Shawna says, and hands me a rag. I feel a bit out of place, but Shawna is grateful for my help, and asks, "Will you greet the arriving guests?"

As each participant enters, I smile. "Glad you're here. May I hug you?" I ask.

With each hug, I feel a deeper level of welcome myself, and by the time we circle around, I'm at home and open to what's next.

We begin the opening circle. I let go of little hiccups in my psychology. I prefer the concept of being present in the moment, releasing rigidly held beliefs that shackle me to the past. One of the elder women, Tanya, leads the opening ceremony by calling in the Cardinal Directions. She started with the south. The element of water was familiar to me along with emotions and the child, but she assigned the color black to the south. Why didn't she start in the east with the fire, after all, that's where we enter, and where the hot rocks come into a sweat lodge during ceremony? Black was always in the west with the earth. So many properties she assigns to each direction are different from my years of spiritual practice. Judgment is pulling me out of the present moment, being here is the purpose, so I let go. I observe an old pattern melt away—there's no right or wrong way to call in the energies of Cardinal Directions. So much is transforming, all before Tanya even gets to the East. I'm pleased to realize how flexible my being is with the change.

The journey around the circle is a wild ride, witnessing each member as she shares what is alive in her heart, or head. One woman is going through a brutal divorce, another's mother has been deathly ill, and one's children are failing at living on their own. Each speaks and then passes the talking stick. My heart opens deeper as I listen. When it's my turn, I say, "I can relate to many of the things spoken into this circle. I'm grateful for the transparency, and to be embarking on this journey together."

Each woman is unique, yet proclaims universal situations. She speaks in a way that's relatable, melting layers of chaos. I witness icy walls melt from the stoic divorcing woman when fiery tears pour down her cheeks as she voices her angry at her husband and their broken dreams. Disappointment is expressed as the vulnerable daughter talks about how her mother's failing health brings up her own mortality. As individuals unravel and open, they become more present, their eyes become clear and they nod and sigh with more interest in the next person's share. I feel united with the cohesiveness of the group.

Doubts creep in. Why am I here? I have so much to do, money to be made, people to catch up with. My mind tries to find a reason to escape, beating myself up for wasting time. About to glance at the door, I take a deep breath, while reality becomes clear. I've made the choice to be here. I exhale and commit to immerse myself in this place and time.

"Get your pen and paper," Tanya says. The main exercise begins; I've done it before in a workshop, in a different format. I could go into how it's wrong because it's different than last time, but I don't. Tanya poses the first question: "Who are you feeling resentment towards?"

I review the people in my life and continue searching into past relationships. As I look inward, I see an old concept, related to Grandfather sun in the East of the medicine wheel, only this one is everywhere—*Grandfather Time*—giving and taking life as it passes by us. Time, time, time, I'm resenting time. Yes, I just had another birthday, and am feeling time chasing me. I relax into not knowing if I'll ever own my own home, and stop worrying about whether I'll have grandchildren someday.

"The first part of the assignment is to write your intention for doing this process," Tanya says.

My mind conjures a sarcastic response, but as I put pen to paper, my higher self takes over and my hand writes:

#1. My intention in writing this letter is to live in love and happiness, and continue to let go of any resentment of time passing too quickly.

That seems reasonable, and more constructive than all the other competing thoughts racing around in my head.

A bit sticky at first, not making much sense, my hand keeps on writing.

#2. I feel hurt by time. I feel afraid that time will run out and leave me behind. I feel angry that I get caught up in the illusion of time, and that my body gets affected by my mind's obsession. I feel sad that my default is not always the present. I appreciate that in this fascinating dimension where I live, exists the concept or thought that time passes. I accept that my body can be a still point, and I can create how I react to this concept. I love time!

The words I write next touch deep, as if I'm in passionate union with almighty time itself. This evokes total presence in my expanded state. My resentment of my concept of time softens. Relaxing into recently discovered confidence, there's an allowance I haven't experienced since being an innocent carefree child.

#3. I accept that time is alive, and I flow in, around and with time.

The following questions help anchor this new cognizance into my cells.

#4. The deep desires of my heart are: to be present, love, be happy, and continue to blossom and flower in beauty.

#5 What I'm asking for right now is: please help me slow down, seek center first, then be the love, balance, happiness, presence and beauty I am.

My request is instantly granted, as if there is no time.

#6. I'm grateful that I've experienced time, over and over again, in a variety of ways. I'm grateful that time continues to exist, that I may be with it, move with it, and sit still within time.

Time becomes my sweet and dear lover, ever so gently holding me in its huge loving arms. The final question is presented. My hand continues to flow, as my blissed-out mind joyfully welcomes the streaming ideas.

#7. My loving and powerful intention going forward is to gracefully welcome each moment in time with open arms and a grateful heart.

"Let's go around the circle and read what you're comfortable sharing," Tanya instructs the group.

I'm deeply compassionate, holding space for each to release any resentment left from her personal situation.

"Cheri, you're next," Tanya says.

I stare at the page and realize most of what I wrote doesn't make a lot of sense. It's cut short, not quite thought out, but the point of the exercise is to clear held resentments. As I read, witnessed by this circle of diverse women, I feel the truth of my realization sink into my being, like hot chocolate soaking into a sponge cake, so sweet and good. *Grandfather Time* is no longer an object of my resentment. He's now a significant lover. I've entered a constant dance, relaxing into his graceful arms. Slowing into travel-between-time, I experience space where time is standing still, and times where I'm standing still within the chaos of society's concepts of time—get up at sunrise, eat at regular intervals, do my work, bank closes at 5PM, don't make calls after 9PM, practice guitar for 10 minutes each day, go to bed to get 8 hours of sleep, weekends have different rules, repeat every Monday, except holidays.

Later that night, after hugging each woman and saying goodnight to my sexy host, I drive away and soon after fall into Timmy's captivating arms. We haven't seen each other in weeks, and my desire is overflowing. We have our way with each other, over and over, for what could have been hours, or weeks, or lifetimes.

The chapter could end here, except the next morning my delicious Timmy takes me out for breakfast. We chat about our troubles, wins, and share stories of new lovers. I admit having a huge crush on Shawna, and he smiles.

After finishing a Yerba Maté, Timmy walks me through his art exhibit at a neighboring shop. I'm impressed with his life-like wrought iron ocotillo cactus with red tips, and huge palm tree structures. Then he surprises me with a drive up to Shawna's land.

"Welcome, sexy friends," Shawna exclaims, greets us with hugs, and then invites us into her cozy cuddle space.

After talking and giggling together, I suggest, "Let's try a three-way kiss."

Shawna raises her forehead with a wide-eyed grin, and in a sexy voice says, "That sounds fun."

"I agree," Timmy says.

The attraction between the three of us is obvious. Our lips press together; his strong jaw and her silky skin make my head swirl. Our tongues explore and the juices meld. We spend the afternoon blissfully connecting. I slap her heart shaped ass, creating a chain reaction of him grabbing mine, as she bites his neck. Ecstasy flows through our bodies while, once again, I feel the total delight of knowing there's no place I'd rather be. Time seems to stand still, but life is constantly moving, some say in circles.

EXPLORATION #11

What is your relationship with time?

_____

_____

_____

Time is a relative concept, measured naturally as our planet orbits the sun, yet is uniquely experienced by everyone.

What is your homework on the topic of time?

_____

_____

_____

Examples:

Write down five things from your past, five things on today's to-do list, and five things on your bucket list.

Where do you spend the majority of your brainpower: future, past, or present?

When was the last time you experienced a time warp?

Sit quiet for 15 minutes every day for two weeks. Set a 20-minute alarm just in case you lose track of time. Notice if the time seems to go by quickly or slowly.

Chapter 12

Young Love

"I rise to taste the dawn, and find that love alone will shine today." — Ken Wilber

I feel young love in all my relationships. I'm not saying it's there all the time, year after year. Some connections need to build, and don't even have that new love feeling in the beginning. The young love excitement that sparks chemical reactions and puts a smile on my face is felt when I can let go and connect with the person in front of me. I let go of any attachment to them, good or bad, and feel who they are in the moment. Young love is fresh. There's no looking back on memories of camping together, no romantic dates to recall, and no grudges, or stuck issues either. With new love it's all about the present.

There's nothing better than meeting a new love to spark the young love feeling in all my relationships. It's like the ripple in a pond, created by a dragonfly taking a sip. That ripple touches every connection I have ever made, or will make. It reminds me that my pond is not stagnant, and that all my connections are a vital part of my life. New love brings renewed excitement for all the people in my life, and reminds me to see their individual beauty with fresh eyes.

The seductive, siren-like voices of my sweet girlfriends lure me into a cuddle puddle. Outside on the patio sofa, sexy giggling women dressed in imaginative ancient costumes are layered around me, like a colorful French pastry. The party's building momentum, and our centrally located position is attracting attention. We entertain bystanders with our silliness, and welcome friends as they venture outside. From my comfy vantage point I see a friend doing push hands with an unknown beauty.

Bodies move, blocking my line of vision, then clear away again like the tides. At first, I feel the pleasing gratitude of viewing someone who's nice to look at. As the tidal waters recede, and I have a clear gaze at the dancing duo, I find myself beginning to notice curious details. Feathers hanging down in long dark hair, obscuring all, but perfectly heart shaped lips. "An Indian warrior," I exclaim. "Ha, I said that out loud."

A chuckle, from the woman with her head in my lap, is the only response at first.

A line of men, taking turns prostrating themselves on the lawn in front of our oversized throne, are saying the most flattering things about our goddess-ness. Each time another goes down in front, I'm increasingly thrilled to see this mysterious push-hands warrior. Then I shriek with contagious excitement, loud enough that everyone on the couch is now aware of my intrigue.

Still greeting friends and strangers as they arrive, I explore each connection, and sink into the moment with a palpable enthusiasm quite unique to this night. Then I catch sight again, and exclaim, "There's the little warrior!"

"Do you know this person?" Katie taunts.

"Who is he?" Valerie asks.

Finally the intrigue overcomes me, and I approach the stranger, face to face. My eyes search the face before me. Long, silky black hair is covering half of his striking features. I relate to his androgyny, feeling both masculine and feminine within myself most of my life.

"The talk of the tribe tonight is the new mysterious warrior, and it's you," I say.

"Me?" he asks, cocking his head.

Shyly I admit, "I started the stories."

"I'm Logan, and I'm flattered," he says.

We laugh, playfully frolic on the lawn, and explore. He's tall with sleek muscles. His hair smells of myrrh and amber, with skin like polished bronze, but warm to the touch. Discovering we have a mutual friend, I take Logan's strong hand and lead him through the crowd, introducing him along the way. We reach our shared companion and embrace with big smiles.

Throughout the night, as I connect with friends, Logan finds me in the crowd. He snuggles in by my side, just to touch for a moment and say hi. We go our separate ways, and engage again, each time for a little longer, and with more intensity. This intriguing virtual push hands goes on and on, until we find ourselves under the stars, watching the black sky fade back to blue.

The next day I'm surprised with dozens of messages from friends I'd interacted with at the party, all sharing how they enjoyed our connection. After the first few notes, I realize how the energy of new love is contagious, and had spread through my enthusiasm into all my relating.

Over the next few days, I feel increasing clarity and excitement in all my relationships. I'm light hearted and present with the individual before me. I express gratitude for our united purpose, and feel inspired by our commitment to truth, respect, and connection.

A few weeks later the charming mystery being finds his way back into my arms. I'm filled with blessings, sex, and friendship. Logan expresses being thankful for the depth of our relating, and the gift of instant recognition. I want to share more yummy connection, and create together.

The smile on my face is becoming permanent!

EXPLORATION #12

What is your relationship with sharing?

_____

_____

_____

I experience sharing as the opposite of selfish. When I share new love energy with others I'm not keeping it all to myself, I'm spreading the love.

What is your homework on the topic of sharing?

_____

_____

_____

Examples:

Recall the last time you had a crush on someone. How did you share that excitement with others?

How do you feel when someone shares something fun with you?

Line up four people. Randomly give a gift to three of them. Ask each how it feels.

Plan an exciting day trip, but don't share it with anyone.

Chapter 13

Wipe That Smile Off Your Face

"Not everyone is lucky enough to understand how delicious it is to suffer."
— Katharine Hepburn

Living from a place of integrity, and staying open through life's occasional curve ball, can be challenging. I push my body into physical states of suffering at the gym, up a mountain, or in the ocean, but rarely want to indulge in emotional suffering, mostly because it affects those around me. They may misinterpret my emotions and perceive me negatively, creating unwanted drama. I don't maintain a state of bliss all day, but coming back to center as quickly as possible is a practice I've established in my life. The philosophy, *it's not good or bad, it just is* helps me stay present.

Challenges come when I least expect them. A little trigger gone unseen can escalate into inappropriate reactions. Compounding reactions become confusing and can snowball into frustration, sadness or anger. For many years anger was my default. If I didn't want the overwhelming pain and sadness to consume me, I would reach down and stir the anger inside me so it would bubble up and suppress the tears. When I was confused I felt angry, if something triggered me I felt angry, when something did not go the way I planned my instant response was anger. Many years of pleading for my heart to open, and stuffing the anger so it wasn't the first thing I felt was the path I chose. Eventually the repressed emotions, mounting out of control, forced me to make different choices. It felt better to let go of resentments and anger as they arose, and avoid having to back peddle through sticky shit I spewed on someone.

Staying open and feeling everything has become one of the most thrilling adventures of my life. At times I felt like a toddler, and yes, crying a lot was a big part of the initial process. I experienced Bliss as a deep acceptance of emotion, any emotion, but usually one emotion at a time.

Once, in a sweat lodge ceremony, I experienced deep sadness, far beyond my own. The shaman requested red hot lava rocks, directly from the fire, to be placed in the center of our blanket-covered dome. With each round of prayers more rocks were brought in, round after smoldering round. My fingers reached deep into the earth beneath where I sat, searching desperately for a morsel of cool dirt. I found no relief. With the direction of my focus pointing downward, I began to sense the connectedness of everyone who walks on this earth. As I felt my own vulnerability, I began to feel the sadness of all those who were connected through the earth. I tapped into the collective sadness and suffering so completely that I became peaceful bliss. I couldn't be anything else; I was allowing so much sadness to flow through my body that it was actually pleasurable.

In unknown situations and relationships when anger or fear arose, my natural conditioned response was to fight back or leave. I thought something was wrong with me when I felt these strong emotions. My desire to have healthy relationships, and experiencing many breakups from both sides, helped me release this severe self-judgment. I learned that most humans suffer from judgment of self and others. I began asking myself if taking the right action occurs to me before the much easier wrong action has been mindlessly done. If I pay attention to when making a good choice occurs to me, then I have more time to stop myself from the inevitable bad choices. This practice taught me compassion and patience for others and myself.

The fight or flight response is a primal chemical reaction in our bodies, and was vital for survival. Elements of this are still present and important in modern times.

When the *fight* response is triggered, rather than physically attacking, there is an opportunity to verbally debate. During an argument we often determine that one is more right than the other, so we learn and evolve together.

When the *flight* response is triggered, rather than sprinting away, it may be a sign to stay and work out an issue. Sometimes it's better if I leave, but rather than bolting I attempt to negotiate in a healthy and mutually beneficial way. I can take responsibility to untangle our relationship in a respectful way, while communicating my appreciation for the other person's point of view. This process of de-escalating relationships with grace hasn't been modeled for most of us. It's as important to practice restructuring and break ups, as it is to practice seeing if a relationship is going to be productive and healthy before getting caught up in it.

It's a rocky ride since coming home from the sex healers conference. I feel like a roller coaster car, struggling to get to the top of a mountain. Then I realize there's a pulley system in place. I don't need to be doing all the work to get what I want, I just need to allow the ride up to be its own adventure. Working with other people utilizing healing modalities, role-playing, and orgasms, all assist in my life discovery. In contrast, some people like the philosopher Ken Wilber go into solitude for three years to gain clarity.

Things are starting to pile up, and I'm more shut down

than I'm accustomed to. I'm still letting go of remnants of anxiety from a fight with my beloved Jacy. My entire world isn't in harmony, because I haven't allowed parts to be heard. It's a cold winter's evening in Southern California, somewhere below 60 degrees and hinting at rain. Trying to get to a spin class at the gym that I'd missed the night before, I'm also on the phone doing my best to support Katie through a mini crisis with another lover. While time-stamping a parking permit to place inside my car windshield on the dashboard, with my head to the phone, I motion to the stack of green cards on the counter and mouth the words, "Can I have a pass for spin class?"

"You can't take the pass outside," Tiff, an easy to like, bright-eyed girl says.

Not fully understanding what she meant, because I'd been taking class passes outside for years, with my hand over the phone I quietly ask, "Are there any passes for spin class left?"

Tiff repeats, "You can't take them outside."

In my other ear I hear a heart being poured out, not a great time to interrupt, but Katie hears the commotion and asks, "Are you at the gym already?"

I take that split second to say, "Ya, hold on just a second." Holding the phone behind me I look right into those big blue eyes and ask, "Is there a new rule?"

"No," Tiff says.

Calmly I continue, "It's custom to give the passes an hour before class." Looking at the clock I say, "Class starts in 20 minutes, and I just need to put my parking permit in my car."

Quickly returning the phone to my ear I say, "Okay, I'm with you."

The cute girl behind the counter appears strangely less attractive as she shakes her head no.

There's a whole stack of passes, Tuesdays are rarely full, it's not the popular teacher, and there's ample time before class starts, so I walk outside. Sitting briefly in my front seat,

I place the parking permit in the window, complete the phone conversation, answer a text, and check that my flight itinerary for an upcoming trip is in my email. I grab a bottle of water and my towel then head back in. As I walk up the steps I see a woman coming out carrying a green pass, and feel a twinge in my gut. Optimistically I think, maybe Joy, the pretty blond girl who always cheerfully hands out the passes, came in while I was out. Or perhaps this girl I just passed was a bit more discreet about coming outside with the pass. As I approach the desk the same unfamiliar, but now slightly militant girl wearing the nametag reading *Tiff* is standing alone behind the counter. The twinge stirs slightly. I hold out my hand asking, "May I have the pass now?"

"There's no more passes," Tiff replies.

But the girl walking outside with the...? I was just here, and early for class! The confused, now dumb looking, big eyes stare right at me; I'm about to boil over. I whirl around, walk directly to a cluster of gym employees, and ask for the person in charge. I watch, seeing each thought in his head as if in slow motion. Darren stands up and points me in the direction of the office, but then looking at the rage on my face he says, "I can help you."

Slightly comforted by Darren's immediate attention to my plea for help, I calmly begin to explain the situation. My irritation continues to rise as I say, "I'm a longtime member, and have taken passes outside for years, as long as it's within the rule of one hour before class." I'm not getting to the core; I'm not feeling any better. Suddenly, a deep desire to be honest surfaces. As I allow myself to express, I feel it—the truest feeling of anger, while facing another, that I've allowed myself to feel in years. Oh dear, here it comes, all this out-of-control rage. Then I look Darren in the eye. "I feel so angry, I feel like punching her right in the face." I say, with surprising composure. Even though I'm fully revved up, I notice I also feel a deep compassion for the new girl behind the counter, trying to follow the elusive rules.

Darren's cool brown eyes, looking right back into mine,

widen. Then, as if somewhere buried in the twisted darkness of his psyche he can relate, he gives a slight micro-nod, almost appearing to agree.

"I'm glad I expressed this to you, instead of Tiff," I say. There's an unfathomable gratitude for the one fully listening to the rage expressing through me, and an ecstatic joy as I realize I'm calmly observing this whole experience.

Darren apologetically says, "Tiff's new here." Then writes my name on the reserve list for the next four classes to attend in the future. I realize this is only worth four dollars, but there really isn't much else to offer me.

"Thank you, I appreciate the impromptu therapy session," I say.

We laugh. Walking toward the locker room I notice it's the exact time for class to start. Any unclaimed reserved tickets are to be given out at this time, if there are any no-shows. I turn toward the desk, asking in a kind voice, "Are there any passes left?"

"Yes, but there's a waiting list," Tiff replies.

I blurt out in response, "I'm not even on that list!" Did I say that out loud? I catch myself, and realize trouble isn't my goal. I'm still feeling it all, and even though my words are short, I'm not yelling at her. I calmly say, "Okay." I think to myself, I can just do a weight resistance workout again tonight since I'm here.

Then I hear Darren's voice say, "Wait."

I look around to see my latest therapist point at a green pass, and motion toward Tiff. She hands me the last pass, saying, "Someone on the waiting list didn't come back."

I smile. "Thanks for not overreacting to my anger," I say.

Tiff says, "I'll put names on the list as people arrive next time."

"That's a good compromise," I say. I feel like hugging her, but think better of it.

Then Tiff puts her hand on my shoulder. Whatever's said after that I can't recall, because I'm feeling the genuine connection of her hand on my skin, and it means it's resolved. The challenges don't end, but the remnants of suffering from being run by anger are completely gone. I've responsibly expressed my anger without repression, and without creating a mess needing cleanup.

I walk into class, where everyone is already on their bikes. Being the first week of New Year's resolutions, the class is packed. There's no extra bike for me. Completely at peace, I fully surrender that if this class is mine to attend it will happen. If not, well, I had a "prepaid" reservation for tomorrow's class. The instructor sees the bright green card in my hand and announces, "A pass is required to take this class."

A newbie without a pass surrenders her bike, learning the rules of the gym. As I mount the bike and begin to pedal, I look up and realize I'm positioned directly in front of the instructor. As she bends down to grab her handlebars my eyes light up, and I can't stop a brief smile. There, before me is the most perfect rounded cleavage, bouncing like two delicious apples on a branch in front of a horse's nose to encourage and reward.

I'm not sure I appreciated the nurturing nature of breasts before. I only have limited experiences with them since I was raised during the era when women were convinced that breast milk was somehow bad for their babies. Just observing the natural way they rebound as she pedals, calms all the tension of the day. Providing a pleasing focal point, as I push the pedals around. I can't help but appreciate how all bodies are intriguingly unique. The woman before me isn't afraid to show her alluring body, and seeing it makes me happy. Even when the sweat begins to soak her shirt, and her breath quickens, she has a delightful smile. I ride my ass off for the entire hour, to avoid becoming the schmuck who didn't deserve the last bike, and I feel curiously rewarded.

EXPLORATION #13

What is your relationship with anger?

_____

_____

_____

I experience anger as stuck frustrated energy that wants to fly out of my body and make others feel bad, in order to be seen and released.

What is your homework on the topic of anger?

_____

_____

_____

Examples:

Recall the last time you felt angry. How did you deal with your feelings?

Write the words, "I am angry because," and see what spews out onto the paper.

Interview seven people you have felt angry with at some point. Ask them for honest feedback on how you handled your anger.

Next time you feel angry or frustrated make a new choice.

Chapter 14

Burn The Man

"It is not the strongest of the species that survive, nor the most intelligent, but the one most responsive to change." — Charles Darwin

Cycle class at the gym is about to pay off. The journey begins three weeks earlier, when Jacy and I involuntarily move our entire home makings to a storage unit. Daisy was a pleasant enough landlord, but not a savvy investor, and is forced to sell her townhouse we called home. Looking for the upside, I think– we're getting the boot so we can upgrade to the quaint little beach cottage near the park. The realtor doesn't like the self-employed box checked, and another applicant gets to live at the beach. Daisy isn't alone; with so many folks losing their homes, the rental market is saturated, and we find ourselves sleeping at a friend's house. It's not all bad. We welcome the change of pace, and freedom; besides, we can do our work from anywhere.

The couch owner doesn't own a car, and is heading to a gigantic festival in a few weeks. I've wanted to be included in this yearly *bonfire* ritual since I heard the original story back in the 90's, and the timing is finally aligned. We're able to give back to our gracious host by driving him up past Reno, Nevada, to the playa. Many years of diligently minding my karma is paying off. My willing and eager guide Fritz, a ten-year veteran *burner*, is exactly what a festival virgin like myself needs.

One last trip to the storage unit for bikes, swimsuits, long coats, shorts, hats, homemade moccasins, and a couple of blankets. There's minimal room for luxuries, so I leave the pillows. The plan is to gear-up in Reno with enough food and water to last 40 days in the wilderness. Jacy stays in Reno for an extra day, to pick up friends flying in from Oz for the event, while I head North with Fritz to stake out camp.

Heat rising from the highway creates glassy mirages, and from my vantage point I see a portion of the playa, with the mountain range miles in the distance. The vast flatlands stretch further than imagined—acres of soft, powdered clay earth. "What's that?" I ask, pointing off in the distance, toward a mysterious grey cloud forming from the ground up.

Fritz replies, "It's playa dust, stirred from the long line of traffic entering the gates of the temporary man-made city."

"I've heard stories, but I didn't imagine it would look like this," I respond.

No amount of groundwork could prepare me for the next hours, or the next days, that deeply affect the next months of my life, influencing the next years of my growth. As we creep along the snail trail, I see a lone sign that reads, *EVOLUTION*. A miniature-looking man on a motorcycle next to the sign gave a perspective on the vastness of the backdrop. Appropriately, the theme for this year is evolution, and I'm about to take a quantum leap in my personal progress.

For the next few hours, we inch toward our destiny in the long, single-file line of cars. The Indian-summer dusk casts surreal patterns across the landscape. Beyond the sign I see an old rounded camper bus, shaped and painted entirely like a snail. I begin to feel a bit like Alice, entering into a strange land indeed. Time begins to warp, slightly at first, in and out of speeding up and slowing, *way* down. Part of the distortion originates from the optical illusion of spatial distances. I've never been on an open plain of this magnitude; my mind has no bearing on how long it should take to get from one point to the next. Other warping factors are the odd caricatures we encounter along the path, urging the mind to search for a reference, but usually creating a new one, anchoring a new beginning point, rather than finding the sought stability.

We munch on snacks all day, so hunger isn't keeping time for me. However, the most ancient of timekeepers is pitching long shadows, and my bum is tired of sitting. Time to venture out of our little air-conditioned capsule. I roll down the window a fraction of an inch, and what slaps me in the face is much more unexpected than the unbearable heat we witnessed through our protective windshield. Instantly I gasp for air, feeling panic come to the surface. My deepest level of survival instinct tries to help, and pulls my shirt up over my face. I gasp again for a second breath, but there's only dust, fine dust, and not enough oxygen. It violates my nostrils, straight through all my natural filters, down my esophagus, and is causing the tiny air sacs in my lungs to jump to attention. My eyes widen, as I feel myself about to suffocate.

Searching in his bag for the air masks in the back seat, Fritz advises, "Close the window."

It was already up; catching my breath through the shirt I say, "I'm usually the calm one, helping others through this state. It's totally unfamiliar, feeling panic from the inside."

This wouldn't be the only time, over the next few rotations of the earth that my body would feel close to death, and the survivor in me would need to step up and take extra care. Fortunately those around me, mostly complete strangers, offer assistance at every opportunity. Before entering the gates, a dust-covered man at the ticket booth hands me a little box of hard sour candies, and says, "These will come in handy while you're here."

I nod. As I put one in my mouth I feel a calm pour over my body. I've been given a *Lifesaver* to help me ease into breathing the adulterated, dry wind.

Finally, dust masks and goggles on our grey powder-coated faces, and tickets in hand Fritz and I arrive at the gates as shadows merge into darkness. No escaping the *virgin dance* and initiation ritual; I enter Burning Man for the first time. I'll never pass through these gates with innocence again.

Over of the next few days, I open my mind, allowing judgments to rest quietly in the background. My only task is to stay alive, observe, and process the challenges at hand. I have an opportunity to change the way I respond to stress; I take it. When I feel any kind of anxiety or strong judgments I breathe deeply, to expand my chest. This gives my heart more space, and I remember to relax into the feeling of openness and love. From that place it's easier to identify the stress. If it's fear, is that fear warranted in the moment or is it a reaction from a past trauma? Do I need to take action, can I resolve the issue at hand, or do I need to relax? Sometimes the stress is simply my body telling me to get out of the sun, drink water, get up and move, or eat some nutritious food to stabilize my blood sugar. Listening to the wisdom of my body, I'm able to address the feeling of stress before it turns into a chronic habit. When I'm relaxed, I can trust what I'm feeling, and get out of the way of danger when needed. Judgment, like fear, is designed to keep me healthy and safe. When I respect it, and pay attention to what the judgment is saying, I take appropriate actions.

Over 50 thousand people are coexisting in survival mode. These circumstances are for a limited time, and most have security in knowing they'll return to abundant homes, but the hardship in the moment is real. Freely giving what we have, I even give away precious sour candies, greeting everyone as if they're old friends. No matter where I am at mealtime, there's free food. When I'm thirsty, and miles from camp, strangers share their water. Everywhere I go I'm gifted anything I care to accept—free beer and shots, places to nap in man-made shade, free love, hugs, concerts, art shows, indescribable entertainment, free bikes, and free rides on art-cars, like themed parade floats with flashy lights and crazy music.

Muddy road under my feet, freshly sprinkled by the water truck, I walk toward center camp, with approximately two hours of sleep in as many nights, my mind drops into contemplative relaxation. This is the first time in my adult life that I feel completely free. I don't need to filter myself or alter what I say. I'm not pretending, or hiding, or trying to impress anyone. None of my teachers, siblings, clients, parents, students are here to judge me. In this place, we're in the same boat: dirty, mostly naked, sleep deprived, too hot or cold, some are a bit intoxicated, but we're here to experiment and explore this alternate reality. I don't need to report to anyone or do anything. Even Jacy and Fritz are off with friends and not wondering where I am.

It's limbo, a peculiar quality of limbo, the kind that borders on boredom, a concept I know almost nothing about. My mind slows, matching the pace of the days. I have lengthy conversations with an array of strangers (philosophizing and discussing experiences) often ending up naked in a steam bath, rocking an RV, or sitting in a leopard skin bar, miles from where we began.

I find my way to one of the most famous spots in the village, second only to the large wooden structure shaped in the image of a man. Center Camp is an espresso lounge under a gigantic circus tent, with straw-bail benches and a ring for performers of all descriptions. Curiously, I'm drawn to a comparatively conservative, older Canadian man. He has no real attractive features, but he's what I imagine a sugar daddy to be. The thought of him in this mysterious position intrigues me. I carry two hot drinks across the obstacle course to my darling Jacy, who joined me at the meeting place for the most luxurious experience available—to recline under the shady tarp and sip a favorite chai latte coffee. The attraction intrigues me, so after delivering the coffee, I run back across the chaos to ask Stan to join us.

I'm grateful to find him in the sea of people, and pleased he agrees to follow me into a delightful discussion about fathers, and sons, and relationships of all descriptions. I experience a fascinating combination of brain activity and forced relaxation, like a caffeinated hangover, slow, yet oddly clear and flowing with a detailed focus. Stan's captivated by the open nature of my relationships, but I'm hesitant to even consider mentioning my sugar daddy fantasy.

Jacy and Stan are caught up in a deep bonding moment, as their words meld into the ramble. What would I need to do if I wanted a sugar daddy? A few friends have sweet (usually older) men, who take care of their bills, buy them expensive things, and most attractively these gentlemen pay for their home, but each situation is quite unique. One doesn't do much for her luxurious estate in the hills, and use of an almost new SUV. She sees her *sugar daddy* a couple of times per year when he's in town, no drama, they just have fun together. She doesn't have many bills, and has her own money so she doesn't need a job. Another received a new sports car for her birthday from one of her *boyfriends* with no strings attached. Just last week, I spoke with a friend who travels all over the world on someone else's dime.

I've judged this lifestyle choice as a form of slavery, and never *really* considered it for myself before now. It's fun interviewing women with positive experiences highly recommending it. Interesting that this man sitting next to me is provoking these thoughts. Stan is kind hearted, and accepting of our open relationship, which are essential qualities if considering this option. Back to the question—what would I need to do if I wanted a sugar daddy? Sitting next to this new friend from Canada, I try to feel if I'm sexually attracted to him. Being this close to the possibility of being taken care of, I realize maybe it isn't like slavery at all, but simply one form of love and caring for another.

Wow, a human/animal is released from a cage on a tight tether. All of our heads turn toward the exhibition. The mannerisms are that of a large feisty cat, looking to attack, if it gets the chance. Distractions interrupt this train and remind that I'm fully capable of working with others to create abundance without looking to a sugar daddy. I realize it's fun to be taken care of, and I get that need met by reliable friends and family who *have my back* when I need them. I'd rather be an equal partner, contributing to a higher purpose.

The coffee keeps me from being quiet for too long, and soon I'm back in the conversation. Most of the topics focus around self-responsibility and freedom, which contradict my earlier thoughts that I thankfully kept to myself. The open lifestyle experiment we've embarked on is a lively topic, provoking an enticing exchange. Before long a group of young English artists join our circle.

"When responsible individuals find synergy with others to manifest abundance, there's less need for detailed governing rules," says Jacy.

There are responses from two of the newcomers, and then I say, "It appears we share common goals of working with a variety of partners to co-create in the world. It isn't necessarily just about creating babies, as the world is populated."

I describe our family dynamic of encouraging individual talents, and desires so that we function harmoniously together. The one sitting across from me questions the security of such an unconventional way of living. We all agree that marriage is an illusion of security, simply because it can fall apart anytime due to a bus wreck, divorce, or one person changing their mind. Our community thrives when the individuals are sexually free, happy, self-responsible and collaborating with others. I toss in the idea that sexuality is a renewable energy and can be used to keep a community flourishing. If each person is able to follow their attractions without shame, guilt, blame, possession, or restrictions then they can be fulfilled and motivated. A community of sexually responsible people has more creative energy to solve the dire problems of uneducated, wars, and destruction of resources currently threatening our planet. When my needs are met, along with a feeling of freedom, there comes an inexhaustible desire to give and share the excess of energy and love with others. Being fully uninhibited is like discovering the fountain of youth.

More questions stir when I mention my latest relationship thought experiment, "What if kids aren't raised with the idea that they need to find one person? If individuals don't couple up, this might eliminate the pairing frenzy and the fear of scarcity."

"'Fear of scarcity' sounds more like food shortages than a relationship issue," the cute, little redhead comments.

Those of us that heard her, laugh. "There's a large population of people who don't know how to meet new lovers because of being an introvert, or working alone, or not having a community of friends. A few bad dates, time goes by, and panic sets in," I explain. "Their feeling of scarcity causes them to couple-up immediately when they get the chance."

Stan says, "Theoretically, self-responsible people become successful and create extra resources, to then help others prosper."

"Scarcity can be healed in all areas of life. In this model, natural attractions could form complex relations, meaning more than two interconnected in a core relationship," Jacy says.

"Not to be confused with complicated relationships, where two people attempt to become one, then try to include other individuals into their dyad," I say. "When there's an abundance of love and support, and it's not about finding the one to meet all your needs, then I imagine groups of all sizes can be more inclusive."

Jacy adds, "These relationships can therefore be more like family, no need to break up with one in order to include new love into the community."

Stan nods and says, "With a focus on giving, supporting, sharing, and including others, there's less scarcity and selfish, possessive relationships."

We all agree that the temporary community we're involved in for the week is a great example of an alternative reality; yet there's question of chaos and instability if the population is unable to find benefit in changing to a new paradigm.

"I can see it being a graceful transition as role models are emerging, and television and media are becoming more supportive of new relationship dynamics." I continue, "In my experience there's been a shift from controlling marriages, moving towards allowing individuals to be free. Partners are learning to negotiate and work together instead of domination and dead-end fighting."

Jacy agrees, "With this level of freedom we're able to be present to what's needed, allow individuality to shine, and trade or give with increasing generosity."

One of the English artists next to me says, "We're using the term paradigm shift, as if we understand what it means. There may be scientists who have evolution mapped out, but that's not me."

"Nothing stays the same," I respond. "From here it looks like we're learning from these changes." We discuss thought experiments on equality of men and women. If partners are equal, they can't continue to live together in the old ways, where a person surrenders to another person to live their life as if they are one. It's vital to recognize we're all whole individually, and it takes two whole individuals to make an equal relationship. It's still valuable to surrender and relinquish control to the highest good. To be one, as they used to say in weddings, may mean something different than what society or religion once taught. I wonder if we're one with everything, as well as one with ourselves. People are realizing it's okay to be different, and marriage is unnatural when people suppress themselves to make it work. I cringe at the thought that a woman better find a good husband because she's going to be living *his* life.

Another existence is that of a kept man, suppressed and under a woman's control. What if she wants both a submissive man, and a strong successful man? This is similar to a man who wants a wife to dominate, and a strong, successful mistress to put him in his place once in awhile.

"I would fear losing relationships, how do you deal with

that?" asks the woman sitting next to me.

I reply, "It's a real possibility that the one I love will fall in love with a monogamous person who's unwilling to share. That thought hurts my heart. The way I see past that fear is to remember that no one is mine to begin with. I don't own anyone. Even if a lover chooses to make a home or a baby with someone else, I know we'll still be connected in some capacity if it's so destined. When I stay in the flow with what is best for everyone involved, then I'm not afraid of *losing* any one person."

She smiles and says, "I agree."

"If a lover chooses to not be with me, that creates space in my life to spend time with others and develop new relationships," I add. "If I'm patient and allow lovers to have complete freedom, not only does it free me, but also there's more available love, and people wanting to be involved in the loving. Often, that same lover will return after realizing they were caught-up in *new love* energy, remorseful for failing to share the bliss with all the lovers in their life."

Stan poses the question, "What would you do if you only had two months to live?"

Enchanting singing interrupts us, coming from the center of the circus ring. The performance our new comrades are waiting for is about to begin. As they depart, Jacy gives a juicy, long hug to one of the girls. That's exciting!

My intrigue resurfaces as the Canadian talks about wanting to invest in property in the south. He's contemplating California. I can already see myself as the caretaker of his monumental estate, tending the exquisite gardens, and driving his pastel aquamarine Aston Martin convertible to the beach. We each chime in and topics leapfrog. I'm filled with compassion as we talk about our fathers, and his son who recently ended his own life. Not sure how many hours pass, but eventually we exchange email addresses, and with warm hugs say our goodbyes. Aspects of our connection linger, pre-shadowing the events that lead to my transformation over the next few days.

Later, when alone, I ponder the unanswered question. It intrigues me as I already feel time speeding up, and want to live with purpose while I still have this body and consciousness. I suppose, if I only had two months to live, I would even more intensely embrace my love affair with time. I wouldn't sleep as much, but that is a double-edged sword because dreamtime is a vital part of my consciousness. I would want to connect deeply with a beloved most nights. So, maybe I would be able to stretch out the inevitable by not eating as much. As I further contemplate I probably wouldn't waste time keeping this body young and healthy. I'd drink coffee and maybe get fat. I'd make recordings in attempt to pass on something to benefit others. I may, or may not, let loved ones know that I was on my way out. If I include everyone in on the pending doom, we might spend all our time processing thoughts on death. I'd want to make sure the ones who need extra love knew they would always be loved whether I was there or not. Oh heck, maybe it's a misdiagnosis and isn't true, so I'll remain healthy just in case. I don't have to know that I am dying to strive to be present in every moment with each person, transmit love and connect deeply.

As first-timers, everything is a new discovery. One evening Jacy and I venture out to see The Man up close. He can be seen from miles away, when the sky is free of windstorms. We pedal our bikes through powdery soft dust, until dark descends. The foundation is built in the form of gigantic flames, sharp and jagged, coming up from the earth toward the sky. We lay our bikes down and walk in. Looking up, I'm impressed at the gigantic support structure we're standing under. The vast surface area on 2x4s and beams create a colossal dome above our heads. Taking it all in we begin to notice details. Angles and designs of the framework, and script—thousands of messages recorded on the soon to be blazing wood. Before long we're dumping our psyches onto the planks. Work stress, taxes, and unmet goals we scrawl onto planks with a black Sharpie. Jacy adds, "Soon they'll be released in the flames."

As each day passes, I discover what's vital for surviving in such an unforgiving environment. The simplest gesture from a passing stranger can make all the difference. When someone offers my weary body a place to rest, or fills my water bottle, I can go from empty and meditative, to feeling included and ready to give. It's profound for me to receive without any expectation of money or exchange of any kind. I see how the beauty of giving freely can only be fully experienced when there's someone willing to receive freely. There's beauty in graciously receiving a gift, without guilt or pressure to repay. This reduces power struggles, manipulating, and buying another. People contribute to the whole in their own unique way, eliminating the need to judge how much, or what is being gifted. It's a flow that simply works, as it is equally important to have receivers and givers in every exchange. With the community open to receive, I witness an increasing generosity of giving, as if the vast expansiveness of the desert is reflected in our actions.

I shed shyness, self-judgment, along with most of my clothes. One day I set out in search of a latex paint artist to decorate my body. Nudity is commonplace; it's too hot for elaborate costumes. My trusted bike seems to know its way around, and takes me right to the perfect camp. Latex painted Sunflowers with heart-shaped leaves and vines, wrapped around in a creative design, cover my vital bits to avoid sunburn. Stripped down to the bare essentials—goggles, dust mask, bandana, boots, hat and my painted body, I ride toward center camp to meet up with some of the clan for a coffee or hot cocoa. I pass an open canopy with about twenty people sitting in a shady semi-circle. They take turns heckling passersby, trying to stimulate impromptu entertainment.

Andy Warhol says everyone gets fifteen minutes of fame, and mine started accruing early in life. At the strange age of five, I appeared on TV for about forty-five seconds. No lines, just a lot of dramatically acted moans and grimaces. It was a staged school bus accident drill for the local hospital, and twenty kids were strewn all over the town park lawn. I must have been making the most noise because the paramedics rush over to me, put on and pump air into big trauma stabilizer pants, and put me on a gurney. I was taken out of the ambulance, still making a big fuss, and the camera crew caught my performance as I was wheeled into ER. Since then I've accumulated about fourteen and a half minutes of airtime over the years.

This peanut gallery doesn't offer an opportunity to be recorded, but it's an international audience with an amphitheater awaiting a performer. I love a good laugh, so I take the bait, hook, line, and sinker. Apparently, I step right into a joke-off. I remember a couple of jokes, and am able to steal the punch line from one of the loudest contenders, causing a roar of laughter. I scamper away, smiling, only to return later with one of my biggest fans and an outrageous performance.

As serendipity would have it, after my café mocha, I squat over the seat in an outhouse, looking up to read an anonymous smutty scribble of nasty profanity. Equipped with my outrageous performance, and the element of surprise, I head back toward the unruly circle. Running into Jacy, I beckon him to join me. We pull up to the stage area and hear, "Ah, she has returned!"

I look over at my mate and say, "Watch this."

Jacy has no idea what I'm doing, or that I was here earlier, or anything about these people. I proceed to recite the rather disgusting, lewd potty poem. During the final line, a heckler in the audience yells, "You just wanted to say ass fucker!"

We all burst out laughing. What a freeing experience to be completely sober, have no inhibitions, and simultaneously be a wild success in front of a provocative audience.

Throughout the week I experience extremes, like the temperament of the environment expanding and contracting. There are dark cold nights of scrounging like a wild animal, eating scraps off a chicken carcass. Other lovely, warm evenings with an invitation to sit at the royal table, feasting on tri-tip steak, fresh salads, fruits and expensive wine. I appreciate it all, and don't expect any of it. No inherent resources, water, shelter, shade trees, plants or food of any kind, yet this community living experiment is about to reset my entire life.

Long evening shadows cast playful images of random

sculptures, and figures with funny hats on bikes, as I ride toward the temple. I haven't ventured out this far yet and it's time. I'm pedaling, while everyone else in our group is walking; so I take off on my own. "Meet you at camp for dinner," I announce.

"Okay. Watch out for bunnies," Jacy warns.

As I approach the triple-decker wooden temple I feel reverence. Ornately carved wooden panels line the ascending walkway and stand 15 feet tall at varying degrees to obscure the view around the exterior, like lacey partitions. The railing on the second and third floors is also hand-carved screens with the light streaming through the designs. I'm humbled by the detailed craftsmanship in the construction of this building, with the sole purpose of being a sacrifice. It too will be burned in a few days. From the second floor rising another 20 feet above the roofline are large curved boards in the shape of an unfolding lotus flower, or flames dancing in the wind, it was difficult to tell which. As I walk up the graceful spiraling ramp, the energy becomes increasingly penetrating, but I'm entering *it*. I sense everything around me, as if it *is* me, and my heart syncs with the heartbeats inside. I pause to witness orange and pink clouds melding as the sun dips below the horizon.

Continuing up the incline, again I notice writing. The words *Daddy* and *Father* catch my eye at every turn. I pass a woman holding another as she cries. On the second level I see a woman dressed in a flowing gown sitting with a spread of Tarot cards on a scarf laid out on the floor. She's reading one of the cards to the person sitting cross legged facing her. As I slowly walk past there are more tears, and I sense flashes of the pain from loss and abandonment. I feel an urge to write just as my hand passes over a green pen lying on the railing. I look up to see an open space on the overcrowded wood, and the green pen engages. I release all my Daddies. I feel the deep rooted cords attached to my father, stepfathers, adopted fathers, and father figures in my life; from the one who conceived me, to the Father who lost his son that I just met yesterday at center camp. I feel the anchors of each chord release, and effortlessly flow through the green ink into the fresh cut lumber.

By the time I climb back down the ladders of the towering sculpture, recede down the ramp, and find my bike, it's dark. I feel every tear and deep emotional release in and around the mother goddess temple for blocks as I make my way back toward camp. The wind picks up and soon the dark cloak of fear is adding to my blindness. Within a few minutes I can't see anything, and am so disoriented that I'm not sure which direction I'm going. Fear is one perspective I've a hard time accepting. Fear can be destructive, and if others are involved, contagious. I find it best to identify the shifty trickster (fear) and choose another perspective as soon as possible. As I pedal aimlessly across the dirt, I'm deep in survival mode, letting go of everything but movement. Nothing left to do, but keep moving forward. I see the fear and relax into it. In this process, I let go of suffering and struggle. There's greater potential to evolve in all areas of life when I'm free. Survival fears can be stagnating. Even with a nice place to live, or a healthy relationship, I can still be stuck with fear in different areas of development. Evolution can happen faster when there's less suffering. I can evolve in all areas of life, if I choose not to suffer over perceived hardships, and walk (or pedal) through the fear.

I continue pedaling, not giving into the paralyzing fright. Suddenly, I see a flicker in the distance. The faint light disappears as quickly as it appeared. I head toward it anyway. I catch the flicker again, but this time I am closer. It's an art car, with headlights! My legs go as fast as they can to keep the light in sight. I'm feeling immensely grateful for all my spin classes at the gym. Eventually the light leads me to a giant woman statue, made of chains, tools, and spare metal parts. Not only did I recognize the goddess with a burning flame in her metallic hand, but also she's within blocks of my camp. I'm free. That art car could've gone in any direction, but it guides me to the perfect point in the 360-degree clock. I make it back in time to share the warm curried rice that's been heating on the car dash all afternoon.

The night of the burn is the beginning of the grand finále. A sea of people gathers, surrounding the giant wooden structure. Jacy, Fritz, our friends from Oz, and I rush to find a standing place near the front. We miraculously run into friends, and eagerly wait for ignition. An explosion, followed by another; flames shoot up. The life stresses to be released have been written on The Man, and now we watch them burn, emancipated with the smoke—a prayer to Father Sky. Burning the image of the man we think we are. The crowd is chanting, gasping; I sense everyone's connected breathing, hear their sighs, like one pulsing mass. I'm in the middle of an external, visual, tribal, masculine experience. In this unified modern tribal ceremony, the mental projections are symbolically cleared for the whole community.

As the outward structure of a man goes up in flames, my *impression* of myself is burning away. The sea of interwoven humans is all one, and my perception of what I think others are, melts away. Energy continues to build, and the *mob mentality* is contagious. Safety police try to contain the crowd. Enormous burning planks fall to the ground, as someone breaks through the barrier, and runs toward the 50-foot high inferno. Firefighters and officers corral him like a wild horse, bringing him back within a safe distance. Unexpectedly, the flaming man crumbles to the ground, and the urge to break free overtakes the crowd. The entire sea of people stampede dangerously close to the flames; but just like a gush of water from a dam break circles around an obstacle in a river, the crowd circumnavigates the falling timber, avoiding casualties.

This body is just a shell, animated by my idea of who I think I am. Burning The Man symbolizes letting go of physical struggles, mental stress and my judgments of others. Burning my tax worries, business stress, and the panic of needing to find a place to live.

The Mother's Temple will burn tomorrow but Jacy and I are not staying for the last day. As we drive away I feel as if the energies that were written in the temple are being pulled out of me. I release my emotional goo and the feeling of needing a father. I let go of attachment and fears of abandonment. The temple reflects the feminine part of my internal experience.

Waiting again in a long line, the wind stirs a dust-colored sky with patches of blue. It's our first time alone together on this road; Jacy and I sit in a mostly meditative state. Then a vision of what it might be like when the Mother temple burns down flashes in my mind. The foundation turning to flame, room by room igniting, until it lay in pile of incinerated ash on the earth's floor. I wail.

Backtracking the way in is easy as we follow a single-file string of cars, vacating the place we called home for what seems like months. My eyes have now adjusted to see all the colors of each car through the grey. Still covered in dust, this now familiar, extreme reality is vastly different than anywhere in my past. The basis of this community is giving without expectation of anything in return, and simply taking what is offered from a stranger without fear. Living in gratitude, feeling truly blessed with the flow of creativity. I give selflessly to others, knowing that I'm taken care of, because the 50,000 people in this culture are committed to unconditional giving. There's a special kind of love in this place of chaos, with very few rules. As each person learns self-responsibility and becomes self-sovereign in the difficult climate, they are less likely to be controlled by fear. In this place, government's threat of a tax audit, or taking away more rights, or religion's imposed terror is no longer a viable way to control others. We're exploring cooperation and freedom on an equal playing field, giving and receiving unconditionally, and loving openly.

Sitting quietly next to Jacy as he steers to keep us straight, I review the transcendent week. One of the striking features was the communal nature of the festival. We lived in camps, shared toilets, and traveled by foot, bicycle or open art cars on the playa. There was no cellular reception; talking face-to-face was the norm. My reward for giving to others was receiving what I needed, usually before asking. I like traveling in convertibles back in the *default* world (as we affectionately call every place other than here, during Burning Man week), so I can be less isolated, and shoot the breeze with cowboys at stoplights.

Limitless time to philosophize while inching along in our dust-filled chariot, the most tangible feeling that permeates my soul is peace. All the *problems* in my life now feel insignificant compared to surviving the harsh conditions of dehydration and low caloric intake due to the 100 plus degree beating sun, and sleep deprivation from non-stop deafening music and repeated firebomb explosions. My life's had a complete reboot. My standards are revamped, and what was previously important or worth my attention has now been reset; my life is a fresh slate. We equate our microcosmic experience at Black Rock City, to the macrocosmic global potential. World peace is possible if humans live free, practice self-responsibility, and help each other.

Topics were sparked by our week's community experiment—like the benefits of volunteering, bartering, moneyless economy, and philanthropy versus the pitfalls of socialism. Jacy comes from a medical family in a socialized country with waiting lists for medical assistance, and restrictions on which health products are allowed. I was born in a capitalist country where Medicare can be helpful to the person without money, but doesn't allow for the doctors, or hospitals to get sufficiently paid. Socialized healthcare for everyone is like having Medicare for everyone. I also come from a family of healthcare providers; it's hard work caring for the sick. Education's expensive and exhaustingly long, so if the medical profession isn't compensated adequately, they will go out of business, and I don't know how the system will survive. Even without socialized medicine in my homeland, I know doctors who've worked their whole lives, and died penniless. Many factors go into financial success or failure: family patterns, cultural beliefs, the willingness to work, physical and intellectual ability to master a chosen skill, environmental conditions, as well as unforeseen circumstances.

In the silence between our discussions my ideas still

flow. I follow one train of thought until another intersects, usually derailing. It's not like me to choose sides on any political topic. Instead of arguing opposing extremes, I like to see the pros and cons from both sides, and collaborate to find functional solutions. The thoughts become too overwhelmingly big, then the obvious pierces my heart—peace starts within. Stop. Take a slow deep breath. Yes, there it is, the perspective of peace. I can feel it right now! The peace inside is always here.

Knowing I'm at choice over which perspective to engage, becomes obvious when I'm this slowed down, yet I must choose it. All perspectives are in me, and sometimes it takes more effort to keep the destructive perspectives out of the driver's seat. While coming from the perspective of peace, how can I support the positive perspectives in those around me? During the last few days we gave to everyone, unconditionally. Yet most people were slowed down, open, and fairly peaceful. Everywhere I turned, people were giving as well as the receiving. Everyone here was in similar conditions for this limited experiment and we had a common purpose, but how do we apply what we've learned to the *default* world?

I recall a time when I went for a drive after pulling weeds all morning in the little plot of land where I spent most of my time. Noticing a man with a beggar's sign, in the same place I'd seen him so many times before, I thought, I'd probably give him 10 bucks if he'd just pull the weeds from the cracks in the pavement, or pick up the trash he steps over 600 times per day as he paces up and down the median—anything to contribute back to society, or do some work for the donation. On second thought, paying the $10 might be misinterpreted and encourage him to bring more trash to pile up to look like he'd really been cleaning. Then he might leave it there to use again the next day, as he brings even more. Perhaps it would catch on, starting a trend for other beggars. If I give to a random person on the street, am I supporting a victim perspective? How can I help cultivate self-responsibility? Did Mother Theresa and Gandhi judge the ones they gave to? Does their model of unconditional, peaceful giving apply to today? I don't know the best way to help the population of people who seem to be unable to thrive on their own. There are many reasons why a person is caught in a pattern of asking for help without giving back to society. Perhaps they *are* contributing by providing an outlet for others to feel needed when they give. It is equally as valuable for those who are abundant to practice sharing with others. Through experiences like Burning Man, maybe it's possible to employ the ancient concept of compassion, redefine how to apply it to modern society, and EVOLVE.

After driving all day, Jacy and I stumble upon a tiny hole-in-the-wall motel next to Lake Tahoe. Two of Fritz's roommates from back home, where we stayed prior to *the Burn*, are checking in ahead of us. Surprised to see them 500 miles from home, we rejoice in each other's company. We had the same desire to take a few days to decompress before heading south. After leaving the harsh safety of the chaotic playa it's perfect to hold familiar beings that have just completed the same arduous journey. Sage and Abby invite us to their room for a bite to eat, and then we all walk across the corridor for a cuddle pile in our room. We melt into the comfort of companionship and shared experiences.

In the morning we have an unexpected treat. Our companions take us to a secret beach just around the bend from our retreat. At Bliss Beach we meet Abby's friend, who stayed the extra day to witness the temple burn. Naked on the warm sand, Brook describes the temple burn exactly as I'd imagined. All the grief, emotional words, tears, despair, green ink, angst of connection to the father melted when the luminescent structure crumbled down. As I listen to Brook's story, I feel emotional baggage carrying feminine wounding of dependence, attachment, and fears of caring too much, bubble to the surface. Tears wash over my inner burning temple until the flames are quenched. Complete exhaustion, I fall into a deep sleep. I awake with a clear mind and new hope, noticing shade from the tall pines at the edge of the shore making its way across our bodies. I'm able to meet all men with fresh eyes, No longer holding on to disappointed, abandonment, or betrayal from any of my daddies.

This life-expanding adventure leaves Jacy and me a desire to experiment with how to restructure our personal relationship. Over the next five months we move around, living with lovers, or staying in hotels, while we contemplate finding a house. We play with ideas of including other lovers in a community style home. Jacy and I have compersion and don't experience jealousy with each other. I feel secure in our connection being strong in many areas and the love we share is based in something more than our sexual love. With our routines and familiar distractions out of the way, we're able to get clearer about our relationship and how our lives fit together.

Communication is what I'm working on with Jacy, understanding what's conveyed, and how to fully express my truth. My interpretations of what's expressed are kept in the moment, differentiating between past events and what's desired in the future. I stay present and feel all that's being communicated to me and from me.

One day I'm nearly fooled by a familiar urge to leave as Jacy goes into a difficult period. It's easier to think only of myself, but I don't want to abandon him in his time of need. I'm challenged by the instability, but I choose to stay present. I'm self reliant, and have a supportive community that meets most of my needs, so I don't *need* anything from him. My interpretations of what's expressed are kept in the moment, differentiating between past events and what's desired in the future. I stay present and notice a practical application of giving and receiving without expectation.

We make *mistakes*, learning valuable lessons—the importance of figuring out what I want, and what I won't tolerate. Jacy and I learn to clearly communicate boundaries, ahead of time, so the other doesn't step on a landmine. It causes unnecessary upset when unspoken lines are crossed. The invisible line may have been a bottom line boundary that wasn't clearly explained, or perhaps not even seen by *either* person. Each relationship dynamic is different; therefore the guidelines that preserve trust are unique to that relationship. I clearly state my boundaries so that we can be completely free within those guidelines, and maintain trust. It's better to risk upsetting someone by being honest about what's important to me, than have to cleanup an emotional mess later.

My favorite saying is from the 1984 movie Buckaroo Banzai by Earl Mac Rauch, *No matter where you go, there you are.* Finally, Jacy and I settle on being financially responsible for a house together, on our own, but making sure it's big enough to include our live-in lovers.

Our new home, affectionately called *The Village*, is a live-in laboratory for implementing some of the new principles that we experienced on our break from life as we knew it. This includes releasing the old ways of rising to the top by stepping on others and cutting out the middleman to save money. We practice new relationship compositions including a few months with nine friends, family and lovers living under our roof. One thing we try is having an exit strategy for new roomies. It's a big commitment to move in and fit into a community, even a small one (three or four people), especially if we're working together too. These agreements include a trial period to make sure it's a win-win, and a specific amount that we will donate to moving costs if it doesn't work. There are growing pains as we shift from familiar routines into the unknown. Cohabitation with multiple lovers and friends is an area Jacy and I've practiced our entire relationship, but now we're living on a property with a real community feel.

It's the simple things that present challenges—honoring each person's unique tolerance for keeping the kitchen clean is an example. I prefer keeping the sinks and counters clear, washing dishes and placing them in the empty dishwasher to dry. Jean prefers a more leisurely approach of letting the sink fill with dishes before loading them into the dishwasher and pressing the button. Willing to compromise, we agree to put dirty dishes in the dishwasher at the time of use, and then run it when it's full. Jacy agrees with Jean, and says he feels too much pressure to keep the sink empty. The topic's discussed during a house meeting. The house is divided. Three like it clean, three like a relaxed approach, and three are on a road trip. The easiest thing to do is nothing, the dishes pile up, and the mice invade. Definitely not worth fighting over, so the three that value the clean kitchen take turns keeping it that way. The others are asked to take over other responsibilities so that resentment doesn't grow.

Jacy and I attempt to avoid hierarchy, but it becomes evident that humans are similar to animals—there are alpha male and female Chimpanzees who are naturally more dominant, and the others prefer to have things done for them and prefer to follow a leader. The difference is often times if there are more than one dominant leader then they will fight for the lead position.

The three of us who are more dominant in nature, like to take charge and get things done properly the first time. We value being efficient and can step into the leader's shoes when needed. While the others prefer to do things in their own time, and let someone else lead. The second, less aggressive group may not even notice that by default if they don't take charge, someone else will do the work. This may sound good to those who value freedom and choosing when and how they give, but it takes a team to run a village. These kinds of personality differences are challenging because both sides have negative and positive aspects and usually each side only sees their own positives and their opposing side's negatives. Jean and company thought our group was bossy and couldn't relax, and we thought they were lazy, and selfish. Our judgments were reinforced when she failed to find a way that she could contribute, and resentments began to build.

Chimps need to learn how to be liked by the others and how to give at least as much as they take from the group. If they don't develop the ability to bond with the others and want to be a part of the tribe they risk alienation, which is dangerous in the jungle.

Soon Jean discovers that gardening is meditative, and pulls weeds, waters the vegetables, and picks the herbs for our meals. Eventually everyone finds things they liked to do, and learn. Those of us who tend to do whatever needs to be done, learn to be patient and engage the others in a kind way that helps them develop an interest in new skills. Jacy begins getting up early to make breakfast for everyone, and Jean wants to learn how to follow recipes from the Internet.

Equally challenging is finding a new financial model for getting wealthy, or just paying all our bills. First we employ more *middlemen* to create jobs for everyone, the opposite of how we used to think about saving money. We encourage collaborating, profit sharing as partners, generous gifting, and sharing to assure that each one is taken care of. After embracing lack and frustration, we let go of doing everything ourselves, and realize there's more than enough when we all contribute and work together. We support one another's strengths and co-create harmony. When we recognize how each of our talents creatively fit together, there's greater success for all.

The most challenging, yet helpful, lesson is appreciating feedback from others. At first when Jean said I was a neat freak I wanted to defend my position. I listened to her perspective and was able to understand because I don't like doing dishes, or anything else, unless I'm in a happy mood. If I had felt like someone was making me do my dishes I might not like it either. The closer I let another into my intimate space, the more our differences rub up against each other. These conflicts help me see areas where I'm stuck in how I think things should be, which holds me back from living in harmony and being free.

I don't always know what I need, but can feel that something is discordant. It takes listening to others, humility, and reflection to discover my needs. When I see how my needs aren't being met, I take care of myself and improve my mood, then I can find joy in just about anything I'm doing, even dishes. Living with multiple intimate relationships is like a crash course in seeing my blind spots and noticing when I'm inflicting my will onto those closest to me. One way to foster accord is to show respect, listen so everyone feels heard, and state my requests clearly (after I know what they are), so they understand what I need. I value a clean kitchen more than some people, but that doesn't make them wrong. Their values lie in other areas that I might not think are important, until I listen to their reasons and apply them to myself.

The benefits outweigh the challenges of group dynamics. Living with more than one other person provides variety, companionship, and it's easier to maintain a house and a business with some help. For the least amount of drama it's wise to discuss the order of values, how each person finds their own joy, and each one's ability to negotiate differences before deciding to live under the same roof. By the end of our full house period, our friends from Europe returned to their country. Jean decided to make a responsible decision and return to a prior commitment with a land-share group, in the north, where she was a part owner. When we parted, I was grateful for the learning experience I gained during our experiment, and I had a feeling that we'd both continue to benefit from it in the future.

My Burning Man experience permitted a break in my view of reality, creating space to make a shift in the way I choose to live. If I get caught up in drama, my thoughts aren't based in a desirable reality. These crazy thoughts create overwhelming emotions, and when I'm on the verge of crying I find it most helpful to take a break—just stop before something breaks. Take a deep breath; connect with the all-stable ground, perhaps help with the gardening and get my knees dirty, and check-in to see what I need.

When my emotional state slips from rational, I slow way down to see each thought individually and decipher what's based in concrete reality. It's easy to be reactive, and it's a more difficult choice to remain mindful—that's why it's called a practice. If a *real* situation is causing my upset, I stop and assess my options—I can walk away, act to change it, or surrender to what's happening in that moment. When multiple people have their own interpretations of reality, it's vital to remain cognizant of my reactions.

One day, before completely emerging out of my post burning man existential crisis, I attend a gathering with a group of friends. We have a practice where everyone sits in a circle and one of us at a time gets in the center and shares what's in their heart. A girlfriend accuses me of repressing my emotions.

In my mind I react and I think, yes, I stuff them way down into hell. But, when thoughts and reactionary emotions reach the inferno they burst into flames, creating a bright light. That light is clarity. Peace washes over me so I can feel again. Not just feel like crying, running, fighting, or shutting down; I can feel all of it. I respond, "Yes, perhaps I'm choosing not to risk being judged." In saying that I realize I was judging her as an unsafe person. That isn't the perspective I want to let in my driver's seat. I then say, "Thank you for mirroring the areas where I wasn't looking. I don't want to judge you as an unsafe person, that makes both of us feel excluded."

"Thank you, and you're right, I was feeling distant and disconnected," she replies.

Instead of taking responsibility for what she was feeling, she blamed me for withholding and being introspective. When my capacity to feel is expanded, I can allow emotions; those judged as evil, as well as desirable ones—feeling all of it is my Bliss. It takes vigilant practice to feel the vast array of emotions simultaneously, and not attach to any single one of them.

My spiritual practice consists of decreasing the length of time it takes to go to *hell*, and back to *heaven*, when I get too caught up in any one earthly perspective. My personal view is that enlightenment is an ongoing process of observing all perspectives at the same time, being all those perspectives without compulsively acting on all of them. There's conscious choice as to which perspectives act and speak through the body. I've recognized I'm all of it, and you have too. When we're both in a blissful state it's like God talking to God, reflecting all of creation.

Tonight, from the contentment of my home, I watch this year's Burn, on u-stream, for the first time since I was there years ago. It seems to crumble faster. One arm falls, then a few minutes later, BOOM, it collapses in on itself and he's down. Moments after he shoots his wad, Annie Sprinkle (the Ecosexual Queen) writes on the streaming chat. In the excitement I scramble to sign-in and send her a quick hello. I'm fully aware of my lack of significance to this celebrity, but for me, we're *one*. Annie and I married the moon, along with a few hundred others, during her and Beth Stephen's purple wedding a few moons ago. I revel in the power of symbolism. This drawn-out chapter is a good representation of the painstakingly deliberate journey that the observer endures as it integrates the lessons from the microcosm of the burn, to the macrocosmic default world. This distant attempt to connect with Annie is the perfect closure for this leg of my journey. As I re-live the burn of The Man, I release all notions of owning any. I am free. The moonlight flickers on the pool outside my bedroom window, and I'm grateful for all of it, including my comfy pillows. I smile.

EXPLORATION #14

What are your thoughts on hitting the reset button?

_____

_____

_____

I experience a reset when I go into nature and release the stress of daily responsibilities. Sometimes a tantric lovemaking session can do the same thing right at home.

What is your homework on the topic of hitting the reset button?

_____

_____

_____

Examples:

Make a date to walk in the mountains, on a deserted beach, or your favorite secluded nature trail.

Write all the things in your life that are stressful, then burn it.

Invite two friends to join you on a vision quest for three days of solitude in nature.

Draw a line in the sand. Make a declaration that as you walk over the line you are starting over fresh.

Chapter 15

Hidden Pools

"Our survival as a species depends on our ability to recognize that our well-being and the wellbeing of others are in fact one and the same." — Marshall Rosenberg

It's a sweltering summer's long excursion to the healing waters of a hidden natural springs resort. We're a group of friends with a good excuse, and perfect timing, taking a coveted long weekend away. Wishing one of my sexual lovers could've come along, but knowing my inner lover is always with me, my need for connection is about to be met by my beloved Nature, and these delightful human friends. Expectations are low, as this is a virgin voyage for me, so I can easily stay in the moment, where most adventure happens. The question pops out of my mouth, "Are we *here* yet?"

Amused, Skyler says, "We're here."

We all laugh, as we recall hearing a mother tell her children those exact words just a few hours earlier when our plane landed in a new city.

"Where else would we be?" I had said to my friends as

we unbuckled our seat belts.

Soon we are soaking in the mineral waters, sinking into our new surroundings. The healing waters penetrate my nearly impervious defenses as I let go of stress. The unwinding begins, making room for the next incarnation of healer, teacher, lover that I am, to enter and express itself through me—ready to explore what this part of the world can show me. I reflect on the year, which I consider the most challenging of my life. In the pool under the shade of a huge fig tree, I reconsider. Was it really the *most* challenging year of my life? The challenges were unfamiliar, but would they be challenges if I'd experienced them previously?

I've seen pain before, and survived unearthing the related shame and repression. I've explored the perceived duality between freedom and connection while experiencing both. Once, I thought an experience was *healed*, but until everyone has healed all of the collective human experience, there's room for more liberation. My personal trauma rarely causes me upset anymore, unless another person suffers from a similar ordeal and shows me a unique, unexplored perspective. This new view of an old trauma is an opportunity to know more of humanity, and therefore free more of myself.

As I merge with the warm water, and the others in the pool. I observe how the stress from the last year is related to my distant past. Painful teen pregnancies, ending in abortions, are related to my desire for freedom as well as deep connection. The past bubbled to the surface because recently Drake was in his own process around not having children, and in an angry moment said, "I don't want to be with a woman that would kill my baby."

I think back on all the shame I felt for having sex, getting pregnant, and getting an abortion—that was a lot for a teenager. I was so shutdown from my own pain and shame that I didn't even consider how the other partner in this crime might be feeling. It was all about trying to hide the fact that we were having sex. I see how sexual shame is a core wounding—we came from sex and it's at the root of the animalistic need to procreate. It's no wonder my passion is helping society release sexual shame.

I know that if confronted with pregnancy now, I wouldn't consciously kill Drake's baby, or anyone's baby. If I was really threatened and forced into a fear reaction, I may even choose another life over my own. What about killing? Can keeping the peace, and killing to prevent war be the same thing? As I feel into life on this planet, it's difficult to see how I could kill anyone, if I'm aware of the whole picture. I wasn't aware when I chose to abort the beginnings of life inside of my body, I felt it was the best choice for my survival, and I valued my life. I remember how I didn't even see it as a choice between my life and my baby's life. It would have been the end of my life as I knew it. For advice I looked to my mom, who had her own fears, shame, and tainted opinions; I didn't have any comparisons for computing consequences at that inexperienced age.

My uneducated choice to have sexual intercourse at the fertile age of 14 changed the course of my life. I liked sex from the first attempt, but unaware that excitable young girls can drop eggs like a farm bird, soon I was pregnant. After repeating the experience twice more I realized that killing the growing cells inside my womb wasn't a choice I wanted to make ever again. I promised *God*, and myself, that if I became pregnant again, even if still in school, I'd make a different choice. I'd acknowledge to the world that I was a sexual being who indeed had sex out of wedlock, and to some that would mean I had *hell* to pay. I'd welcome the inevitable change, and devote part of my life, for the rest of my life, to an externalized version of my DNA.

I dunk my head under the water to baptize away that nearly forgotten promise, and all the stirred up reactions. My reaction to Drake's words showed me I still have judgment from my past. His words are uncomfortable, but I no longer need to hold any pain in my body, and I'm now capable of making educated decisions. I'm not a biological mother, but ever since that promise, my mothering instincts developed. They became the driving force behind my education, in preparation for all that

I'd give birth to and nurture in the years to come.

As I think back to years that were perhaps as difficult or harder than this last one, I see that in some ways life is getting easier. I'm learning to use tools that help me feel all of the emotions that arise during hard times. These tools include breathing, clearly stating my intentions, and identifying perspectives inside—like the victim perspective, for example. As I float around the pool, I'm entranced by the melodious sounds of trickling water. Memories surface of waterfalls in the pools near where I lived when I was fresh out of college. I drift into a daydream, or nightmare depending on the perspective, reminding me that last year was not necessarily the worst year of my entire life. There's an overwhelming similarity in this moment, to years ago with the sounds in the pools, warm sun and cool water, and the feeling of relief that I'm through the worst of it.

I remember years ago lying in the warm sun, listening to the waterfalls, and thinking I'm on the upside of the worst year of my life. I'd spent all morning at the gynecologist's office, making sure I was all right, after a date gone horribly wrong. A few days later, I found the courage to tell my neighbor I'd been raped. His response was both helpful and unexpected. He asked me why I didn't yell for help. His question initiated a deeper contemplation of the depth of shame and secrecy around sex, along with the lack of self-worth because I didn't want to create trouble for anyone else. Untangling the experience was complex.

From my dominant, responsible perspective, I'd flirted with the handsome stranger a number of times at my apartment common area. Attracted to his physical appearance, I failed to admit that I sensed an underlying anger; I overlooked the warning signs. Racing home from Palm Springs, in his Porsche, we were pulled over by police. I remember convincing the officers not to arrest him when he argued with them. His ugly hostility was beginning to seep through his appealing physique. If he had gone to jail, that night would have ended differently. Did he deserve to go to jail after he disrespected me? He ignored when I said *no* to his sexual advances, and didn't honor my request when I asked him to leave. Was I wrong for not even thinking to call the police, or yelling to a neighbor? There's a part of me that wanted to have sex with him. Had I been as clear as he needed, when I changed my mind and chose to say no?

I flirted with him during our date, and secretly admired the sexily dressed women who appeared to be escorts at the restaurant. I was naive about how this profession has an agreed upon exchange of energy—their companionship for money. He bought dinner for me. Was he expecting sex in return? I was 23 years old and even though I'd had many lovers in school, I didn't have the *street smarts* to understand about other forms of sexual exchange, or dating strangers. I wondered the significance of what I create with my energy, and if my intention was unclear from the beginning with this man. I didn't understand that my fantasies became desires which created attraction. I thought I wanted to fulfill my fantasy, but as the night went on I became less attracted to him. Still undecided by the time we got back to my place, I wasn't clear; and I'd been drinking.

When I did say *no*, he sounded disgusted and his last words to me were something about fickle American prudes. His reaction caught me by surprise. I immediately thought, he must have had some bad experiences with women, and I better ask him to leave. Well, he didn't. I was fortunate in that he didn't hit me or take out his anger on my body. It didn't take him long to get what he wanted and rush out the door.

A couple of days later I learned that he had left the apartment complex, and I never saw him again. I remember thinking he must have known his actions were wrong.

Taking responsibility for my part of the situation, I learned to be aware of my surroundings, my desires, and the intentions of others. I learned the importance of a deeper connection, to pay attention to the big picture, and to be clear with everything— from my thoughts, my actions, to my requests. Sex should be between consenting adults. That means asking for consent, and getting a verbal *yes*. Non-verbal communication is confusing and conflicting, and is not a reliable way to reach consent with another person. Communication happens energetically—thoughts are expressed through facial expressions, body language, chemical pheromones released, pupil dilation, heart rate and breath, and more. I become more aware of the primal undercurrent of this interconnected non-verbal communication.

The evolution of society is in a difficult transition period—women are speaking out against a history of abuse and demanding respect, men don't have examples of how to verbally ask for what they want either and are also wanting mutual respect. People seem to be at odds. I like to start at the basics—treat others the way we want to be treated, listen, be self-responsible, give others the benefit of the doubt, command respect by being respectful, and learn to verbally communicate with each other.

I don't speak much about the incident, but when anyone tells me it wasn't my fault, I disagree. I'm not going to allow the victim perspective to dominate. The victim perspective will use any excuse to lurk in the shadows, like a vampire waiting to suck the life out of all others, if left unrecognized. I allow that perspective to be expressed, be heard, and be loved. The way to stay clear of being blindly dominated by the victim perspective is first admit that I was a victim. I breathe, feel into all of the perspectives present, and once again, expand my capacity to feel even more simultaneously. The victim is always the victim, and is always there, which is why I still call that experience *rape*. Like the victim, the responsible one, the student that learns from experience, and the leader that makes changes, are also always there. Each is present, but I can choose to acknowledge and learn from each one. Observing them all, I allow only the highest perspective to speak from my mouth, because I know these words shape my future reality. I feel compassion for myself and for the one who didn't know how to stay present with me on our first date.

My most difficult moments are hard to talk about. Not because the wounded perspective inside me doesn't want to be reminded of past hurt, but because it may trigger painful reactions for others who have experienced similar things. In searching to communicate these grievous experiences there are no *right* words. Everything has the potential to be misinterpreted by someone. He was wrong to force himself on me, but my only regret is that I didn't know how to educate him so that he doesn't act out his aggressions on another naive girl. Since that night I have helped hundreds of men learn how to listen, take out anger in a healthy way, and how to get what we're all looking for—connection. Thousands of hours of therapy are spent on these topics, but the bottom line is all we have is our actions, behaviors, and thoughts from this moment forward. I want to choose highest right action for the greatest good from today forward.

Sipping cool lemonade, I rest next to the soothing pool. Relieved that I can recall these past experiences without residual distress. I'm filled with hope, realizing it's possible for others to release blame, anger, and destructive habits too. I want to teach the underdog how to optimize safety and be smart, and teach the bullies how to find happiness, feel included, and be a constructive part of their community. For the past 25 years I've been diligent to instruct people about listening to their inner thoughts and validating what other people say. When children haven't been respected, they're more likely to disrespect others. But this is difficult when the parents weren't revered, disciplined, and didn't have positive examples in their upbringing. To break this cycle, start by honoring yourself, and commanding respect from others. The next step is sometimes overlooked—respect other people.

A little leisure, along with extra therapeutic touch from friends, is exactly what I need to move forward. With relaxation comes the release of emotions held inside from stress. Compared to the suffering of others, or catastrophes on the news, I don't have much to complain about, but it's still more than I can process all at once. As tension unwinds, the overwhelming conglomerate of stress begins sorting into separate issues, in a linear order to be seen and felt, and become part of the known instead of the frightfully hidden.

It started just before the New Year, when a lover calls me with symptoms of gonorrhea. He and I haven't engaged in sex for over three months, and we always use condoms as a precaution against pregnancy, or passing potential infections. I feel healthy, and mutual friends and our other lovers don't have any symptoms, but we all get tested just to be safe. Only six, myself included, receive positive results, out of over fifty that were tested (each of our circles of lovers and their sex partners). The business, financial, and relationship stress I've gone through these past few months has compromised my defenses. A few primary partners of the known infected ones chose to receive treatment before getting their test results. Strangely, the final results reveal that none of the primary partners test positive for the bacteria, even though they had unprotected sex during the *potentially* contagious stage. Each of us does due diligence, contacting everyone we had sex with since our last negative gonorrhea test. It was four months since my last visit to the STD clinic, but I call everyone I've had any physical intimacy with for the prior year. Each one of my lovers from the past, reports they're in good health, and haven't had gonorrhea.

However, there's one lover I can't locate. Last time I spoke with him, he was in good health, but what if he's unwittingly carrying the bacteria without symptoms? He left my life abruptly, after betraying my trust one night during sex. He asked me if we could have sex without a condom, and I clearly told him no, it wasn't okay with me. He agreed. I have such a deep desire to trust and be trusted that I didn't even consider he would dishonor my request.

One night, during an intimate connection he slipped off his condom, and I immediately stopped him. Alarmed, and not sure how to communicate the gravity of his behavior, I didn't want to disrespect or shame him, but I told him that his actions were not acceptable. He left that night and we didn't speak again. I could've avoided months of vexation if I'd handled that night differently, or cleaned it up sooner.

It's my policy to get a recheck after any condom slip, so

as a safety precaution I got tested beyond my regular bi-yearly clinic visits. It's been many months since my all-clear results, but I'm still unable to get the thought out of my head. Had he infected me? What if I infected him? I'm responsible to inform him that he may have been exposed to bacteria that can live undetected in the body, and eventually cause harm. What if he unintentionally passes it to others? I need to find him and be sure. I contact everyone I know connected with him, and explain why I'm so insistent on finding him. Finally, after making no progress I speak with a private investigator. Even this is a dead end.

I'm angry with myself for not listening to the signs, once again. It's been many years since anyone has betrayed my trust like the rapist in the Porsche. At least this time I stopped him, but why did it get to that? I should've seen this coming, and been a better judge of character. Was he similar to the one who hadn't listened to my *no*, years before? When he asked me about not using a condom, wasn't that a huge sign? Why did I give him a chance? We initially had a number of dates without any sexual play, as if that made him safe. My anger's talking, and it isn't helping. I'd been enjoying getting to know him, until he ignored my clear boundary.

I've given my best attempt to find him, to make sure he and his future lovers are safe. There's a part of me that wants to apologize to him for not knowing how to communicate better at the time. I wish I could show him, and all people who don't respect others, that it's better to talk about the shame that comes from hurting others. It's better to forgive instead of running away feeling guilty, misunderstood, misled, or wronged in some way. Communicating needs, boundaries and negotiating desires, then acting with integrity, creates harmony. Learning to implement this in my life, I attract more clear and conscious people.

(Years later, by chance I ran into the untrustworthy one in a crowd of hundreds at a festival. We finally talked and cleared the strange energies between us. He'd gotten the message I left with his former landlord when he returned from an overseas pilgrimage. It was a relief to see he was in good health.)

After the gonorrhea scare, I began to identify with Job from the Bible stories. The timing couldn't have been worse because I was scheduled to travel with Drake. It was our annual birthday/anniversary trip and it didn't go so well. We were going through a stressful period anyway, and this was the straw that caused us to take a break. Sometimes I cry when I'm angry. I wonder if I'm letting go, or if the tears are about feeling sorry for myself over not expressing what I need clearly? Or, am I attached to my *perfect* life, trying to hold it all in place so nothing will change? I'm afraid that change will leave me behind, stuck in my chosen hell, alone.

Antibiotics, along with shame and the stress of testing positive (or was it a false positive since I had no symptoms, and my partners tested negative?) catapult my body into a cascade of reactions. At first I assume the itching is a side effect reaction to the antibiotics, but it won't go away. I return to the doctor, who tries to convince me that my hormones are changing, and I'm not contagious. A month goes by, and it continues to worsen. My hormones are changing due to stress, and lack of sex, so I go to a dermatologist for a second opinion. He says I seem to be stressed, but we need to rule-out scabies to make sure I'm not contagious. I do the toxic treatment three times, but the now insane itching continues. Nearly six months go by, with almost no physical contact. During this miserable period of no human contact, I slip into early menopause. My hormones drop to being almost nonexistent, and I feel deprived, scared, and hopeless. Even my sex drive is waning. Finally, I go back to the dermatologist. He assures me I'm not contagious, and I'm indeed having a stress response, and that my hormones will settle down after menopause has stabilized.

I'd abandoned sex and hugs, getting a haircut and teeth cleaned. So I begin to schedule much needed appointments, and consider hugging my friends again. Before the itching completely subsides, I discover part of the back of my front tooth is discolored, and a small piece breaks off at the roof of my mouth. Distressed, I make an emergency call to my dentist, who's out of town.

Meanwhile, one of my long distance lovers is in town, and gently initiates me back into the world of the living. I don't remember ever feeling so vulnerable and fragile. I'm as sensitive, as if a virgin again. I estimate about 60% of my attention, was going to managing the pain and distraction of my irritated skin; my body hasn't been a comfortable place to be.

"Let's lay naked together," René suggests.

"Yes please," I say. I'm verging on overwhelm and gasp, as the long-awaited hand touches my skin. Excitement comes quickly. Gentle caresses, René's eyes witnessing me, and eager kisses, creating a building energetic orgasm. Our bodies undulate together in a rhythmic cadence, becoming ridged then release with shivering kriyas running up our spines. Time disappears as we explore ecstatic sensations. As René's wand of light enters me, the rolling energetic orgasms explode into life.

"Thank you," I whisper from the little spoon position.

The next week, at my scheduled dental cleaning the dentist discovers a rare resorption of the discolored front tooth. This occupies my attention for the next 6 months. I undergo a front tooth extraction and dental implant, which consists of major dental surgery with bone augmentation, and extensive gum and skin grafts. All of this followed by a second surgery, and placement of the artificial tooth. Beyond the surgeries, I endure over 30 stitches, and to control the bleeding more than three vials of Novocaine injections in my face. I quite literally can't smile, even if I wanted to.

Not only is it as if I have been punched in the mouth, I now need to rehabilitate my face in order to smile again. Months later, parts of my face are still numb, my nose doesn't work right, and I can't smell or taste much. My jaw is angry from holding my mouth open for hours, so I have to wear a night guard to keep from grinding my teeth when I sleep.

The worst part is I'm incapable of giving a reassuring

smile, or a quick *hello* smile, or a *thank you* smile, or an *oh-silly-me smile*, or simply greet someone with a smile. I notice some acquaintances don't recognize me without my smile. I see how much I rely on smiling as a way of greeting people. I communicate many things with a flirtatious smile, from acknowledgment to appreciation; even some questions can be answered with a smile. I didn't know how much I communicate with my smile, until I couldn't! There's also no kissing or giving any variety of oral pleasure, for the remainder of this hellish year.

This year feels all jammed-up inside me, and I need some help to keep things moving. After my long soak, I arrange a session with one of the resort's highly recommended craniosacral therapist. This allows my head, and face to begin unwinding the stressful pain from my dental procedure. He's good at paying attention and listening to my body. After the session I painstakingly re-live the agony in each cranial suture, releasing the aftermath from the jarring trauma suffered during my tooth extraction. The next day, while considering more bodywork, an unassuming man walking timidly past Lola and me, offers, "My name's Jon, would you ladies like a free massage?"

"That's just what I need," I reply.

So, here I am, practically naked at a stranger's hotel room. As Jon opens the door he asks, "Do you want your massage later tonight, instead of now?"

That's a suspicious question, but I still feel confident that I'm not in danger. "No, now's best for me," I reply. Does this man have unspoken motives for getting me in his room? Does he want to have sex with me? I'm not afraid of sex. I'm clear that I'm not attracted to him sexually, no confusion on my part, no mixed messages from me.

"Okay, welcome," Jon says, and motions me into his room.

How did I get here? Is this one of those stupid positions

I was warned never to get myself into? His room is at the end of the building, with the door around the corner from the others. Can anyone hear me if I yell? Will I yell if I need to? As I slip my clothes off, and lay on the massage table, I feel surprisingly safe.

I'm not trusting in this man, because I don't know anything about him; I trust myself, and the safety this resort provides. As Jon works on my sore, needy body, and I begin to relax; I don't let my sexual needs seep out. I stay in my responsible professional persona, and ask, "Why did you offer me a free massage?"

"I take a massage workshop here, every year," Jon replies.

"Do you have people to massage at home?" I ask.

"I'm married to a *closed* woman that I love very much," Jon says.

"Aw hum," I groan through the face cradle.

He offers, "I had a powerful psychic reading earlier today, and was told to do something for myself."

As he continues to talk, it becomes clear why there's no need for money exchange today. He's healing me, but I'm about to offer him something of equal value in exchange. Jon asks, "Are you part of the Polyamory group here?"

"Yes, many of my friends here practice honest, open relationships," I say. "We are transparent with our partners about attractions and experiences with others."

By this time he finishes working on my back, and I turn to a supine position. His skillful hands are well trained to stay within the lines. I'm able to completely relax, and feel entirely comfortable. I may have even dozed, because before long my massage is complete. He's standing just next to my right hip, with his hands still on my body. Politely he says, "I feel like kissing you," gesturing toward my groin.

Equally polite, I say, "I don't need that at this time." I feel no desire to grant even the smallest of sexual favors. Based on our conversation it's clear that it isn't in his, or his wife's, highest interest to cross that line between healing session and sexual experience.

Then the magic begins, and Jon opens up even more, saying, "I thought your friend would accept the massage, but I didn't think you were going to say yes."

It's truly my destiny to be in this position, with this vulnerable man at this peak moment. His hand still gently touching my hip, I explain, "I practice honesty in my relationships, and I have a variety of connections in my life. Earlier I heard you talk about loving your wife," I continue, "If you want to stay with her, I encourage you to be open with her."

"She's closed," he says.

"You may be surprised at the things she's ok with," I say.

Jon agrees, "She has been, surprisingly supportive of the massage classes, and says I've become a nicer person since I started my massage business."

Very softly, Jon moves his hand to my outer labia and says, "I've never seen a grooming like yours before." He continues, "I've been married to my wife for many years, and only dated a couple of women before that."

Observing his hand, and checking in with my body, to my surprise, there's no sexual energy moving through either of our bodies. In that moment he appears young and innocent, even though his body is at least half a century. He's simply exploring a part of the female body that he has little experience with, and is highly curious about.

I notice when he speaks he often closes his eyes. I engage his eyes, and say, "Maybe there's more than one meaning to the psychic's words."

Then, as noninvasive as he started, he lifts his hand, his eyes open wide, and he agrees, "Doing something for himself could have multiple meanings." Jon says, "There are many things I can do for myself."

I watched him transform, choosing self-responsibility and realizing he can give to himself without taking from another. "Would you like a hug?" I ask as he starts to turn away.

Jon nods.

I reach up and pull him into an embraced, saying, "Thank you for the much-needed massage, and for being transparent."

"Thank you for showing me new relationship possibilities," Jon says.

I hesitate to get dressed, because it feels natural to walk out naked. We have both given during our session, been vulnerable, and it's proven safe in this place where our worlds meet. I leave feeling taken care of, by me and by this man who is no longer so strange.

Night falls, creating a new wonderland with sparkling lights in the trees reflecting on the water. The slightly cooler breeze is an extra treat. Skyler comes around the enormous fig tree, grabs Lola's hand, and motions for the rest of us to follow.

Harper asks, "What is it?"

Skyler calls over his shoulder, "You'll see."

Hand in hand, single file, we wind down a grassy path, under a wisteria arch to discover hidden pools of varying temperatures, surrounded by fragrant flower gardens, and candle-lit altars. Trickling water falling on stone fountains creates a delightful music. The moonlight reflects on my naked, levitated body. Surrounded with hands positioned under to gently float me, supporting my complete surrender. My heart is overflowing with gratitude for life.

That night as Lark, Harper and I make love, I see something I've never named before. It's the way Lark smiles with her eyes. She presses her juicy body up against mine, as I lean against Harper's strong chest behind me. I take those eyes in, and as the chaos of the world slows to just before standstill, I think; note to self, learn how to use my eyes like that. Even after the smile fully returns to my mouth, it's a beautiful thing to have a backup.

The next morning we dined on the resort's restaurant patio. Jon waves hello, as he walks past with a new confidence. There's no hint of creepy, undefined agendas. He's a healed healer, with integrity and gratitude, full of joy. I stop mid-sentence, and call-out, "Thanks again."

Jon turns and smiles as our eyes meet for the last time.

Driving home is remarkably different. It's still hot, but each of us is somehow changed, and way more relaxed. Conversations meander naturally with a silly playful twist. I say, "The salt of the ocean is no different from the sweat on my butt."

Laughing, Skyler says, "Let me look that up."

Even with the smartest of phones, none of us are able to access the origin of it. I'm sure I didn't just make it up. None of us mind being squished, bumping body parts as we round corners. The return jaunt to the airport feels twice as fast as the journey to the hot springs just days ago. Gratitude and joy are flowing, and though my cheek muscles are sore, it's good to feel the smile on my face.

EXPLORATION #15

What are your thoughts on community?

_____

_____

_____

I experience community as the chosen family I share my gifts with, and allow to support me when I'm in need. When I keep my body and mind clear from stress and trauma, I am able to share my strengths with the people in my life. It's a constant process and we all need each other to survive and thrive!

What is your homework on the topic of community?

_____

_____

_____

Examples:

List the people in your life who feel like family. Send them a love or thank you note.

Think of a time when you needed support. Did you ask for what you needed? Can you ask for support now to clear any post-traumatic stress?

Invite a group of friends to join you on an outing to a museum or camping.

Invite a friend to tea. Discuss your strengths, and ask them to talk about theirs. Explore how each of you contributes to the people in your lives.

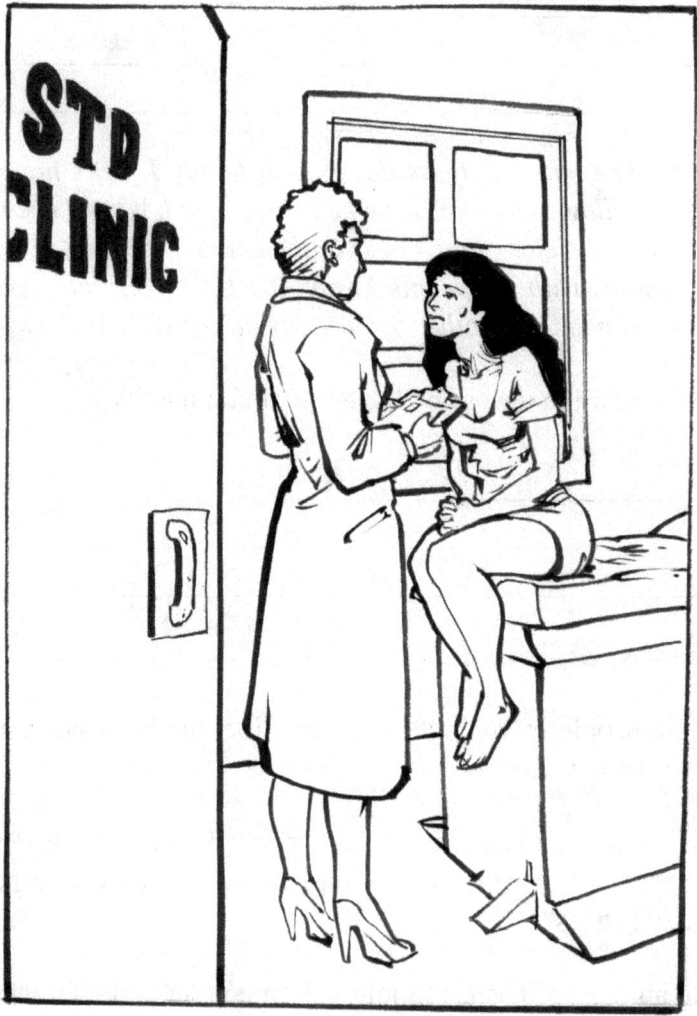

Chapter 16

Clinic Visit

"Being honest may not get you a lot of friends, but it'll always get you the right ones." — John Lennon

Invariably, it's appropriate to ask about STDs when dating more than one person. When I was fresh out of college I almost got married, just to avoid worrying about risking my health by having multiple partners. I thank my more rational perspectives, and being introduced to radical honesty for helping clear my misguided confusion on this topic. I remember the day I learned it was imperative to have an STD conversation early on in just about every new, potentially sexual, friendship. If the conversation is up front, then I can make an educated choice about whether to take an offered taste of a beverage, or borrow lip balm, or kiss. Many people are ignorant about sexual health, and even more are uncomfortable talking about it. With a short check-in I can gather just about everything I need, about how health-savvy a new person is, and how risky it is to consider engaging sexually with them. When having this safer sex conversation with a new potential lover my favorite question is, "What does sex mean to you?"

It's an appealing beginning to a tumultuous relationship. A few days after the fall of the New York towers, life seems surreal. I'm attending a gathering in the pines above Palm Springs. I go on my scheduled trip, even though it might be canceled, as I'm not much use to my clients in this state of mind. It's a touchy-feely group that I've started to identify with over the past few years, yet because of the shock I find it painfully difficult to connect with anyone, even though I'm in nature, being fed deliciously healthy food, and surrounded by caring people. Everything's unsure and grey. Our world has just been shaken up; I'm also going through a personal struggle, and just can't get the negative thoughts out of my head.

It's the final event on the last day of the retreat. It's a simple exercise, where some stranger leads a blindfolded fool around, introducing the trees and rocks and dirt. Here I am, blindfolded and trying not to stumble, in my disconnected body. Then it happens. The divinely-guided being holding my hand stops. Lowering slowly, he places my palm on the sunlit ground. The moment my fingers feel the warm soft dirt, I bust out into unexpected tears. Flashes of reconnecting to the very thing that provides stability, then it hits me like a bulldozer running over my butt—I've been stunned by the events of the week, and had fallen into an alienating fear. Immediately I see that once again I can trust the earth as a safe place to be. The Earth is at the root of my physical being; it's where I live. I feel the sun warm my body, and the connection of the strong callused hand in my hand, and dirt in the other.

Time slows to a perfect rhythm. I bless the physical experience of being an integral part of the heaven and earth dynamic. With eyes closed, I walk through a sea of hands stroking my hair and body as voices whisper, "You are loved."

The next one says, "You are beautiful."

Another voice says, "Thank you for your smile."

Tears wet my face. The final anchor, a large person with huge arms wrapping around me with a tenacious squeeze, voices right into my ear, "Welcome home."

As the arms slowly release my awakening body, I feel the first deep breath enter me since the morning of 9/11. The hours following that breath seem timeless. The glowing participants share watermelon and laughter, while playful lips steal grapes from my belly button as we move to the music. In this elevated state during the last moments of the event I meet Don, the man who'll change my approach to dating and honest communication.

Our first date is normal enough. Pad Thai from a ma and pa hole-in-the-wall for lunch, followed by a walk down a meandering path through the changing leaves in a park. We sit under a tree on a blanket talking about nothing much, each trying to get a sense of the other. Don feels good to me, and I'm impressed with his intelligence. I like his strong masculine face. Don asks, "How do you bring up sexual health with someone you're interested in dating?"

Before I could answer he proceeds to tell me detailed intimate things about his sexual history and current health status. He talks about his relationship status, and agreements with his partners, and that he uses condoms in all intimate situations including rubbing genitals together. He tells me that he gets tested every three to six months, and he was tested four weeks ago. He proceeds with a detailed list of all the tests he had done. "The results for each of these tests is non-reactive, meaning I'm all clear," he says.

When he pauses I say, "I usually just say, I've been tested, am clear and healthy, then inquire about them."

The moment of truth, he actually becomes angry at my response. That should've been my clue that this would be a tumultuous relationship, but there's a stronger force drawing us together.

The lessons I learn from our experiences, over the next year, are invaluable. Things like explaining my relationship dynamics, and my safer sex agreements right up front. I still practice telling the person I'm getting to know when I was last tested; specifically for syphilis, gonorrhea, chlamydia, trichomoniasis, HPV, HSV, and HIV, then asking them the same questions. I now see the value of having this conversation before things get heated, to allow the other person the best chance to tell the truth. Before that day I'd never considered that someone might lie about such things if they were sexually aroused, because they want to *get off*, and don't want to deal with physical or emotional rejection if they admit to being less than *perfect*.

My life is so much simpler now, because most of my friends and lovers openly share their health history and get lab tests on a regular basis. I practice self-responsibility and open communication as I don't want to perpetuate the spread of any illness by a careless kiss or a condom break. Birth control pills disrupt the body's natural hormones and missing one dose can interrupt their protection against pregnancy. Additionally, the fear of unwanted pregnancy is good motivation to use female or male condoms, which also protect against the spread of unseen infections. When I think back to how it was in school, I feel blessed. Really, like an angel prescreened each potential lover, only allowing the safe ones close to me, keeping me healthy.

It's not always the easiest path to be radically honest. Often there are obstacles to overcome. A shame filled experience during 6th grade sex education where they separate the boys and the girls and we're expected to keep secrets about our bodies, or *the talk* from an embarrassed parent, or internalizing the terrorizing forces of religious dogma we heard growing up, or the lack of positive guidance around our changing sexual bodies, could be the basis for developing shame and many are left thinking sex is wrong, dirty, or evil. It's not the norm to be honest about sexuality with others, or even with the self.

I used to tell myself I was monogamous, but as I learned the meaning I realized I hadn't been monogamous since age fourteen. The definition of monogamy was *the practice of marrying only once during a lifetime*. To me this meant having one love, and not only was I on to my second love by then, but I still cared deeply for the first one. I also loved my family, and girlfriends, and even a few of my teachers. Being honest about number of loves was only part of this challenging and radical honesty.

I also wanted to be honest about improving my exercise habits, making more money, and cleaning up my diet. If I knew eating sugar and processed carbohydrates was an unhealthy choice, but I ate it anyway, then I wasn't in integrity because it fed unwanted candida, and zapped my energy by spiking insulin and crashing my blood sugar.

Radical honesty might be too radical in some instances. Too much detail, or when my way of doing something is completely different from those around me. Religious conservative thinking expects everyone to conform to the norms of the past, but this would go against the natural process of growth. The world has experienced rapid change with mass media, and now the Internet exchanges multi-generational ideals with a blending of cultures like never before. When sharing, I use discretion, and keep my focus on the highest good for everyone involved. I'm aware that spreading negativity is sometimes easier than sharing uplifting information. Being radically honest with myself is a safe place to start. Then as I communicate with others, I watch for new areas where I can improve.

My New Year's resolution is to be impeccable with my word, so I spend the next nine months learning what that means. How and when to tell the whole truth can be tricky.

September, time for my biannual clinic visit, and I'm apprehensive about the possibility that my perfect status could change. On my drive to the clinic, I reflect on the past six months since my last wellness screening. I've been more sexually active than usual. There's the excursion with the young college boys, but they're vibrant, and because I'm a family friend there's little chance that they lied to me about their sexual health. I feel tired, but I have lots going on, and I've gotten up early too many mornings in a row. I think I'm okay.

There's plenty of time to contemplate while waiting in that room so appropriately named. Is my definition of safer-sex safe enough? It starts with keeping my immune system healthy. Closely followed by getting tested regularly to catch any virus or bacteria before I can spread it to other people, and if detected, treat it while the count in my blood is still low. Of course I use condoms with everyone unless I've agreed to fluid bond with a partner and all my other partners are aware of this trusted connection. Near the top of my list is having my safer-sex conversation with any potential sexual play partner before things get heated up.

I sit silently. The room filled with regular looking people, all waiting to get their clean bill of health. Sex is taboo and many people don't talk about it, or maybe they assume getting tested is only for prostitutes and drug addicts. Whether I have sex with someone or not, it's good practice being comfortable talking about it. When a person initiates a safer-sex conversation, and their level of comfort and attention to detail is proficient, it's encouraging to me, telling me about the maturity and trustworthiness of this potential sex partner. I like to be relaxed, aware, and sober when connecting with a new lover. I look at their physical body. I notice if they're run down or overly tired, because the health of my sexual partners is critical. My health is vital for continuing to be a good lover and enjoy life.

Sexual repression in our society creates shame and judgment around *sexually transmitted* illnesses. The common cold, or flu virus can be transferred by close intimate contact as easily as syphilis. Because of my nursing background, and science degrees, I geek-out on health a little more than the average non-health professional. I wonder if the handful of bacteria and viruses that are included in an STD test are simply because they can sometimes go undetected for years if not tested. Maybe these tests need to be reevaluated, adding other hard to detect, potentially destructive things like H pylori, skin diseases, tuberculosis, or intestinal parasites. Perhaps adding tests for diseases for those who live with specific animals, or in certain parts of the country. For me this is why annual physical screenings for general health are also an important part of being responsible.

To avoid unnecessary complication, I fill out the

paperwork as briefly as I can. Finally I'm ushered into a little white room, to wait for the physician's assistant (PA) to come. Eventually, she sits down in front of me looking at my papers, and begins the questioning, "When was your last period?"

"August 20th," I say. As if this is a test to see if I remember what I wrote.

"Are your periods regular, have you noticed any hot flashes, or vaginal dryness?" she asks.

I want to go into the reality of how juicy I am when I'm sexually and emotionally aroused. I want to say, the only time I experienced vaginal dryness was ten years ago, when in a relationship with a man who wanted to suppress and control my sexual expression. I felt shut down and thought it was normal to conform to society's idea of what relationship was supposed to look like. I want to tell her, the only time I get hot flashes is when a lover surprises me with a hot text or phone call, or when I feel the desire of a lover after a few days of being apart. I begin to realize that what I used to think was normal is shut down, and I'm awake again! But I just answer, "Yes, no, and no."

Her next question catches me off guard, "How many sexual partners have you had in the last year?"

I hesitate. I know it's not appropriate to tell the truth; it would be like requesting to go to secondary inspection at a border crossing. My mind jumps from subtraction to division, and then abandons the idea of truth, and searches for the number that won't flag an alarm. I tell her, "Four," but as I look up at her face I realize even that is the *wrong* answer. This is the point in the interview where the questioning turns into interrogation.

"How many were men, how many women? Did you use a condom, or female protection barrier?" she asks.

The answers are quick and easy so far, but then she asks a question and I feel the need to lie. Not because I'm ashamed of the answer, but because the reason she's asking doesn't apply to my lover. "Have any of your male partners had intercourse with men?"

I tell her, "No."

She asks, "Have any of your partners shared needles?" (Of course that's a no) but to get more specific she adds, "or use IV drugs?"

Again faced with an honesty dilemma, because he frequently has a vitamin C nutritional IV, but never shares needles. We use natural medicine, and for the most part don't take pharmaceuticals. Best to keep things simple. "No IV drugs," I say.

She looks back over the numbers with a furrowed brow, and I feel the need to explain myself a bit more. For the first time in a clinic setting I proceed to explain a small portion of my family constellation, the four I've admitted to. "Two of my lovers are a couple that I've been close with for nine years, and we've only had sex a handful of times. I live with one of my partners, but we haven't had intercourse for seven months." I continue, "One is fairly new, I've known for almost two years and we have sex two or three times per month."

I might as well of had horns growing out of my skull just for admitting to having more than one partner, but I feel less judgment coming from her after that description, as she realizes I'm probably not a walking Typhoid Mary.

One of my partners once made an impartial observation, that I had as many lovers in the past year as he had in his whole life! Intrigued with my chosen lifestyle, and half admitting he was a slow starter. After learning more about societal norms, I realize I'm somewhere in the low-range, on the sexual activity scale: from the six percent of the population at one end of the scale with no sexual partners in a lifetime, to the six percent on the other end who have many thousands of *sexual partners* in a lifetime. For me it's not about a number. I would need a clear definition of what is meant by sexual partner, and then I could count the people I've had sexual contact with. I have platonic friends, and other people in my life that are non-sexual. However, I unrepentantly admit I like sex, and find it a valuable way to connect with consenting adults who also love sex. It's also a powerful way to move creative life energy. It's important to express myself at that depth with others who consider their physical, emotional, and mental health as significant as I do. I value self-responsibility. When everyone involved is self-responsible there's less risk of creating a mess, or drama.

There's a subtle shift in the room as I open my heart by sharing a piece of truth, and in her listening a real connection's made. I'd like to clarify the question, and tell her all of my sexual details; if only there were a legitimate purpose to counting how many people I've connected with in the past year. But there's no reason to expound any further and I'm at peace knowing that what I convey to this PA isn't creating distance, or alienating me into some high-risk category. Instead my heart opens, I relax into a comfortable experience, and get my usual clean bill of health.

As I leave, the PA goes the extra mile to find female condoms for me. I'm not sure if it's because that is her job, or because a genuine human connection has been made, and she's as touched with my honesty, as I am at being able to speak it. Even though it's only part of the truth, I'm able to speak 100 percent of the truth about those four lovers.

So much has changed since that clinic visit. I now do my best to give an accurate ballpark of numbers, and my health history because I know we're all learning that living a sex-positive lifestyle doesn't need to be a risky lifestyle. The truth is that there's less risk of cheating, lying, withholding, passing infections to others, holding shame, suppressing emotions, or contacting an illness when we're open and create safety for the people around us. When I look back on that visit, I see that it was the first of a burgeoning pattern of leaving the clinic with a smile on my face.

EXPLORATION #16

What are your thoughts on honesty?

_____

_____

_____

I experience layers of honesty. We're taught not to lie, but telling the truth is also part of honesty. What about little white lies and withholds? I must be honest with myself, diligent with the words that escape my mouth, and aware of the meanings and possible misinterpretations of my words.

What is your homework on the topic of honesty?

_____

_____

_____

Examples:

Sit with a partner and take turns saying the words, "Tell me something you want me to know." After a few rounds of sharing then take turns saying, "I am withholding (fill in the blank.)"

Make a list of all the times you have had sex or sexual intentions in your life, and then share it with a partner.

Plan a date with a partner to go over all the details of your sexual health.

Make a list of all the lies, white lies and withholds you have done in the past week.

232

Chapter 17

Healing through BDSM

"Out of our vulnerabilities come our strength." — Sigmund Freud

I'm experiencing fear; what if my beloved chooses to stop spending time with me after getting to know the *real me*? I'm working on being my authentic self. Letting go of trying to impress, and only showing the parts I think will be liked. Now I realize I'm working on the wrong part of this problem. I can't lose my beloved, because the beloved isn't mine to lose. When I completely release control of another, I'm free to live fearlessly. From the other side of fear I gain clarity, and am able to command higher integrity from those around me. Newfound bravery is felt when communicating with potential beloveds, who are inspired to discover their truth and clearly share it with me.

I want to spend the majority of my intimate time with people who have the capacity to love many. Sharing new love energy with all their lovers, and spreading the love is beneficial to all. It can be hurtful to anyone involved when a lover chooses to be with only one, and *breaks everyone else's heart*. It was all backwards in the old paradigm—most believed that when they found an exciting new love, the honorable thing to do was to break it off with other lovers, selfishly keeping all that life enhancing flow with only one person. As I learn new ways to relate, and love, I'm grateful to experience how having compassion and loving everyone is a service to those in my life. Instead of continuing to break hearts every time I have a new attraction, I become aware that there is room for more love, and I expand my capacity to share.

Being myself is the best way to attract those who truly appreciate me, and want to be with me as I am. After years of wondering why someone is head over heels about me when I'm not really attracted to them, and when I'm insanely interested in someone they are repelled, now it seems obvious and simple. It was easier for me to be myself when I wasn't trying to win affection or manipulate them into wanting me. I don't own anyone and I'm not looking to be owned. Being honest about my true nature in each moment is attractive to those that will be good partners for me.

I'm selective with my valuable time. I typically don't break up with anyone, and I continue to add new love into my life. There may not always be enough time in a day for multiple lovers, but there's enough time in a week, and even more time in a month. I stay current by negotiating what's working and not working in all my relationships, and value how we fit into each other's lives. As I keep my heart open and allow others to live their lives, there's a natural flow to our rhythm. Some break it off with me, but even that can be an easy transition. It's a process maintaining clarity in loving, including, and negotiating relationships.

Breaking up now seems like a foreign concept, but only after years of contemplating what love means. I used to think I would someday find someone that I would love more than everyone else in the world. A number of times I tried to pin that title on one person, only to be disappointed when it didn't go the way I'd imagined. They didn't live up to my expectations, or I didn't live up to theirs; either way, it was heartbreaking.

I returned to the reality that I have many amazing lovers in my life, each mirroring back different parts of myself, revealing a more complete, whole me. We all have the dark and the light within us. Each person has masterful qualities, and each of us is a student in areas of developmental lack. Shining good traits, as well as twisted aspects, and also not so nice parts of the psyche, all blend together in unique ways to make each personality. How could I possibly choose just one person to love?

Love

True Love

Unconditional Love

To LOVE another is to see the other as they are, without wanting to change them. But I must also see myself, so I won't project hidden agendas onto the other person. I want to avoid projecting who I want another person to be, blurring my perception of who they truly are. I want my connections with others to be real.

I want the smile on my face to be based on truth and reality, not rationalizations or avoidance. In my formative years, Mom couldn't love all of Dad, or maybe he couldn't love all of her, and for most of my initial romantic experience, lovers projected their perfect ideal onto me. I grew up learning to love partially, and to be selective with what part of myself I showed. As a young person, I thought love was about focusing on someone's potential, but what happens if they fail to live up to it?

I didn't know anything about kink; anything that was out of the ordinary felt uncomfortable and was usually avoided. It's difficult to pretend to only see part of another person, and trying to show only part of me was an impossible struggle. I was 30 years old before I explored kink or any kind of BDSM. I watched another person have sex in a group of people and thought I might actually vomit. I had only seen porn for the first time a couple of years before that, and was still traumatized from watching the actor Jodie Foster getting raped in the 1988 movie *The Accused*.

I knew I liked to be tied to the bed, but I didn't know that was kink because it was just something exciting that a lover gently introduced me to, and I found it relaxing to be forced into surrender. I later realized that kinky things don't seem kinky to the person who likes it, only to those who haven't tried it yet.

After observing that first introduction to kink and BDSM, I began participating in group-sex; I liked the new experiences and excitement of facing the unknown. A couple of new friends from that first group sex experience introduced me to other ways of being submissive and following commands. I found a secret kind of freedom in surrendering control and trusting the one who tied the ropes, or cinched down the corset on my bare breasts. I found a whole world of strange experiences, and much to explore within myself and in others. Imagine the relief when I realized it was okay to love all of someone. It was tricky opening to others and allowing them to see all of me, because I judged some of the things I liked as unacceptable.

What if love is about acceptance and consideration, giving and receiving, as well as releasing expectations? If I don't expect someone to like the same things I like then it's a surprise to find someone who likes it. When I accept and allow all the perspectives that are in each of us to have a voice and be seen, I can be truly interested in how they may be different from me. At first, this seemed like a sickness. Aren't we supposed to hold, obey, and keep our *other half* in line? Such outdated thinking doesn't allow for accepting all of anyone. In intimate relationships, psychology considers it codependent or enabling to allow the other person their full expression to do whatever they want. Somehow if my partner does something *bad* it becomes a reflection of me. It's so much pressure trying to control the other! Instead, I can allow them to evolve, grow up, and be free.

Most people are doing the best they can. I'm responsible for myself, and I can be a good example. When I focus on being my best, and improving myself, then I attract others with matching vibrations who are doing the same. Allowing the other to love freely, and be who they truly are, we can choose each other from free will. Our union can be filled with joy and desire, instead of guilt, pressure, or trying to control the other.

As I know myself better, it becomes easier for my intellect, intuition, logic, and my feelings to align. My heart and brain stop fighting to prove which is more right. My feeling nature and intellectual side can see one another, and become calm. Love can't be forced, just like a fake smile isn't felt inside. It's about allowing all of it, loving the shadows and the sunshine.

Loving myself allows me to see and love others. I choose to love those who control their mate, are afraid of darkness, or judge the sticky parts of life. I feel fear as I dip into the shadows of my being, and all beings. The result of these explorations is my glowing smile—a reflection of the freedom I feel from seeing deeply, and knowing I can choose to express the most appropriate thing at the right time. Remembering I have a choice usually helps me to make one. Sometimes I get lazy and don't make the highest choice, but even then, I'm doing my best not to slip into complacency.

I had a long and jagged introduction to understanding the oneness of everyone and everything. After working for many years in psychiatric hospitals, I remember seeing a former long-term patient walking down the side of the road. Seeing them in a different setting, on the same street I was driving down, forced me to reevaluate the barrier that had previously divided us into patient and nurse. As I drove by, I had a clear realization that it's a very thin line between that person and me. The phrase *there but for the grace of god go I* suddenly had new significance. My understanding of humanity shifted and I felt gratefully connected with all of it. I related to this person walking along the road, who had previously expressed their inner hate by cutting their arms and threatening to harm others. I've touched my own dark shadow parts, and I can choose not to hurt myself or others with that darkness inside. Once it has been seen it's no longer in the shadows, and I'm at choice. I like to be positive, reflecting back to others, so they can feel the acknowledgment, and allow the dirty shadows to be bathed in light.

Running along the path at the Bay, just a few months before meeting Don, I admitted to my running partner that I was in conscious denial. It was no secret that I wanted to have children. But because my family leaned toward Christian conservatism, I decided it was best to get married, to a man. I found a kind and able man who already had an older daughter, and was willing to make babies with me. We functioned well at creating a home together and began our happy life. Soon my new husband added that we should also become monogamous. I was caught up in my 35-year-old eagerness to bear a child, so I agreed. I turned off my sexual life force energy, to keep it from leaking out to those around me because I didn't know how to guide or direct my energy.

We had a good sex life, but my vagina was no longer wet when we made love. I thought it was just what happens when the body gets older. What a lie! It's what happens when I'm shut down and not fully expressing myself. I truly wanted to be with him. I just didn't want to be with *only* him. Then I started to feel like I was dying, but I didn't know why. I loved the man I was living with, we played house together so well, but I'd made promises I couldn't keep. I had layered lies around a man I wasn't legally married to, but because we had a wedding and agreed to monogamy I felt trapped. I liked a part of our life together, but the rest of me felt like I was dying, far too fast.

One evening I went to a concert where a former lover of many years was singing. After the show he hugged me and I felt my body gush with sex juices. My body wasn't old and dried up any longer, and I shared juicy sex with my husband again. I presented multiple ideas of what would work for me in our marriage, but we couldn't agree on opening up our relationship again. I was choosing to live in denial, afraid of losing him by being honest. Yet I felt a deep human need to have both real connections, *and* to be truthful.

The affair that ensued was a lifesaver, but neither my lover nor I wanted to live in a lie. I'd created all of this mess in the name of wanting to have a baby and doing it the *right* way. Even that was a lie—we were never going to have a baby together. I was trying to force too many areas into some sense of normalcy. I knew I had to undo it.

Running may have saved my life. By the time I'd gone from never jogging more than four miles to running 13.2 miles, I went from total denial about my marriage to conscious denial, to clarity. Each week as I ran with my running coach, I blasted through new personal boundaries, and each week got closer to realizing I needed to live in truth. All was ready to change; as my body got stronger so did my mind, and as I broke through physical limitations, I broke through the unkeepable promises into truth.

The thought of undoing everything seems overwhelming, yet for me it's the logical next step. I want to revert back to the beginning of our relationship (before we made unreasonable agreements) but that's impossible. We need to untangle some parts, but it's a transition into the next phase of our relationship. I can't go back, only forward! I'm not sure why one would say the words *'til death do we part*. If feeling like dying is the only way out of a commitment, it isn't a good choice.

Freedom from the burden of deceit was a relief. We split and remained friends. Unfortunately, when marriage doesn't work (or works for awhile but then stops) it feels like failure. It was another decade before my former loving husband understood the benefits of polyamory and confessed that he wished he'd listened to my requests when we were together.

One of the jagged parts of my past that helped me learn to see all of my beloved, not just the soft skin or shiny hair, was a yearlong bond with Don, a dungeon master. It was more normal than it sounds. This time, my surrender to another's will is consciously chosen. I had *tried* to get pregnant, look normal, and suppress my energy. None worked for me. I'm ready to see beyond what I thought I knew and wanted, and who I thought I was.

I'd grown up with spankings, and sometimes seemingly unnecessary parental punishments, so having a relationship with a dominant felt familiar and nurturing to me. I received a deep muscular Rolfing massage that released pent-up fear in my gluteal muscles, held as memories since those childhood spankings. Don helped me instill love, strength, and personal power back into those muscles. The amount of directed attention I received from this teacher was intense, and divulged my inner makings like an x-ray. At times I didn't exist, and other times there was so much of me, I couldn't be contained. One thing was undeniable; none of who I am could hide or stay in denial any longer.

After that first date with Don, realizing there's much to learn, I go underground and spend the majority of the next year in a dungeon. At first, I try all my usual tricks of avoiding conflict and showing only the sunny side of my disposition. I want to please, and Don wants to punish. I feel like nothing I have to offer our relationship is good enough, but it becomes clear that he wants to see my dark side. It's a skirmish between trying to let down my defenses, and trying to hold on to all the layers of who I think I am, and what I show to the world. It feels like death when a part of my personality is asked to step aside and allow what is authentic to come through. My face is wet a lot.

When above ground, I dress conservatively and walk calmly so as not to draw attention. Sitting in an uptown diner, on rickety old converted church pews, Don says, "We need to be discreet and keep bite marks below the neckline."

I nod as we share a bowl of vegetarian chili and a butter burger.

"It's important to be grateful and stay positive," he adds.

Just before walking to dinner, I'd been crying and then rocked in his arms until I felt safe. It might have been easy to slip back into emotional release if I wasn't paying attention. I understand the dangers of getting arrested if there were any hints of misconduct or unwanted abuse. We agreed to only play the roles of dominant and submissive when in private. I see the importance of not making a fuss about the inevitable bruises on exposed body parts while in public.

In the hardware store, we didn't purchase everything at once to avoid appearing suspicious with a shopping cart of chains and restraints. Complete presence, and choosing only to participate in activities when I'm ready, are vital to my wellbeing in the months to come. Not saying no to something beyond my boundaries, or saying yes to being hit with canes, which is too much pain for my body to process, can be physically and psychologically dangerous. He asks my permission before we begin each BDSM scene, and I trust that he will listen to my no and my yes.

Being told what to do takes on a new sense of freedom for me. I'm taken care of in every way possible. I spend most of my time with Don, practically living with him. He pays me to do the shopping and help with his accounting. Don made his money in real estate, and I save him over $1,000 per month just by cooking some of our meals. Our daily lovemaking is healing. All the brainpower that normally goes into the hundreds of choices I make for myself every day, is now freed up to focus intently on just one thing.

Concentration and directed intention are new for me. In the past, I learned to expand my mind, and take in more information. The challenge here is to slow my mind down in order to be present with the one thing in front of me at any given moment. I begin doing chores only when I want to. Not just to get them done, or have a sense of accomplishment, or to build momentum, but to practice being fully present. I only cook when I can clearly see the nutrients necessary for that day, and infuse the food with positive intention.

It's actually nice not having to make many mundane decisions. Don't get me wrong, this isn't a time to luxuriate, nor is it a game for the lazy. These series of days include some of the most stringently detailed, deliberate unwinding of the conditioning in my consciousness, I've ever undergone. My energy is spent staying present to every reaction and pattern that surfaces when my body is subjected to new sensations, or when Don toys with my emotions. At times the only thing that keeps me from dissociating, or trying to escape, is the reward of comforting sexual pleasure. In fact, it was the lure of really good, focused sex that drew me under to his dungeon in the first place.

We haven't made love yet today. Here I am, in Don's bed, after choosing the riding crop he will use in our next scene. I know the impact is going to penetrate the barriers that shield past trauma, and the embedded beliefs concealed in my body will soon be stripped down to the bare origin, hopefully without stripping away any skin. As Don enters the bedchamber, I smile in a flirtatious way. Just being in his presence is challenging, yet magnetic. Apprehension turns to anxiety before culminating in nervous fear. This familiar pattern of emotion dominated so much of my life. I begin to feel the room closing in, becoming darker and condensing until all that exists in my outer awareness is what's on the bed.

Don forcibly takes my wrists, and with one swift move binds them together, hogtying them to my ankles. Resistance is futile, but I push against my quietly raging anger. My exposed backside quivers as I hear him pick up the chosen tool. "Are you ready?" Don asks.

"Yes," I say.

Don presses his thick, muscular chest against me till I feel the slow steady rhythm of his heartbeat, then he pulls back. Heightened anticipation mounts, slowly at first, until he snaps the whip and I feel panic.

"Stay," he says.

I'm not a dog. I'm not submissive; I'm in control. Then a loud pop stings my left ass cheek, and interrupts all thought. Again. This time on the right side. Is it too much? What is wrong with me for needing this treatment? Self-doubt broadsides me. As the judgment subsides, I feel so much hatred, and it isn't coming from him. The stinging slaps are repeating faster. My lips curve, forming the shape necessary to utter my safe word. Before I make any sound warmth surges up my spine as his loving hand touches my welting skin. Don pulls the end of the rope, instantly releasing me. I feel the angst channel from my body, through his and into the ground. Here comes the self-judgment again; am I using him for my grounding? Am I able to stay grounded on my own, and be an open channel during challenges?

Soon the magic takes over. I surrender to the sensations, allowing the flood of endorphins to soothe the reactions. "Stay with me, I'm right here," he says as his strong hand presses down between my shoulder blades.

Something has shifted; the familiar feelings I associated with fear and anger are changing. Am I dying, or am I letting go of what I once thought was me? Then I become aware of my capacity to feel all the repetitive old patterns, as well as knowing that these familiar reactions are no longer viable. I can never react to panic in the same way again. I'll be forever aware of my ability to dive into the unknown, and choose life in the midst of darkness.

The inside and the outside of reality seem the same. There's no sense of time. He wraps his arms and legs around my body and begins rocking gently side to side. I feel high from the sensations and hormones released, and it's unclear where my body stops and his begins. I feel small, without any thoughts left. I burst into tears.

"Let it all out, I'm right here," he repeats in my ear until I sleep.

It's a beach day, so I pack the towels and a lunch. Because of all the stimulation, I have less stagnation and bruises heal quickly. I prance into the surf with an unfamiliar acceptance of my body in a swimsuit and a new confidence in my step. I pause as the receding froth exposes my legs again, strange, there's no angst or wishing the water would return to cover my seemingly unsightly thighs. I'm not judging by body for the first time since I was a gawky 11 year-old, developing awkward shapes on my hips, upper legs and budding chest. What shifted the perception of my body? Don had given focused attention to every inch of my skin pouring adoration into my fat, cellulite, misplaced hairs, scars, freckles, poor posture, and asymmetrical parts. His complete confirmation of my body was contagious, and I felt comfortable in my exposed skin for the first time in my adult life.

Trust is building between us, and each experience we create allows deeper confidence to develop. Facing fear is one of the benefits of playing at this level. Both of us come face to face with the edge of too far. I want to take more, and he wants to give more. Testing the edge of danger and self-judgment.

One morning we decide to literally push our personal edge with knife play. I've always had a phobia of cutting flesh. I remember refusing to shave a man's beard in nursing school, for fear of slicing his face. The deer-antler handle, combined with the Japanese steel and leather strap, make this the most unique cutting tool I've seen. The 5.2" blade is sharp and cold as he grazes it along my arm. I become aroused as he alternates the touch of his blade with pressing bites and soft kisses against my skin. "I've never played in this way with a dangerous weapon," he says.

I wonder how far he'll push it.

We enter the state of timeless trust, and soon the pandemonium inside is harmonized with exhilaration. I want to feel all of him. Inside I become aware of a vast space, not quite empty, but almost. The edges are blurring and the ornate extension in his right hand fuses into one. Opening, wanting, his left hand slowly slips in and out of my excited vagina a couple of times, deeper than either of us have gone before. I'm ready, fully surrendered, open, his right hand up against my labia as the warmed steel rests against my inner thigh. Slowly his blade glides past my gateway, into the depths of the abundant bliss that flows through my river. My body melts around the blade as it descends, but with everything relaxed there's no tension to cut against. I feel a warm gush of amrita as the steel recedes.

I face the unknown, and the veil that was blowing in the breeze between familiar and unknown is no longer there. He slashes at my fear until it blows away in the windstorm we create. When my eyes open, all of my distress is gone. We walk down to the local diner for a burger, and share an ice cream sundae.

Throughout the year I'm completely cared for and supported by Don. Even when my eyes are seeing punishment, and my body is feeling pain, I'm present and aware of being completely loved. Shown deep fear inside me, up close and in my face, I make friends with the pain of that fear. I release the suffering about the fear.

I'm not alarmed by the darkness, as if I already knew I had everything inside me. I am possessive, controlling, grateful, manipulative, sincere, hateful, peaceful, confident, angry, joyous, and I recognize myself in the void. I truly am one with all of it. I have learned to love others the way I want to be loved, but am I free of the unconscious desires to control, manipulate, or possess others? My actions are with awareness and choice, and staying committed to this level of consciousness is a lifetime practice that I revisit often.

I celebrate the day my teacher permitted me to restrain him. The trust I felt with Don was mutual, and I was the first lover he allowed in like this. I showed him the same level of respect and focused attention he had given me. I covered his eyes with a silk scarf then tied his strong arms and legs securely to the bed frame. I'm able to keep him engaged for hours, and give him the experience he never surrendered to before. At one point he asks, "Please, may I be untied to go pee."

"No, you may not," I say. Since he's blinded, I take the opportunity to invite him into an even deeper surrender. Like a magician, I'm able to fool his senses, but instead of smoke and mirrors, I use sensation and a big gulp cup. It takes some encouragement, but he's able to relinquish control, and completely let go, fully convinced that I'm swallowing his pee.

BREAKUP POEM

He wanted to see her dark side·
He hates it, but once Pandora's Box is open,

it demands to be experienced·
It must be played all the way through,
until her full expression is released into the eternal
abyss·
Back into Bliss,
left unexpressed no longer,
reintegrated into the wholeness of her entirety·
The dark and the light blend into beautifully swirl-
ing,
creamy colors, appearing subject and spicy·
A new beauty fusion, waiting to be born, adored,
and tasted by the connoisseur of perfect chocolate·
He left,
she cried, "He wanted to see my dark side!"

When our time was up, and my teacher left, I cried. He had become the all-seeing, all-loving, beloved; but then again, so had I.

EXPLORATION #17

What are your thoughts on shadow work?

_____

_____

_____

I experience shadow work as an invaluable way to become a conscious person, and one of the best ways to learn true compassion for everyone.

What is your homework on the topic of shadow work?

_____

_____

_____

Examples:

Make a list of unacceptable traits you see in others. Notice how they apply to you.

Make a list of three behaviors you judge as bad. Then write about why you don't like them, when you were told not to like them, and the good side of them.

Ask a friend to tell you three behaviors that you don't know you do, followed by three strengths they see in you. Ask them if they would like you to do the same for them.

Choose an archetype (like the ruler). Then look at the extremes (like tyrant or coward) at each end of the continuum that this admired being could act out.

Chapter 18

The Beloved

"The moon stays bright when it doesn't avoid the night." — Rumi

I know you've tasted enlightenment. I saw it in your eyes the first time we met. All I want is to look into your eyes forever. I too have seen it. From here I make a conscious choice to also experience being human. Being all of it, the sacred light of life, as well as the darkness is part of my sacred path. When I acknowledge my darkness, then I am aware of more options and I can choose to shine my light on the world around me.

My most consistent teacher has been nature. She taught me to observe until I understand enough to begin when I cross a river, climb a tree, or hand feed berries to a blue jay. Much of my childhood was spent outdoors, in the Pacific Ocean, exploring the Rockies, or on a horse. All were much bigger than me, so I had to learn to respect and relate. My earliest memory of swimming was at age two, racing the neighborhood kids from the deep end of a pool. They gave me the diving board so I could have a head start because I was the youngest by many years. I was riding horses at age four, and skiing in the Rockies by age five. It was a gentle and natural way to learn about relationships. I'll admit it took me a bit longer to learn how to apply that wisdom to human relationships.

At a very young age, I briefly experienced fear when I heard my parents frantically call my name as I wandered away from our mountain camp following my older cousins. But later, when I started kindergarten, I undeniably was afraid. Nothing was familiar, so many yellow buses to choose from. I was new to being on my own. Why can't my sister come with me, like she did in preschool? I eventually adapted to my new environment, and by 2nd grade, I was fascinated with the diversity of human interactions. I observed how some kids have a special friend, while others get along with larger groups, and some are loners, similar to different animal species.

When it came to the differences between boys and girls, I didn't understand. In the animal world, we often couldn't differentiate male from female unless we looked at their genitalia. I remember chasing boys, but didn't know what to do when I caught them. The next year, boys tried to keep girls from playing baseball. Girls were supposed to bring their dolls to school, and sit under the trees combing their hair during recess. That was fun, for about two days, and then I was back out on the field asking to play sports. Finally, our 3rd grade teacher organized a baseball game with all the kids. First time up to bat, I hit a homerun, and that was the last time I had to fight to play sports with the boys. I earned respect for my skills, instead of being judged for my gender.

As captain of the 4th grade baseball team, I befriended an awkward girl who was left out, the way I used to feel. I thought it was strange when the kids accused me of picking her for our team so that I would look better.

In 5th grade I was shocked to win every award except perfect attendance—returning from my Dad's house after winter break, a snowstorm caused me to miss a day—so Chip Chiporelli got that one. The award ceremony was in a gigantic auditorium, filled with the entire school. I had to walk all the way up onto the stage, in front of everyone, to receive my award, four times!

I felt small and confused because I didn't know why I'd been chosen.

In 8th grade, I experienced a similar confusion when my entire class nominated and voted me class president. Why me? I hadn't even known I was in the running. The thought of having to get up on stage in front of an audience, to give the president's graduation speech, was too much. I convinced the kids that my math buddy should be president, and I became the vice-president. Later our wise teacher helped me push through this fear. He announced that the vice-president had to give the welcome speech, which put me on stage once again. This time I was prepared.

Then came the summer of Love. I was 13 and had just experienced my very first kiss with a 15-year-old boy named Dave. We spent many long hours, slowly exploring kissing. Our kiss was simple, just lips, tongues, and pressure. We never explored with our hands, or any other body parts, we just sat next to each other with our mouths joined. He gave me a mother of pearl ring, and our song was *On & On* by Steven Bishop. This was my first romance, so I had nothing to compare it to. A few hot weeks into our budding relationship, I had to return to my other parent's house, 300 miles away, to go back to school. He was learning to play guitar, and sing John Denver's *Leaving on a Jet Plane*, which he performed for my sister and me the day we left. We exchanged weekly, handwritten letters through the mail. Sometimes I could almost hear him playing guitar for me, as if he were in the next room.

Then the unthinkable happened. Early one afternoon, scrubbing the dingy yellow walls of the apartment attached to the garage we'd rented to a smoker, Mom handed me a fat letter from Dave. Excited as always, I ran outside to open it. As I read, I didn't understand. Why did he have to get rid of me? I wasn't in his way. I wasn't even there! Had I been longing for something that wasn't ever real? He wrote that he was seeing another girl now. My eyes blurred, filling with water as I sank down to the ground, ashamed at my reactions, and confused by the unfamiliar emotions. Not knowing what was next. When I'd left at the end of summer, at least I knew I'd see him next vacation. I never saw Dave again.

I began to transition between childhood and adulthood. I felt lonely at school, and often asked my classmates if I was weird. One morning I was late to class and two large, tough-boys cornered me up against my locker. My initial response was confusion, then fear, and then anger took over. I threw an undercut punch into the belly of the unfortunate boy closest to my fist. As he doubled over they both stepped aside and I walked briskly to class. I was taking a crash course in standing up for myself.

The following year, I experienced my body as nature when I almost became a mother. My focus shifted from innocent ignorance to discovering a deep desire to be a better person, and become a good mother when I was actually ready to have a child. Being uprooted from such a natural state of being (motherhood) at such a young age left me feeling disconnected. Following nature's example with each species of animal, plant, or bug connecting in a different way, I began to recognize the beloved in many forms. I fell in love with philosophy, psychology, physiology, anything related to the human body, art, and spirituality (not necessarily in that order). Studying in so many directions was like nature, spread out all over the world, but every molecule is connected. I was searching for the true connection.

Somewhere I read that death and misery unite everyone. Death is such a seductive mistress. Don't we all want to be there sometimes, sooner rather than later, just to end the misery? Death has been romanticized in tragedies like *Romeo & Juliet*, as if it were the deepest form of love. I found facing the misery in life, and exploring the Bliss in love were greater challenges, and ultimately more rewarding. Discovering I'm at choice, I choose to let go of suffering, and allow misery and death to be part of the larger sea of perspectives that we all share.

I'd rather say we have sex in common. Sex is the foundational source of creativity within our bodies. Sex is a celebration of life. Strange how there is so much taboo and censorship around sex and bodies, yet violence and destruction are publicized freely. What if our world was sexually uninhibited and we shared our bodies freely with others? If sex was viewed as a positive thing, would we be more cooperative, creatively stimulated, and peaceful? Would we be more connected and willing to share resources? Does our human conditioning affect my interactions with the beloved, and the world? I can only see through my lenses, or can I also see you through another's eyes?

One of my deepest practices of sexual union is meditation—a solo experience of sitting before the beloved within. Sitting before a beloved outside of myself is an equally important way to reflect on all of God. During my explorations, I discover the following idea: perhaps we're all more connected than we know. Not only do we breathe the same air, walk on the same earth, and drink from the same water, but we also think the same thoughts, and feel the same energy. So how could connecting alone with the self, be separate from a deep connection with another? It becomes more complicated as we add two brains receiving and filtering data, or three, or more; but what a powerful challenge it is.

I long to sit fully open and aware before you: knowing I am love, one with everything (including you), and needing nothing. Our potential is infinitely greater together. Connecting with you is the cosmos making love—Mother Earth coming up through our feet, and Father Sky entering down through our crowns, uniting in our hearts. Being with you ignites our purpose, inspiring creativity and bliss. Our relating uncovers the hidden shadows of the psyche. It also illuminates our brilliant ideas. It's always an adventure inviting you inside.

Through my years of exploring relationships and discovering that I'm connected, I begin to learn the importance of clarity. My practice is to move through uncomfortable emotions on my own, in order to show up whole and without agenda when I connect with others. Sometimes communicating can help me move through a stuck place, and verbally sharing common struggles can be one way to feel connected. However, speaking something out-loud for others to hear may potentially create momentum in a direction I don't want to go. So, if thoughts that I don't want to manifest are spoken, I ascertain that anyone listening is able to completely release all meaning, remembering these words are only spoken to move through them. These words aren't all that I am, and I don't want to move toward manifesting them.

By observing nature, I learn about the calm within chaos, and the flow of life. There's always more than one thing happening at any given time. The violence in nature can make life appear antagonistic. Eddies in the Colorado River force any living thing down to its watery death. Yet that same river is a source of life, sustaining farmlands that feed us. When I suggest river rafting to a couple of friends, one may think that's a lovely thing to do on a Sunday afternoon, while another may feel scared and think it's a dangerous proposition. I value having others understand what I intend, but the listener will interpret what is spoken through their filters.

We won't agree on everything, but I desire to share myself authentically, and create safety for you to open up. One of my favorite things is exploring life-force energy through a sexual connection. I prefer stimulating this creative energy with others. I practice keeping it flowing on my own using my breath, intention, or self-pleasuring, so I don't desperately need an external lover. This awakened life-force energy can be directed to heal (emotional, mental, physical or spiritual) pain. This energy can infuse a desire or project to manifest into reality with ease, or the healing intention can be sent to others like a wish or prayer.

My energy often supports others, and their projects. The good news is there's an endless supply. Healthy sexual energy truly is a renewable source of energy. A blissful state can continue indefinitely; when I give to myself and live a balanced life, the ripple effect to others is endless. Creative sexual energy is vital for a productive and harmonious existence.

It's exciting for me to find purpose in making love, other than procreation. Something that makes everyone involved feel good isn't a bad thing. Coming together to enhance our lives, raise the vibration in our bodies, and stimulate creativity, are just some of the benefits of sex.

The age of texting and social media is upon us. Unlike the days of letter writing, the turnaround time is almost instant, and it's easier to stay current with more people simultaneously. I wish to find more inclusive vocabulary, and ease suffering. Besides the risk of misinterpretation, sometimes I'm challenged by my own opposing perspectives, like thinking, what I wrote is weird, and different is bad, or that I shouldn't *rock the boat*— thoughts that want me to mold into whatever you want me to be, so you will like me more, and ones that don't want to push the send button at all!

With a smartphone in hand, I begin to push through these communication challenges by contacting Drake after a great weekend together. I write:

I'm feeling contented peace—deeply loved and free simultaneously (that's new). In the past if I focused on one person, my dualistic mind wanted freedom, and when I was unattached, I longed to be one with a beloved. Now I see that I can go deep and stay free.

I hope our exchange is mutual, I vitalize more than hinder, and the thought of me excites you. If not, at least one life is greatly improved by our connection, and those around me appreciate that. Our adventures and conversations inspire my art, knowing you're interested in my projects is invaluable.

Still juiced up from my weekend with Drake, I hike down a cliff to the beach with Bobby and Harper and share my good mood. I have an abundance of friends, and if one doesn't understand or appreciate all of me, there's always another who can see those other parts of me. We reach the sand, strip off our clothes, and run into the cool water. The waves are stronger than usual making bodysurfing a blast. I swim as fast as I can to catch a big wave that takes me all the way to the beach. I stand up to see Harper on the next crest, heading my way. Bobby catches the last one of the set, and I jump out of the way to keep him from bowling me over. Exhausted, we rest on the sand, laugh at our wave wrestling stories, and rehydrate before hiking back to civilization.

A few weeks later Drake and I joke about our evolving, long distance dynamic. I send:

You're a fucking fuck, and fuck you for not wanting all of me all the time, but what a fucked up delusion that would be.

Drake calls immediately and says, "Your timing is perfect; I needed that." He's walking through a dark LA neighborhood, cooling down after a run.

We both laugh.

Our conversation goes on late into the night. After hanging up I text: *I like how we're fucked-up on the same page.*

The beloved is always here, and concurrently nothing but an elusive illusion. Drake and my relationship grows in its own time with sporadic visits and our own rhythmic cycle. We may not speak for weeks, but I feel everything. Our opposing energies spark while the current builds, nothing can keep us from pulsing rhythmically together. When the stars align, he's available for me and I'm available for him, our purpose is stronger than the forces of nature and our magnetic polarity draws us together.

When I see Drake's brilliant blue eyes, we explore which energies want to be expressed, depending on what's arising, and where we synchronize. Today, I surrender into my feminine sitting on a pillow next to his feet. Drake bends down placing his hands around each of my arms lifting me onto his lap. As his masculine takes over, I feel small and light—such a fun dynamic for me as an older sister who's always felt bigger than most women. Suddenly my energy shifts, I grab his shoulders as my mouth pins him down at the nape of his neck like a mother cat. My masculine and feminine tenderly loves his masculine and feminine, and sometimes not so gentle. His feminine flirts with mine, while my masculine respects, and is honored to be friends with his masculine. My masculine wants to be fucked by him, and eventually, it all melts into oneness.

After hours of emotion-moving sex, hurt from past relationships surface and he talks about letting it go. Upon returning home, I write:

Beloved, I still feel you inside. I'm both fully satisfied, and insatiable. I'll take as much as you'll give, and I'll give more than you can take. When you're before me, nothing else exists. Sending a wish that tonight your dreams are gently assisted, cutting cords and releasing painful memories, so that tomorrow's waking dream is seen through fresh eyes. I appreciate your generous presence, the way you share the love that you are, the way you look at me, and the way you touch me with your kiss. Thanks for lighting me up. I Love You.

I Love You.

I've noticed in many of my relationships, these three little words can easily be misinterpreted. The meaning can be influenced by past experiences, the feeling in the moment, or beliefs about potential effects it can have on the impending future. Expecting others to understand what's meant by these words is a mystery. Sometimes the recipient of these legendary words is triggered from a past trauma instead of seeing the person in front of them in the moment.

Love has a variety of ancient meanings. Since language is evolving, I want more descriptive ways to speak that don't trigger past associations unrelated to what I'm trying to express. *I love you* isn't about the future, or trying to turn our union into happily-ever-after. When I say, *I love you*, it's different than most other people's meaning—it doesn't mean I love *only* you. I want to love everyone. Because it's possible to feel more than one thing at a time, I can love those I don't like very much. Each person I love is different. I love the former lover that I no longer engage with sexually. I love the one who's angry, and the one who's cruel. Each aspect of humanity deserves love. Some people use those words to express wanting to live together, and create a family.

When *I love you* is spoken, the one who's had these words dumped on them may be listening with tainted ears, but also the one speaking them is often coming from an unclear place. I realize it's impossible to be inside another's mind, to help them hear without prejudice, so I take it upon myself to be impeccable with my words.

When I say these three famous little words, my intention closely resembles gratitude for being able to express the love that I am. Often, I'm in the midst of feeling uninhibited in a new way. I feel safe to express a part of me that's been in the shadows. If love is who I am, then as I feel encouraged to be fully expressed, past a new frontier of opening deeper, I'm filled with overwhelming gratitude for being seen by another, and the words *I love you* spillover.

Maybe expressing the love that I am is like enlightenment, or being a shaman or guru—one doesn't actually announce it, they just be it. What if Love is the essence of the soul, to be experienced, but not spoken, only felt?

Love is a strange word. I can't help but like it. It's the spark of life in everything alive. Love is at our core. When we open and relax into bliss, that's love. When we let go of fear, the love underneath is exposed. When we drop the anger, we are love. We can lead with any emotion, or we can simply feel what is, and be in love. When I'm being love, and you're being love then our core life energy can resonate to the same frequency. Saying *I love you* is another way of saying, I'm attracted to the way that you expose your inner self in my presence. I feel who we are underneath all the reactions, walls, and stories that surround us. My love likes to feel your love. Love connects all living things.

Thanks for encouraging my love to shine. There are perspectives within me wanting to be heard that have been put down for over-communicating. *I love you* may come from that voice of inhibited stunted feelings, unable to find creative ways to fully express and avoid misinterpretation.

Saying *thank you for witnessing the love that I am* may

still be too loaded. Did I mean brotherly love, love of God, sexual expression of making love, or the love of an object? Has our society lumped it all together as an internal experience for anything on the outside of the self? These words are an acknowledgment that our inner beings are mutually connecting where the essence of who we are is seen, and allowed. Perhaps shared love is when the individuals involved encourage opening while going deeper than ever before—seeing the raw, untamed, and unedited, even if just for a moment.

I can engage the brain, and the feeling body with carefully chosen words to convey feelings, like I feel seen or I see you. When you and I connect as the observer, the present moment is real.

The philosopher Ken Wilber talks about resting as the observer. The I am, connecting with the I am—your higher self (I) and personality (I), connect with my spirit (I) and ego (I). The II:II, or 11:11 is my reminder of this eternal connection. Each night at 11:11, Drake and I make a wish.

One day before I drive home, Drake asks, "Do you feel loved?"

"Yes, very much," I reply. We kiss and I head home.

I want to adopt Drake's perceptively ingenious phrase. It's a brilliant way to verbally express love. Asking, *do you feel loved* is less confusing, and doesn't need a definition.

When I arrive home I send:

I'm feeling connected, seen, heard, appreciated, expressed, free, and so excited that I want to share it. The addictive perspective inside is crazy about us 24/7. The lover perspective always holds you deep in my heart, unconditionally. The healer perspective is continuously sending you love. The controller wants to limit the crazy thinking (obsession) to once a day.

A few weeks later I experience a different kind of Dear John.

Feeling the distance between us I write:

You Good?

He simply replies: Super, talk soon.

I miss his call again the next night. Then I come across a love poem and write it out: *Nothing can shatter this love. Even if you were to take another into your arms my dear, you would still be kissing me.* — Rumi

I hesitate to send it. What if Drake misinterprets it as a sign that I want him to go out with another, and actually put those arms that I cherish around another? Yet, I've gone to the trouble of getting all the poetic words down perfectly and feel compelled to press send.

Drake replies: Good to know.

When I'm in bliss, I know who I am, and have a knowing that everything is exactly as it should be, but when I'm hungry, or tired, or hormonally challenged I can fall from Grace. Old unconscious patterns crowd in and run less than blissful thoughts.

I feel close bonded, open, safe; then, oh god, it happened. He went on a date. I wasn't there, I didn't know. Panic! I judge myself for getting in this situation, considering my primary lover to be someone other than the Shiva inside my own being. Why the fear, and the sick feeling of losing myself? Falling, falling, falling from that sweet spot that I've grown accustomed to. Yet, I feel it all—knowing that *everything's in perfect order* keeps slipping into the spiral of emotions.

We finally speak on the phone. "Do you feel jealous?" Drake asks.

"Yes, I feel it all," I answer. "I'm happy for you. I want you to be free. Yes, I feel jealousy, fear, and uneasy," I quickly add, "I also feel grateful for our connection, there are so many good things in my life, I don't need anything. I like it when you choose to include me in your life, but I'll survive when you make other choices. All I want is a real relationship, and that means truth."

Drake says, "Thank you for your honest reaction, you're amazing."

"I don't want to be with someone who's dying because of my suffocation," I say. I choose which perspectives to release, and which ones feel good, helping me back to where I want to live—in bliss.

Freedom and sexuality stimulate creativity. When my beloved's creativity is turned on it stimulates mine, and when mine is stimulated it benefits others. Sexual energy is the core baseline that moves my life force energy. It's how I celebrate the divinity uniting with humanity. Sexuality enhances the creative flow, and I celebrate when those around me are sharing more love. It's at the root of opening and feeling more. Feeling it all is so new to me. How can I be feeling peace, fear, anxiety, hope, and compersion for a lover who has a new lover, as well as painful jealous insecurity all at the same time?

"I haven't had sex with her yet. I'm grateful to you for helping me. You and I are stable, and there isn't any drama in our relationship," Drake says.

"Thank you for telling me about your date. I want a real relationship that includes honesty," I say.

I remain calm, and we agree that neither of us want monogamy, which would include covering up desires, and feeling suppressed.

Unlike when I was 13, sitting on the floor ashamed and wondering what I'd done wrong, now I'm aware that it isn't all about me. I feel all the feelings and observe, without letting the thoughts take over my process. Even though I can still feel my 13-year-old self getting the Dear John letter, I move through it, noticing that I also feel many other emotions along with the confusion. This time I have more life experience, and understand what I want based on seeing a bigger picture.

I want freedom, at any cost, for everyone involved. Just because Drake's with another woman in this moment, doesn't mean the connection between us has changed. When I'm with other lovers, I still love him; that never changes. I'm always connected to everything, and I'm my own primary partner.

I think of being my own primary relationship, and my breath shortens. Not in a sexy, ecstatic, ready to orgasm way; but in an I can't breath, I'm having a panic attack, I can't feel this much despairing loneliness, this is unnatural, kind of way. I observe my breath quickening out of control, it's racing faster and faster, but no air is getting in. Am I suffocating in my own emotional goo? Just as fast as it started I take a slow breath, deep into my belly, and feel the all-connected air fill my lungs, expanding my chest and releasing the tightness that I held around my heart. I still have a choice, and as I slow down even further, the feeling of panic relaxes to expose many other feelings underneath, including a peaceful, humble gratitude. I remember my warrior spirit who stands so effortlessly with the masculine and feminine within. I feel the heavy pain in my heart lift, because I know I am love, and I want all lovers to share the love that we create together. It's all part of a larger plan to create a space for world peace to thrive.

Felisia, Jacy, Jean, and I take a picnic to our local park. After enjoying an eclectic meal that we pooled together from the food we had at the house, Jean invites us to explore the far end of the park before darkness falls. Theodor had recently told me some of the history of this area and said this land was a cemetery before the school and houses surrounding it were built. Felisia jumped when a bird flitted from an overhead tree.

"Oh come on girls," Jacy says. The four of us huddle as we make our way to the edge of the grass.

"What's that?" Jean says pointing at a crumbling headstone. I feel my heart racing as if a zombie or goblin is going to jump out from behind it. As we walk around the path there is a cluster of old grave markers that are no longer doing their job. We're shocked to read so many of them were from the 1800's. I share some of the stories Theodor had told me, and the thought of ghosts sent a shiver across my shoulders.

That night as I drift off toward sleep, a brief conversation from the picnic comes into focus. Without many examples of having multiple partners, and living with some under the same roof, we are relationship pioneers. One of the benefits is that none of my relationship dynamics and lovemaking falls into rutted patterns because when I make love with a variety of people, I bring new experiences back to every relationship. Each person I have sex with is different, so my body learns to be flexible and orgasm in multiple ways, which means I can show-up for live-in lovers like Jacy and keep it fresh. In my six years of relating with René, we're still learning new ways we can play together.

A few days go by, another call from Drake. I'm proud of myself for maintaining compersion, and a sense of humor through the growing pains with this beloved, as we explore newfound sexual freedom. He's keeping me in the loop by telling me about his experiences. I want to know, I want him to be happy, and I don't want to date a caged, trapped man. I want him to share the love, and to explore his creativity, and life force. Another night, another first date with another woman. He calls me; I miss the call. I text saying, I'll call in a few minutes, but it's too late she's arrived, so we don't speak.

I distract myself for hours. It's half past one in the morning, so I turn off the Gladiator movie on my laptop, just as The Romans are coming to see The Spaniard be a real man, and I roll over. Within a minute, in the dark silence, I begin weeping. Deep sobbing. What the fuck? I was so happy for my life, and being able to share total freedom with an exquisite lover. Why do I have this thought haunting me that he will choose another over me? It feels as if this fear is a long rope, tied tightly around my waist, with the other end attached to something I want to come closer, but it pulls further away tightening its grip.

Thoughts spin around like a windstorm; swirling confusion, in no apparent order. I think of my biological father, who chose his original family over my mother, sister and me. Then my mother divorced the only man I called father, and he chose to adopt his new wife's kids. My other partners are choosing to spend more time with other lovers, so I sleep alone most nights. The evidence is piling. I'm tired; everything will be so much more peaceful in the morning. I realize being real means letting all the perspectives, with all their thoughts be heard, even if it looks like insanity. I assure myself, knowing what I want with all my heart, is to have real relations with everything, including myself, and all of God.

What if the past repeats? What is the truth about the past anyway? What about all those who chose another lover over me; did I choose not to be chosen by them? I'm aware that I don't want to feel trapped or manipulated, and I want to be free to choose my beloved. So, it makes logical sense that I want them to freely choose me.

Maybe I'm not looking at all the truth. I only see the parts of the truth that fit the story that I'm running. I only see as much as my capacity will allow. Expanding and feeling more, my breath deepens and slows as my mind relaxes into stillness. Living a polyamorous life means I have multiple beloveds— my internal beloved, my beloved nature and all of god, and the beloved humans as they come before me.

Life is mysterious. We're born, and at some unknown point we'll die, but in between there are brief moments when the great mystery reveals life's true purpose. My spiritual practice is to share the love that I am with the beloved before me. I'm grateful for the perfection of how our unlimited time unfolds. I love through the pain, anger and the unknown, regardless of what comes back in return. We are bright flames, and when we come together we ignite a blaze to purify, rejuvenate and destroy the stories of loneliness and self-doubt. Tonight I remind myself that I am capable of sharing true love. Life isn't always easy, and relationships are difficult sometimes, but they are my favorite part, so I'm willing to be patient and hold a space in my heart for you to show-up again.

It's easy to cut someone out, draw a line, make a boundary and say that's enough, but at the end of life there's no one left. Patience and truly loving is the challenge. Finding compassion and keeping that room in my heart free of clutter, making it pristine for the beloved to return when they're ready—if I can't learn to do this, who will ever do it for me?

I'm blessed to feel so fully. I know deep inside of my being, I'm the beloved father and the beloved mother; and there are a little girl and boy that are always with their mother and father. The masculine and feminine within me make love through my flesh, while the children blissfully play in nature. The divine connection with all life is one within me, and all I need to do is witness and enjoy.

EXPLORATION #18

What are your thoughts on love?

_____

_____

_____

I experience love at the core of who we are as living human beings.

What is your homework on the topic of love?

_____

_____

_____

Examples:

Find a partner. Make a list of all the possible things love could mean to you. Share your lists.

Remember a time love felt painful. Now that you have space from that event notice how all the emotions got mixed up. Make a list—loss, pain, confusion, etc.

Sit with a partner and ask, "How old were you when you remember feeling love? Please describe the experience." Then switch partners. Feel free to ask a new question each time you switch roles.

Recall a time you felt love. Write how it felt and how you knew that was love. How many times have you experienced love? Is it always the same?

Chapter 19

Becoming One with The Beloved

"Be yourself; everyone else is already taken." — Oscar Wilde

It's Thanksgiving, 1988. Graduated from university, I'm living in a turn of the century Victorian farmhouse on a few acres with Henry. We're about to go visit my family, and I'm more nervous than I care to admit about not knowing what to call him. The intense affection I feel for him doesn't disguise that I'm in a relationship without a *proper* title. Our expanding concepts of spirituality and relationships make it a struggle to remain involved in my family's conservative lives without raising any eyebrows.

Everyone's aware that Henry and I are cohabitating, so we don't expect to be greeted with outright disapproval. However, we're still told to sleep in separate bedrooms, as if our union is scandalous. Since high school (a wild dating and communication experiment), I'd only had one relationship other than Henry where I was able to be honest about wanting other lovers. Yet I still have conflicting beliefs. Maybe I need to choose just one person for potential baby making. Henry supports who I am, but the prospect of seeing my family resurrects all the *shoulds* in my thinking about partnership and marriage.

We arrive just in time for dinner and the smell of fried onions greets us before the door opens. I notice Dad peering down the hall to see if Grandma is within earshot as he gives us the news of separate rooms. We set our bags in the foyer and follow him to the kitchen. Henry pulls me aside and with an upset face says, "We shouldn't have come."

"Ya, I wasn't expecting this. We just drove for seven hours, after we get some food in our growling bellies things will be easier to handle. Besides we can survive three nights apart," I whisper.

Around the dining table: two brothers, three sisters, one sister's boyfriend, Dad, Stepmom, Grandma, and the two *sinners*. This half of my family is much more relaxed and jovial than at my Mom's house, but more conservative. Dad still seems uneasy, and I begin to think maybe Henry was right about not coming here together. I don't have any experience with how to talk to my family about relationships, especially the ones that involve sex.

Henry and I decide to give our feelings a label that my family can understand. After the dishes are washed I call everyone into the living room to make the big announcement. "We're engaged!" I say. Yes, Henry's my beloved, but we're living a less conventional *open* lifestyle, and we haven't even discussed marriage before tonight.

It's a success, my parents relax, Grandma gives a smile, and enthusiastic hugs from everyone. With a little encouragement in Dad's ear from his wife, we put our bags in one room, and are able to participate in the family holiday without feeling the results of their shame.

How do you undo that? The faux engagement stuck. We spend the next couple years exploring meditation, spirituality, sharing our charismatic love, and using the *engaged to be married* title. During this time we're also setting failed wedding dates, and trying to redefine our relationship in a way that we can live with. It's an impossible feat. It doesn't feel like a lie, but it seems unnatural to have this fiancé label with Henry while exploring having more than one relationship.

One weekend we host our friends' wedding in our gardens. From my limited experience, the couple appears ideally matched and is excited to be united as one. All of our friends are there, and I see the expectation of what marriage is supposed to look like. "Henry and I don't have what they've got," I say to my girlfriend Zany. "I don't want that definition for our relationship."

"Ya, to only be with one person, and always want the same things, seems like a rare find," Zany says.

Henry and I aren't aligned in enough areas to stay together forever, and neither of us want to be with only one person. We like co-creating in a few ways together, but there are big differences in our views on politics, finances, and other values that make it challenging to continue with the fiancé status.

I was unable to confront my family's relationship beliefs that were different from mine, and my choices created a pathway between those old ways and the direction I wanted to go. Now I'm faced with how to be in right relation with a man I love, but don't want to be wedded to in the old traditional framework. It takes us years to fully untangle the knots we started to tie on that family visit.

I'm 25 years old when I meet Lex for the first time. Henry, Zany and I are meeting up with another friend, Ken, for a conference on opportunities in the natural products industry. Ken is telling us about his buddy Lex's herbal supplement business in Santa Monica as we leave our hotel room. The doors to the famous Bonaventure glass elevator, open, revealing a man in a stylish brown leather jacket with kind eyes and shiny dark hair. I stop hearing what my companions are saying as this gorgeous being walks toward me with mesmerizing confidence. There's an instant ancestral vision from my ancient past. Who is he? The unexplored concept of a past-life soulmate flashes in my head. I freeze in my tracks; I must see where he's going. We smile as our eyes meet. Then to my amazement, the friends behind me greet him. It's Lex!

The next few hours are a blur, as I try to keep up with so many things happening all at once in my comparatively insignificant world. Not only am I learning about business, a subject I didn't study in university at the school of nursing, I'm also assimilating all new feelings around the concept of finding my potential *soulmate*. Am I meant to find one true beloved? I was unable to choose just one lover, out of the sea of amazing schoolmates and interesting lovers in my past. Sure, some relationships are easier than others. Each has its attractions and repulsions; areas of synchronicity and other parts struggle to align.

It's getting late. My head's full, as well as my belly from an extravagant dinner. Zany and I playfully escort Lex down to the lobby. Any excuse to ride in the translucent elevator, and spend a few more curious minutes with this delightfully unexpected man. Something about traveling downward feels like sinking deeper, and deeper, into hypnosis. The three of us move closer, and closer, as the elevator plummets. Pressing our bodies together, I feel ecstatic energy racing up and down my body, and back up again. With a subtle cushioned bounce, like an airbrake, the elevator stills and the doors begin to open. The bodies begin to pull away from mine.

"Not so fast," I say, as I hit button #35. The doors close around us like lips. We begin our ascent, bodies moving eagerly together. Zany and I are very familiar with running our energies together with another between us. Our love goes deep, and moves smoothly, incorporating Lex effortlessly. As we near the lobby once again, it happens—the anticipated moment, as his face comes close and our lips can't stay apart any longer. It's rare to experience a kiss that perfect, especially between three people.

Ever consider what makes a kiss desirable or deplorable?

I've been contemplating kisses for a long while. One line of thought emphasizes the role chemistry plays in making me think a kiss is a good one. Kissing disasters often involve things like strong perfume, distasteful breath, or prickly facial hairs. Once a man's bristles managed to poke the tender inside of my nostril, provoking an unfortunately timed sneeze. Is the first kiss the ultimate first impression? Did my very first kiss influence every kiss to follow? His face was so smooth.

My first kiss event seemed life-changing because my younger sister had her first kiss at age five, and I felt a bit late out of the gates. At age 13, riding tandem on a horse, my first was a quick, nervous peck on the lips, but I had done it! The days that followed, or should I say, the long kisses into the wee hours of the morning, many nights in a row, that followed, made an impression on my virgin lips. Those first few smooches influenced almost everything I like about kissing. I say almost because, I've met a few people in later years who introduced exciting new sensations. Bringing me to the question: Is kissing all about technique? I don't think this should be excluded altogether. It's helpful to have some practice, know how to read cues from the lips involved, and take turns initiating new moves then surrendering completely into that amazing bliss that arises when a kiss is done right.

How the lips fit together, their relative firmness or squishiness can also influence the kiss. Some may like a bigger lower lip; even the scent of the lover's mouth could be enough to tip the kiss into a spectacular impact. I feel excitement when my body lines up just right to my lover's. What is more delicious than mouths that want to explore, connect circuits, taste, and breathe each other's breath? One of the factors that keep kissing compelling is the variety—it's the *spice of life*.

Lex walks away, leaving two elated beings behind the glass. Zany and I bring these yummy feelings back up to the 17th floor, creating a delightful night with Henry and Ken. We all appreciate the *new love* infusion in the room. Finally, falling into a deep and dream-filled sleep, I'm aware that I have new fuel. A desire to follow curiosity ignites, that will lead me to make life-shaping choices, and ultimately reveal the secret of how to become one with the beloved.

Over the months following that delicious kiss, Lex and I make delectable contact a few times. I see him as my beloved, but with other beloveds in my life, it's unclear why I'm so enamored by this one. Perhaps, a leftover idea of obligation to find the one keeps me in search of something more. Alexander, or Lexandria (if a girl child) became the name I wanted for my first born, (until I met Jamie on the Greyhound to Grand Jct., but that's another story). My attraction for Lex influences decisions, and changes the course of my life. Lex was the first person to introduce me to reflexology, which becomes my primary healing modality for the next 20 years. Eventually, I move to L.A. to be near him. He is a busy business owner, but tells me, "You are not interrupting me. I will always make time for you."

I look to him like the ultimate mirror, following every hint I can glean from our interactions. I see deep into my psyche, and into my emotions as he reflects the intensity of my desire. Even though it's unclear what kind of relationship we have, he is able to meet me at my level of attraction and respect each time we get together. I value his unmuddied, agenda-free heart.

I begin to see what I want in life, and how to get it. Freedom, happiness, productivity, meaningful contribution, love, and acceptance are the clearest of my desires. To have freedom, I must release everything. To achieve happiness, I must be completely happy with myself. To be productive, I need to diligently do my best, evolve, and adapt. To contribute in a meaningful way, I must become the person I'm meant to be. Love and acceptance are inextricably linked. I give these to others, but now I began to give them to myself. The key is to develop compassion and accept myself, unconditionally.

Everything I want to attract, I need to become. I want healthy people in my life, so I need to keep myself healthy. I recall the Biblical story of King Solomon who wanted more than anything to be wise. "What do you want?" Lex often asks.

"I'm not sure why that is such a difficult question to answer," I say.

I don't want anything from him, except exactly what's happening at the moment. So many new things to learn, and I'm in a state of beginner's mind. I've been a student all my life, choosing teachers, but only truly learn as I do the work to assimilate and teach myself. Learning to step into adulthood, I discover that we are all teachers *and* students.

The autumn sun is warm on my back, while the cool ocean air chills my face. I'm about to be introduced to Lex's 18-year-old son for the first time. The three of us meet at a quaint Santa Monica restaurant. I do the math and realize I'm precisely eight years older than the gorgeous blond haired, blue-eyed son, and eight years younger than Lex. I'm literally right in the middle. They're both tall with the same slim, muscular build. Lex's dark eyes, which see right into me, seem to be smiling at the chance to share his son with me.

There was juicy energy between us, but my fantasies went far beyond what actually happened that day. That experience was the first of a few remarkable father and son attractions. It took almost two decades to consummate a related experience, healing past shame, and showing me what's possible when there's no possession or sexual agendas and each person is acknowledged as an individual.

My tango with Lex leads to soulful contemplations, revealing a profound key to love. I gain clarity about beliefs and taboos around sexual relationships, enabling me to accept who I am, and connect with the beloved (or beloveds) before me. I learn to be an adult—taking responsibility for becoming the person I want to attract. The mystery of love is unlocked—I become the beloved.

EXPLORATION #19

What are your thoughts on self-responsibility?

_____

_____

_____

I experience self-responsibility as the way a person acts after seeing how they create their own reality, and each choice is either toward the desired goal or slipping away from it.

What is your homework on the topic of self-responsibility?

_____

_____

_____

Examples:

Make a list of everything you want in a perfect partner. Then look in the mirror.

Next time you disagree with someone, take a deep breath, list three possible ways you could be wrong, and arrange a time to discuss after both parties are calm.

Keep your home tidy, and plant a sunflower to make your neighbor's view brighter.

Slow yourself down, and clear your mind of imagined scenarios before verbalizing an upset.

Chapter 20

Secrets for "Women"

"The challenge is not to be perfect, it's to be whole." — Jane Fonda

These pages aren't just for those who identify as female. The feminine aspect in each of us may want to hear a few secrets. Some people may be less familiar with their feminine side, if predominantly relating from an internal masculine aspect, but each of us has a unique way our feminine and masculine aspects create together inside. As we become better at navigating our internal atmosphere, it's easier to sail the external ocean.

Women are in a changing time, that's no secret. Many of us were raised with mothers who didn't know how to deal with stress in a healthy way. My mom usually reacted to stressful situations with anger or fighting back. In my life, when the pressure of stress built up, anger was my first reaction. My life is different now. I have more compassion for all sides of the story. The event that shifted my perception happened one day when I got angry with my mother for being angry with her mother who was in a wheelchair. I was boiling over with anger at my mom for treating my grandma that way. Fortunately, I got it. I was doing the same thing. That day I stopped allowing this automatic response to cause my emotions to landslide. Since then, unfamiliar situations side swiped me and I reacted with anger, but it only takes a moment to examine my reactions and choose a different approach.

As women's liberation evolves from a history where those with a vagina could not vote or speak in public, to a society moving toward equality of all people, we see a growing need for new descriptive words for addressing humans. The Latin-based languages and some ancient cultural teachings have historically divided our view of the world into male and female. In reality, the sexes are not so black and white.

Studying Native American Shamanism, with the universe mapped-out into mother receiving and father giving, influenced my development, but it didn't take long to see the flaws in simplistic identifications. To give is not inherently masculine, and to receive is not only female, even though a penis cannot physically receive a vagina. This isn't complicated; I simply want to acknowledge that human sexuality is on a dynamic scale from more feminine to more masculine. Many people are fluid on that scale, depending on their endeavors, the person they're relating to, mood, or hormone levels on any given day.

Using the terms masculine/feminine or man/woman is problematic due to its binary nature. I don't wish to exclude those who choose to identify using other designations. In this chapter, I use these ancient terms as a starting point for this conversation that most people can understand, but they aren't meant to be labels.

One engaging human quality is the superhero, wanting to rescue someone in need. I appreciate characters like Superman and Wonder Woman, reminding us that this desire is not gender specific. As a child, I wondered why Lois Lane couldn't figure out that the boring Clark Kent and the exciting Superman is the same guy. They're both lovable, they both serve a purpose, and she can love both. A person can express in any way they choose, whether they want to wear the cape, the glasses, (or any number of expressions in between), but it excites me to see the combination of all the aspects.

I've heard some women complain that there are very few good men. I disagree. I think people are evolving and upgrading the ways we communicate and interact as equal humans. Some people may have difficult antisocial behaviors, but the majority express themselves as lovable and caring. Each body is uniquely different. Those with more testosterone, which is a strong force, can sometimes look angry. I agree that unconscious or unmanaged anger can be destructive, but it's possible to recognize and learn healthy ways to express these strong emotions. Imbalanced hormones, as well as a lack of healthy coping skills, can contribute to overwhelming stress, making it difficult to express kinder qualities.

Regardless of a person's gender, the human brain and body chemistries are delicate. Keeping the body systems balanced will help maintain healthy emotions. Ten of the self-responsible deal breakers for a healthy body, brain and emotions are:

1. Stable blood sugar
2. Adequate hemoglobin
3. Diet that replenishes the feel-good brain hormones
4. Manage stress and nourish the adrenal glands
5. Oxygen to the brain
6. Improve circulation
7. Eliminate toxins
8. Exercise the body and mind
9. Be aware of emotional reactions and release antiquated conditioning
10. Discover how to contribute back to the world

(For more details go to NurseCheri.com)

To engage another person's wholeness, I show up with both my masculine and feminine energies clear and present. This allows them to meet me where they feel safe to express and open their feminine side, as well as let their masculine side feel free. I'm not on the hunt for the one and only when I connect with another. That thought creates an extremely critical mindset, which may not feel inviting, or safe. When I allow and understand myself, it's easier to allow and begin to understand another. I start getting to know myself by recognizing my reflection in everyone I meet. Then it's easier to see the goodness in others, and I can better appreciate all the idiosyncrasies of the one before me.

Only a few weeks left in the year, and we're all preparing for a wild New Year's Eve party. One of my girlfriends asks me to dinner, or more accurately, the new girlfriend of my longtime lover Bobby. Enveloped in flattering lighting, she sits surrounded by ornately carved wood furniture and statues of erotic Thai women strewn about us. Our unobtrusive waiting staff brings us a drink to start the evening. "What's it like to be with a woman?" she asks, adding, "Will you share some secrets for attracting women?"

Her questions take me by surprise. Possibilities, other than monogamy, are new to Clara, so I assumed the evening's topic would be to prepare her for the upcoming sex party event with her new lover. Maybe we'll talk about clearing her potential jealousy or possessiveness of our shared lover.

Before I can answer, Clara says, "I feel very comfortable with you, and can sense you're not competing with me over Bobby."

"Maybe there's no need for competition because we aren't trying to win the one perfect mate," I say. "There's room for more love, and it's fun to share," I say with a bright smile.

"Yes, I'm beginning to see that," Clara says.

"I like to be inclusive with added relationships," I say.

"I'm excited we met through Bobby," Clara says.

"I remind myself of what I want in my life, like the freedom to choose who I spend time with. I also want others to choose to be with me," I explain. Most of what Clara wants to know doesn't feel like a secret, but I'm happy to answer her questions.

"That's a logical approach, and sounds nice," she replies.

"I don't want to be controlled, or to control others, unless it's agreed upon," I say with a wink.

"Ha," Clara nods. "What relationship qualities do you value?"

"Allowing others to freely express themselves, and clearly speaking what I want are attractive qualities," I say. "Not complaining when I don't get what I want, but knowing what I want and what I don't want so we can negotiate what works is also a good practice."

"I like being clear with those around me," she says.

Smiling I say, "I love being with people who allow free expression."

Clara adds, "It's repulsive when someone is bossy to another, demanding what to do and not do."

I say, "Unless it's consensual, where one has agreed to allow another to control them, then it's no longer a battle for dominance. Any relationship dynamic is valid; I just might choose not to spend time with the ones that aren't my style."

I gladly share how valuable I find expressing all of who I am, including my masculine and feminine sides. "Being attractive to the same sex is no different than being attractive to the opposite sex."

"How can I express myself without feeling arrogant?" Clara asks.

"There's value in letting others know who I am," I say with a sense of humble respect. "Trying to be right all the time, or better than others in subtle competition, gets tiresome." I speak with embarrassed humility, "I've been guilty of these behaviors when I try too hard to be liked. Also, if I'm judging others and emotions arise, it's better for me to identify it, and communicate about it if needed, in order to get back to a place of allowance of those around me. Showing all of who I am has its challenges but I crave being met by people who are in touch with all of who they are, and can just be it without feeling the need to prove it."

Clara adds, "Like when someone always has to have the last word. Even when texting they will send one more, well beyond anything left to say."

We both laugh.

The waiter brings a dish of crispy steamed green beans with pieces of bite-size sautéed beef. It almost feels like we're in another dimension experiencing deep focused conversation while we enjoy the nurturing surroundings, and savor our delicious meal.

My dinner partner and I tell stories of when we first felt freedom. I was three years old and had just seen the British film *Born Free*. It was the soundtrack by John Berry and the theme song (written by Don Black) that stuck with me. The next morning, my sister and I got up with the sunrise before Mom and Dad were awake. We went out to the swings in our backyard and pumping our little legs got them flying. The feeling was nothing I'd ever experienced as I listened to the words we were singing at the top of our lungs—*born free as free as the wind blows as free as the grass grows*. It was the first time I can remember feeling so connected to my little world and we were free.

I then tell of a time when I was guarded, and didn't want to express being needy. "I was given the amazing opportunity of breastfeeding for the first time, from the engorged breasts of my girlfriend. Mary drew me toward her, and I pressed my face into her bosoms. As my suckling stimulated her body, the letdown response caused a warm stream to squirt in the back of my throat filling my mouth. It was the sweetest milk I ever tasted. Mary held me as a mother would, so comforting."

Clara set down her chopsticks. With her head tilted back and lips pursed, she uttered, "Mmm."

My eyes engaged with Clara's, as I continued, "Mary

took my face in her hands, and we kissed passionately. Our bodies pressed together while strong waves of energy ran up our spines causing kriyas, and happy moans. Mary needed to be reminded that she was still sexy after becoming a mother, and I needed to feel needy."

"How do you keep that needy feeling from taking over?" Clara asks.

"We all have an insecure perspective that can judge ourselves. The way I keep it in check is to acknowledge that I'm not perfect and that we all have self-judgments, then remind myself of gratitude. It can always be worse. I evoke the part of me that's eternally grateful for what I've got. Even now," I say. "I maintain that experience as one of the yummiest. Maybe it was the sexual energy running between us that was healing us both by supporting me in feeling loved in my neediness, and supporting her in feeling sexy."

Clara nods, "I think I'm understanding how sexual energy can powerfully contribute to everyone involved."

I feel my eyebrows relax as my eyes soften; I'm pleased how receptive Clara is, and that she comprehends. "Back to the question of attraction secrets and being with women," I say.

The corners of Clara's mouth quiver and her chin protrudes, elongating her neck. Her voice cracks as she says, "Yes, my curiosity's bursting."

Humbly I look down at the spicy noodles that had appeared on the table, and say, "It starts with the relationship to the woman inside. Healing my feminine side began in the late 80's when a woman I worked with invited me to a Barbara De Angelis women's seminar. We spent all weekend in a room with 100 women. I shifted from being unsure I could even stay in a room with only women, to loving my female side, and genuinely feeling good to be around women. One of the most therapeutic moments was an exercise where we walked around in a trance state with our hearts open, greeting each woman we passed. I recognized nearly all the women in that room of strangers, as their faces actually looked like my family and friends. I didn't realize a woman was flirting with me until the end of the weekend when she asked me out. I was clueless at that time about connecting with women."

While perusing the dessert menu, I remember a good example of branching out, and a wave of excitement passes through my body.

Clara recognizes my shift and asks, "You can't possibly like mango and sticky rice that much. What is it?"

"Remembering when my judgment about interacting sexually with women did a U-turn," I reply.

Putting down the menu and looking right into me, Clara begs, "This is what I've been wanting to hear, please continue."

Elbows on the table, I rest my head on my hands to align our eyes, and begin, "I met Ariel shortly after becoming comfortable kissing women. I was full of excitement and uncontainable energy. She was a powerful, influential teacher with many students. Ariel liked the way I flirted with her, even though I didn't know I was flirting. When asked, I delightedly agreed to fly to her community and spend time with her. That night, on our way up north, our flight was stranded in San Francisco. Ariel sent her entourage to a different hotel, giving us our first opportunity to be alone. The next few hours in that airport hotel room forever changed the way I experience the feminine dynamic!"

I continue, "This story isn't about the juicy sex details, but after we filled the room with hours of excited pleasure, she curled her perfect body around mine. Holding me from behind, I was surrounded by an overwhelming feeling of safety and comfort. I experienced for the first time with a woman, what I had only felt with men, and until that moment believed could only happen with a man. Letting go of an old outdated belief, I realized I was free from the limiting thought that I needed a man to make me complete. I was shocked that a woman was meeting my needs for touch, companionship, and security. With the feeling of knowing everything was right in my world, I relaxed and sunk into Ariel's arms. Minutes later, from our bedside window, we could see the sky transform from grey to pink as we watched a spectacular sunrise over the Bay." I pause, and look up toward the auburn and rose tapestry on the wall.

With dreamy eyes, Clara says, "Beautiful."

Reaching across the table, I put a perfect bite of mango and sweet rice in Clara's desiring mouth. "The next step for me was discovering I didn't actually need anyone to be a whole person. My experiences with women nurtured and accelerated the dance between my masculine and feminine sides. I cleared the programming and stuck energy preventing me from flowing naturally with all beings," I say. "Nurturing, healing, mother energy is only one of the feminine expressions. Connecting sexually with women is a direct reflection of my feminine side, and brings out my masculine side in a different way than being with men. Dancing with my own masculine and feminine aspects, I learn to perfect the dance with others in their masculine and feminine energies."

"I love the imagery, and agree about the importance of becoming whole. It seems difficult to open yourself to all beings," Clara says.

"I find it helpful to know myself," I say. "When I'm aware of my choice to be fully present, I open my heart and connect freely with the being before me, regardless of sexual orientation or type of body they live in. It's a choice to receive their reflection of me. I practice remaining self-connected while I enjoy discovering other aspects of humanity that they embody, and how they show-up with me."

Before we knew it the restaurant was closing. We had enjoyed an exceptionally tasty Thai meal, and each other's company. The level of depth we shared that evening in a public place, with no public display of affection, was a lovely relationship birth. We parted ways, excited for the upcoming party where we would have an opportunity to consummate our budding connection.

How can each of us help to heal the separateness of humanity? I'm dismayed by the way modern society is structured with one man and one woman, isolated in a house and away from a community, as if it were a sign of wealth, prestige or normalcy. Problems emerge when we couple up and isolate. When two people become one there can be loneliness, enmeshment, control, bickering, frustration, communication breakdown, vulnerability, defenselessness, dependency, boredom, lack of help, stir craziness, failure, divorce, abandonment, destitution, quitting, and the list goes on. Humans need to bounce ideas off a variety of others in order to understand this world, and our minds wants to learn, create, accomplish, and succeed. We need to feel understood, to be touched, to help others, and for me the best part of life is other humans. In a secluded household, the suppressed couple is more likely to keep other attractions in the shadows, and the natural allure between women becomes repressed.

When I was a young woman, not only did I think it was wrong to connect sexually with women, but somehow I thought I was supposed to get all of my needs met by only one man. A big part of healing humanity comes from allowing people to express their feminine in any combination of energies they desire, no matter what gender their body happens to be. I celebrate women becoming more comfortable recognizing their inner Goddess.

Sometimes the female perspective feels dissatisfied or unheard. Needing to process emotions out loud can be viewed as bitchy and needy in the eyes of the masculine perspective. When I take responsibility for my desire to process, or vent, I can simply request a receptive ear. I then need to wait for my venting partner to show up to listen. If I really need to process with an extremely masculine-identified person, it's helpful to have a third person present to help with any miscommunications. I've found more success enrolling people who are already at ease in their receptive feminine to provide the support that they naturally give. It's more successful if I can complete the processing ahead of time, before sitting down with a masculine-oriented person. Then I can have a results-oriented discussion that includes empathy for their point of view as well, space to verbalize my identified personal needs, and have clear requests for them.

It's easy for communication to get sloppy with the most intimate people in my life. I don't want to withhold, assume, or say hurtful things. I want to be honest and transparent. Healthy communication is where the lines get fuzzy, it feels like the new frontier of human evolution, and most of our parents didn't know how to demonstrate the skills necessary to succeed in relationships. It's easy to dismiss people from our stages when their performance doesn't draw applause or live up to our critique, but soon you'll be starring in a failed one-woman show.

In order to love people through the tough spots in relationships, I often felt like I was over-sacrificing and somehow it would be damaging to me. However, once I pulled back enough to see more than just my opinion, and could see pros and cons to both of our points of view, it was much easier to stoke the fire of my compassion. Once my heart is open and I'm not charged about the topic or the person I have an issue with, then I can begin a conversation to see what's working and what's not working for us.

Love is who I am; I don't need to try and get love from someone else. Love means wanting others to be free to express themselves, and there's no need to fear or isolate myself from others. When I let go of competition and comparison, I can connect with women in a non-threatening way. This connection doesn't need to be sexual; it can simply be supportive, but I personally love connecting with sex-positive woman. We can move and share life-force energy together to free the collective creative energy flow, heal guilt and shame, and unblock true liberation.

Listening is a receptive quality, regardless of a person's sex. When I try to force the masculine side to stop and listen, it can turn into a real battle. Frustration builds, and trying to feel heard can begin to look like escalation or drama. Instead of trying to shift the one closest to me into the feminine receptive space, I need to stop. It's better to take responsibility and find someone who already has access to their feminine side, or find a therapist.

I have an opportunity to face my communication conflicts at a Tantric Shamanism retreat, in nature with some of my closest friends. As a student of Shamanism for more than a decade, blending Tantra and Shamanism isn't a stretch for me, but I'm eager to see how others interpret the inquiry. My studies with Shamans did not involve the use of hallucinogens or psychedelics. My adventures with plant medicine involved use for healing, ceremony, and aligning with specific energies— like the tall birch trees are medicine for bones, and the broad tobacco leaves represent grandfather sun. Each Tantra teacher at the retreat is assigned the task of sharing their own personal specialty, and combining it with what they know of (substance-free) Shamanism.

Blindfolded, in a trance journey class, rocking on my yoga mat in the dark, I see how I don't keep my psyche as clear as I prefer. Before starting my day, my long-standing habit is to review my thoughts, clear any worries that crept into my psyche during dreamtime, notice the weather through the window, and bring the new day into my awareness. If I get interrupted early and rushed out of bed, for too many mornings in a row, I notice heaviness in my mind. When I feel uncomfortable, I complain to the closest person in my life. I want to stop this behavior and take full responsibility to empty my own wastebasket.

In my blinded solitude, the clear vision of this relationship-destroying pattern is right in front of me. I feel needy and rely too much on my beloved to rescue me. I sit quietly, looking at my detrimental behaviors, and clear each pattern like a conscious exhale. I don't need to feel heard by another person because I can evoke the feminine within myself, and turn up the self-listening. I want to feel seen, understood, and acknowledged without requiring assistance from anyone outside of myself.

After the session, I take a cool dip in the pool and lay out on the sunny deck to dry. The sun creates a bright orange glow behind my eyelids, and I'm blinded once again; I take a deeper look. As I continue to breathe and undulate my (now naked) body, another layer of judgment dislodges, and wants to move out. I try to let it go, but again feel that I need outside help. It's a struggle, and the thought won't shift. I start begging Great Spirit for release, and to be at ease with all of it.

This thought that I need outside help runs deep. I see how it can be related to taking a long time to orgasm if I look to a lover for that release. This is all related to being self-responsible, and not taking my frustrations out on my closest partners. Needing help from the outside can easily turn into blaming the beloved before me, and other forms of provocative communication. To clear these old behaviors, I need to choose a different action the next time it happens. I wonder if there's a way I can tackle this pattern while it's fresh in my mind.

This morning I was sloppy with Theodor, complaining to him about my neck pain from the Energetic Sex workshop we participated in together last night. I didn't consider that the disconnected way I spoke could've been misinterpreted as blaming him for causing damage to my neck. Theodor doesn't deserve my unconscious disrespectful communication. Lying here I feel embarrassed and want to be accountable, so I make a mental note: I'll apologize to Theodor for my lack of clarity and my sloppy communication. With my next exhale I release the shame and remorse. Theodor may not have heard my complaint as a blame, but I want to be extra vigilant with this old pattern of getting lazy with my communication and taking my frustrations out on those closest to me.

Fortunately, Katie is curious about what I got out of the blindfold experience, so I review the visions out loud with her willing ear, helping my mind find clarity. Next, to prevent this old pattern from dictating how I treat those closest to me, I map out future action steps:

1. Catch myself in the needy pattern when I start to blame the one closest to me.

2. Make a different choice, and remember my connection with the person I'm speaking to is more

293

important than any frustration I need to discharge, or point I'm trying to prove.

3. For the next few times, diligently catch myself when I want to blame my beloved, until the choice to take responsibility and choose love are the new neural pathways in my brain. Then it'll be easier to choose a positive action, and let go of blaming others.

The next evening Katie's upset because she thinks her husband hasn't been completely truthful with her. She makes a concise request to talk with me in a few minutes, then walks away from everyone to take care of her own processing. Soon she returns to discuss her feelings with me. With ample time to evoke my feminine listening, it's easy to hold space for her. She discusses her upset with me and I summarize what she's said, repeating it back to her so she can hear her words. Soon she's lucid enough to speak clearly with her husband. With her transparent communication, they quickly move to resolve. We then continue to have a playful evening together without unnecessary drama.

Healthy vs. unhealthy feminine and masculine was foreign concept to me growing up because I was raised with predetermined guidelines of what a girl is and what a boy does. There are problems with a rigid set of beliefs about gender roles—girls grow up into beings that also do, and boys grow up into beings that also feel. Devoting my life to the study of hundreds of relationships, I recognized that the genders are not as different as I once believed. Both men and women can open themselves up to being more balanced and self-responsible beings. Regardless of gender, most humans are capable of being grounded and holding space for others, feeling to the depths of all things, and embodying the charismatic Shakti energy.

No matter what gender, most people are capable of embodying both Shakti and her lover Shiva. In the ancient story when Shiva and Shakti finally unite, they stay in union, as one, for a very long time. My process of maturing into a balanced human starts with getting past the belief that a woman must take her place as a man's appendage in order to become whole. One way to discover my true self is to live as an integrated human, with the divine lovers entwined within, then walk as steadily as I can with what I know, and observe how others respond to me for healthy self checks and balances. I cherish the knowledge that I have every aspect of human nature within me, and I'm at choice to create my individual expression. When two or more individuals choose to bring their integrated selves together, the true magic of uniting with other whole beings is born into reality.

Once I recognize each aspect within myself, and allow them to freely flow within my psyche, then I'm released from thinking I should play with dolls, only wear dresses, or be married to be validated. Each inner aspect can interact with others at any given time. Examples are: My little girl can play with another's little child. My inner adolescent can flirt with another's adolescent. My adult woman can dance with another's adult man, or woman. My inner adult can even comfort my own inner child! Finally, the aspects within myself unite and strive to interact with other integrated whole Beings.

Growing up I wanted my own identity, independent of my parents, but like most humans I was influenced by my parents. I can see now that they weren't as conservative as they looked, but they still followed many societal norms. Most people will do the same until it feels safe enough to venture beyond *normal*. I'd like to say many integrated people also have the capacity to be bisexual, but I realize this is my own bias. All genders are learning how to relate and communicate with others who identify differently.

Perhaps individuals have their own definitions of what it means to become an integrated person. As a sexual woman, who feels both the divine masculine and feminine within, I love all the combinations of what it is to be human. Most people are doing their best while they learn and evolve. Becoming a whole person takes bravery, and fortunately, there's support available. It's a lifelong journey, so be gentle with yourself, and kind to others.

EXPLORATION #20

What are your thoughts on freedom?

_____

_____

_____

I experience freedom as a state of mind, when I'm not in battle with others or myself. Freedom is when I'm at choice, and I choose harmony.

What is your homework on the topic of freedom?

_____

_____

_____

Examples:

How free do you feel? Draw a line down the center of a page. In the left column make a list of each time you felt free, and in the right list when you felt controlled. Notice which side is longer.

Ask six people if they prefer to control their partners or allow freedom of choice.

Next time a road is closed to traffic, walk (or run) down the middle of the street and notice how it feels. Note: An agreed upon rebellious act is different from rebellion.

Sit with a partner or small group. Discuss if freedom is more physical or mental? Does one influence the other? Ask if freedom is an internal decision, like a state of mind? Then ask how controlling others is related to freedom.

Chapter 21

Secrets for Men Too

"Once you choose hope, anything's possible." — Christopher Reeve

I realize I'm not genetically male, but ask anyone who really knows me, and they'll tell you I have a well-developed masculine side. If I turn my vagina inside out, my cock would be bigger than most; it's simple geometry, I can fit a penis inside mine.

I have the little boy inside that is competitive in baseball, loves to race and climb rocks. I also have the teenager, who wants to fuck everything, and explore excitement and danger. I have the masculine perspective that hates, desires, and loves the feminine. He's a warrior, works hard and is a good provider. I have the mature teacher, protector, and peacekeeper. From my masculine perspective, I understand the challenge of relating to the modern feminine perspective. It calls for greater mindfulness. This perspective must clearly understand the demanding dynamics between the masculine and feminine.

If it seems like I'm always dating crazy chicks, maybe I need to reconsider how I'm engaging her. Does the superhero fear that he'll be seen as boring if he's not wearing a cape? Does he consider that there must be a damsel tied to the railroad tracks, in order to have something to rescue? I'm at choice about which aspects I want to engage; therefore, I can choose how to interact. If I only show up as the superhero, and engage the one who needs me, then that dynamic is created between us. If she responds to the one who wants to rescue her, she must either surrender to being *saved* (forever indebted with her life), or fight (like *crazy*) to get free. Either way, she'll tire of being seen as helpless. And being with a *crazy chick* becomes tiresome.

When a victim finally learns to stand up against a bully…Wait, we were talking about superheroes! How did it go from dating crazy chicks, to rescuing helpless damsels, to being a bully? Maybe the little girl was taught to play dumb/crazy/helpless to attract a hero. Then, because we all have everything inside us, the one who was rescued wants to be free to express other parts. If we don't know how to interact with a strong woman, our attempts to rescue begin to look like bullying. Has she become a victim because women are viewed as helpless?

Perhaps, because we all have everything inside us, we judge the powerless part of ourselves so much that we actually take it out on those who appear weak. Even in a girl body, I was shamed for being weak. When someone would yell at me, *you're throwing like a girl*, I'd become irate. It made me feel like fighting, but it also made me hate weakness. It took a lot of work to not become a bully. I had to learn compassion for my own weakness, and I also spent many years showing timid women how to discover their strength. I had to first get over my urge to *knock some sense* into them.

In the bedroom, my experience of both men and women is we're more alike than I once thought. I hear from men that they want to make me orgasm. I can relate when I feel guilty if I orgasm and my lover doesn't tip over that edge. Even if he is practicing the tantric healing method of purposefully holding on to his seed, I still want him to orgasm and feel the energy release (without ejaculation) during our sexual play. If he doesn't, I may feel guilty. My head knows better—I've learned that we are each responsible for our own orgasm. My job as a lover is similar to my role as a healer in a healing session where I hold space for the other to let go, release, and feel safe.

Secret #2. You are whole.

The fastest way to break the pattern of engaging with unstable women is to see the one before you as a whole person. Everyone has a wounded child inside who wants to be rescued, and that wounded child will always be there. It's important to also acknowledge the powerful archetypes like the survivor, healer, wise one, parent, visionary, and lover. It can be a blessing to hold someone's hand through a needy time to help facilitate healing. Acknowledge their strengths, and allow them to surprise you with their ability to live up to their profound potential.

Did you catch **Secret #1**? We all have everything inside us.

Here's one possible broad sketch of human history— women were seen as the weaker sex, mostly because of size and testosterone levels. As humans evolve, both male and female brains develop. Humans begin to outsmart their predators and become the hunter. Roles become defined as women stay home having babies, and men go hunting. Perhaps as we ran out of things to hunt, the male needed practice, so the female played the role of hunted. That got out of control. Eventually, like a trapped animal would, women began to fight to be recognized as equal with men. Women became formally educated, as only men had predominantly in the past. Pre-women's liberation, a wife was considered a man's property and needed to submissively conform to his world. Now we know that women have the capability to develop *manly* skills and physical strength. Many women suffered and spent time in prison to fight for equality.

Secret #3. Change is challenging but constant, so adapt.

A lot has changed in the dating world over the last few of decades. In the 20th century before the 1990's, men were busy with careers and work, while it was a girl's full-time job to find a suitable husband. Now it seems that everyone is busy with careers and running a household alike. Simply scheduling the time to date can be a challenge. There's also the shift from women being seen as inferior, and being a virgin was revered, to people wanting equal partnerships rather than one dominating over the other. There are even women now that admit they actually like sex, and the pursuit of men.

In the old paradigm, men were thought to own, and were expected to protect, their wife as property while having plenty of other women on the side. Women, however, were forced to live in secret. If it were discovered that a woman had lovers on the side, or extramarital affairs, or premarital intercourse she might be killed, viewed as unworthy of marriage, and considered ruined. In a relatively short period of time women's rights have changed dramatically. It's a challenge for men and women at the forefront of modern interacting to find examples of how to relate. People still protect and care for each other but it has less to do with gender, and more to do with education, talents and each person's strengths. With less defined gender roles, communication is imperative to work out how partners will support and love each other.

Secret # 4. Sex is a mutual experience.

This seems like a natural place to bring up female ejaculation, or amrita as it's called in Tantra circles. A man's orgasmic ejaculation is revered as important. After all, it carries the sperm to populate the earth. Women and men have similar biology, but female genitalia is just a little larger than males, on average, and goes in instead of out. Amrita intrigues me as my body has only produced it a handful of times. The men, I happened to be with during the waterworks, didn't have any detectable thing in common with each other.

The first one was a sexy Chippendale dancer with an above average sized cock. I was pinned down on a small sofa, unable to do any kind of giving back to him, but it was exactly what he needed to relieve his chronic back pain. After a few dates, we learned to prepare with extra towels, as I would probably make a serendipitous mess. The second guy, who aided in my amrita experience, also had chronic pain. He found relief from the endorphins released by our sexual play. Contrary to the male stripper, he was a svelte yogi, and we often explored Kama Sutra positions. I had a number of ejaculatory orgasms while sitting in Yab-Yum, or riding on top. Then there was a third man who excited me beyond words. He didn't have chronic pain, and we didn't repeat any of the previous positions to create my amrita. Years later I discovered lovers who were proficient, with their hands, in techniques to assist in female ejaculation.

Amrita isn't necessarily related to my orgasm, they don't always occur simultaneously. Not so strange because I've seen many men who have orgasms without ejaculation, and don't always have an orgasm with ejaculation. There's an excitement present each time I ejaculate, but that's not the only common condition. Besides, I've been that excited many times without ejaculating.

One night, out of the blue, I squirt with a lover, and suddenly I understand what each of my other experiences has in common. Sam spends an extra amount of time pampering me. I don't feel guilty because I'd spent the previous weeks overindulging for his birthday, and Sam wanted to repay me. I determine that every time I ejaculate, I completely surrender and let go. I feel as if I've unlocked a secret of the universe—a woman's ejaculation is also creative energy. When I'm present with my body, giving and receiving pleasure, I feel peaceful, empowered and creative.

A man once called me a cold, dead fish. I was haunted by those words each time I began to relax in a lover's arms, until I understood my part in that distasteful moment. The truth is that I couldn't feel a connection with him, yet I failed to speak up and tell him. I hadn't received him mentally or emotionally, as I lay there physically inert. Disconnected sex is potentially dangerous and unsatisfying. To engage in a successful sexual connection it's best to get a verbal yes and have aligned intentions for that experience. I learned to listen to my own body language and to slow down so that I can connect with a lover at their pace. Like a DJ mixing music, even if their beat is faster than mine, I slow down to sync with them, then we can let it fly.

Secret #5. If sex doesn't feel right, ask for a *hell yes*.

I dive into my personal sexual freedom, and notice the ones I ejaculate with are different from the *dead fish* guy. I am relaxed, completely still, but not lifeless. I'm turned on, excited, and attracted to the lovers who allow me to just receive them. I still maintain a deep desire to give during sexual play, but I can add total surrender to my dance moves.

A woman who's viewed as equal, may still have a desire to express that she's an independent, free, alive, sexual being. Many women are still learning how to show up as an equal partner, and where to surrender control without feeling fear of defeat. There's historical psychic pain, with fearful memories of fighting for freedom. The next step in this freedom fight is freedom from lies—verbalize what is a yes and what is a no, and be impeccable with how you speak *and* listen to each other.

Secret #6. Stereotypes are lies.

When I was six, I witnessed the birth of a single litter of puppies from four distinctly separate canine breeds, born from one bitch. It was common to see multiple males mating a single female in heat, or see a male mounting multiple females. Men want to spread their seed, mix the genetic pool, and attempt to dominate by having more offspring. The receptivity of the female body and mating behavior is also designed to create genetic vigor by mating with multiple men. This is common in nature and in the animal kingdom. From the perspective that humans have both the masculine and feminine aspects, I can let go of stereotypes that females need to have dinner on the table by 6PM and males need to earn all the money to support everyone they love. Many women do cook the meals and want dinner at 6PM, and many men do make enough money to support others, but to say that of all men and women is a lie.

In postwar America, stereotypes suggested that most men wanted multiple sex partners, while women only wanted one partner. It was common for men to have affairs outside of marriage, but they didn't want their wives to have the same sexual freedom. Many women in the past had secret affairs too. Now that people are becoming more transparent about their relationships and attractions, and there is DNA testing, it is less secret. Couples are learning new ways to communicate their desires and live honestly. Now a woman may be shocked if her male partner says no when she suggests they open-up their relationship. Sexual agency is improving, as our ability to communicate and create equal partnerships evolves.

There's still work to be done on sexual shame and the severe negativity around sex that most of us were raised with. Stereotypes fall away as we learn to honor the inner masculine and feminine within each of us. Sexual energy can still find erotic polarity regardless of a person's genitalia. There's freedom in being comfortable and free to express sexual desires. I value the things that make the sexes unique, and that each person can be free to make their own choices regarding their sexual expression.

Secret #7. Tell the truth.

Be open and honest about attractions that may arise with other people. Be honest, and speak up when things are great and when something isn't working in relationships. It can be difficult to hear the truth from a partner and learn that I'm not always the center of their world. There's fear of losing loved ones if the whole truth is told. What if a Beloved needs to be the one-and-only, and gets angry, or leaves if they hear about other attractions? Isn't it better to know this now, allow them freedom to make an informed choice, and find new lovers with similar ideology?

It feels good to be my true self, and give my undivided attention to each of my precious partners when I choose freely to share it with them. It's an unreasonable thought that I want to only focus on one person, and shut out the rest of the world. There are times when I allow myself a brief period of obsession with only one person, but it's a rare adventure. I desire to be trustworthy, stable, and remain compassionately loving.

Another area of potential challenge is in the realm of

finance. A female partner may earn more money than the male, and there's uncertainty around who pays for dates. Loaning money, or helping a woman financially could be met with resistance, due to the conflicting nature of what those acts meant in the past. She may fear a potential expectation to be submissive in return, or that she isn't being seen as an equal human. Sometimes a woman may love to have her lunch paid for, maybe because she frequently pays for others, due to her job or social status. No matter how wealthy someone is, it's nice to feel taken care of sometimes.

Secret #8. Be generous.

Applaud others for their accomplishments. Pay attention to detail, and praise (not empty compliments) even small behaviors that are going in a positive direction. A healthy dynamic, in most relationships, involves the equal exchange of energy. Ideally, the ones playing the receiving role give value, rather than expect a handout; a welcoming receiver is needed in order for the giver to be fulfilled. Finding value and how each person benefits, is a great approach to the delegation of responsibilities, creating equality. If one has less money, and you want to travel, or want them to take time off work, they need to be clear about what their contribution is. When an individual's abilities and talents are acknowledged, there's a far less chance that giving money will trigger feelings of being manipulated or degraded. Usually, sex is not used for exchange because the act itself is designed to be mutually beneficial. If one partner is not benefiting from the sexual exchange the act may become a manipulation tool, or prostitution, or be considered rape.

Women's newfound voice and sexual freedom, along with the possible dilemma of which one pays for what, are not the only potential landmines in pursuing the modern woman. I find it helpful to remember if the highly sensitive feminine says no to a request, there may be multiple reasons. It's important to hear why she said no, and if she isn't interested in you then stop pursuing. It's a gift to acknowledge that she's being responsible by saying no. You would want her to do the same if the roles were reversed. If she clearly isn't interested, it can be beneficial to self-reflect and see how to improve while making sure not to add it to a list of what's wrong with the world, or unnecessarily take it personally. She is making an empowered choice in that moment, and may need a minute to communicate an alternative idea in response. She may not even be aware of all the reasons she's not into the suggestion, and it may not have much to do with who's doing the asking. Perhaps she doesn't want to do the thing that was asked, but she would like to do something different instead. Listening, negotiation and communication are vital parts of connection.

Secret #9. Have clear intentions.

There are heavy stereotypes, developed over the centuries that can haunt the one who's actively courting. I've felt like the creepy stalker, player, and my personal worst, the *dirty old man*. When in hot pursuit of another, it helps to understand intentions. Be upfront with any agendas. Recognize emotional pitfalls and patterns that can trigger an undue fear reaction in the pursued one. Being aware of myself makes it easier to be responsible, and available for true connection. If the masculine energy is ungrounded, or not cleared of emotional needs and fears, then those emotions may be reflected right back by the feminine counterpart.

When both my feminine and masculine sides are clear, and I sit before someone who's also free from suffering over their inner struggles, then we have a clean canvas to create the experience that arises between us.

Secret #10. Lack is the root of war.

Searching for the one, perfect person can create unhealthy competition, and fear of scarcity. Trying to own a partner can also be detrimental to the relationship. Relate to others as sovereign individuals, without the influences of outdated social ideas unconsciously dictating behaviors. There are billions of people. If we can love, protect, care for, create with, listen to, trust, engage, unite, and be one with as many people as possible, then we may learn there is plenty.

Imagine this ideal, even as a monogamous or married individual. Recognize there's a fluid continuum between masculine and feminine. Swimming between the two gracefully, within the self and with another, is a lifesaver to keep the relationship afloat. Accepting where our partners land on that scale is important.

If a woman works for hours up a ladder pruning trees, or negotiating a business deal, acknowledge her and then negotiate how to create space for her to relax. We all have strengths and we all need to relax. If she spends time on the feminine end of the scale, listening to complaints or nursing a sick kid, acknowledge her and discover what she needs. Being stuck on either end of the scale can be exhausting. Learn to be fluid and help your partners help you find balance too.

Many young men have asked me how to understand the mysterious female. The most helpful thing my feminine side has taught my masculine is to relax around a problem, so the creativity can flow and create a solution. When I'm able to slow down, take a deep breath, and open up around a perceived problem between the sexes, I realize there may not be a problem after all. Perhaps it's as simple as getting to know both the masculine and the feminine within the self, then allowing your whole being to communicate with another. It's vital to get to know a woman as a person, and figure out if you can negotiate all aspects of life with them before considering a serious relationship. Trusting each other and being stable is attractive, and helps to keep the way you relate juicy and alive.

Bonus Secret #11. Compassion, and being love is true stability.

Finding the natural flow in connecting is a practice that continues to evolve. The current may be swift, but if we're in the same river, there's bound to be glorious moments of perfect union. The more attuned to all the nuances of the natural flow, the more ease and bliss there'll be around relating. The old paradigm says: I will love you forever, or until the novelty of our relationship wears off, and I sneak around to find an exciting incipient relationship that replaces you. Not necessarily better, here is the stance of modern dating: I will love you forever, but when a new person comes along, I may shift my attention onto them, and not have enough time to continue our relationship at the intervals you've grown accustomed to. Perhaps the *new paradigm* could be: I will love, forever.

EXPLORATION #21

What are your thoughts on communication?

_____

_____

_____

I experience communication as a dynamic conversation that involves clarifying and understanding as vital parts.

What is your homework on the topic of communication?

_____

_____

_____

Examples:

Sit with a partner and talk for five minutes (set a timer). Ask them to tell you when they didn't understand your communication.

With five or more people in a line, whisper a sentence in the person's ear next to you and have them pass it on to the next. Then that person whispers to the next until it gets back to you. Try the same thing with one word.

Make a list of the areas you feel misunderstood. Then write three different ways you can explain what you want to communicate.

Sit with a partner. Ask them to speak for five minutes (set a timer). Repeat back everything you heard them say. Ask them if you missed anything.

Chapter 22

Fake It 'til You Make It

"Patience is the companion to wisdom."— St. Augustine

My best advice for just about any emotional upset, sports endeavor, yoga position, school assignment, meditation practice, writing project, or new undertaking is: fake it good. Exuding confidence and envisioning the highest potential while maintaining a look of poised, courageous certainty might help you find those exact things. I don't mean lie. Honesty and being a trusted loyal person are in my top three highest values. But, by going through the motions, as if already adept at the situation, the accomplishments often eclipse the original pretense.

Endless examples come from my school days of pretending like I knew something, but when asked to demonstrate for the class, to my surprise, I'd acquired the skill. Acting like a good ball player, and then hitting a homerun! Due to my intimidating confidence, I became the female arm wrestling champ of my entire high school when I was merely a sophomore. Meditation and yoga, I mimicked the teacher until I found myself leading classes. Singing, playing guitar, and writing are similar in that I pretend to be good at it, and the talent develops with practice.

Another area where I apply this practice is calming emotional turmoil by being non-reactive.

If I were a hawk soaring 100 feet in the air, I'd be able to see that the tree was in a forest and my breakfast darted under an elderberry. From an earthbound perspective, it's easy to forget there are a broad range of ways to see any situation. If I were the rabbit, running for my life, I may be besieged by anxiety and think that's my only option. If I were the elderberry, entangled with the forest's root system and our leaves photosynthesizing from the same sky, it would reason that everything is connected. As a human, it can seem that what's inside my body is me and what's outside my body isn't me. I can become over identified with the emotional reaction from my point of view. Perhaps suffering is when I get attached to one perspective, and bliss is that expansive feeling when I relax into feeling *all* available emotions.

It's also easy to think other humans have perspectives that I don't have and begin to feel unrelatable. Thinking I don't possess a certain perspective is denying a part of myself and can cause as much suffering as believing I'm only one thing. This is where I practice the fake it 'til I make it strategy to help me see from the hawk's point of view. If I think fear isn't part of me, arrogance may be defending against it, and I can get caught in this battle of perspectives. To the fearful rabbit, it may feel like suicide to accept that he's capable of a confident perspective too. However, it's easy for a tree to feel *one* with the familiar forest. Humans can learn to embrace both the familiar and the unfamiliar perspectives present. Fear is often a useful tool if I remember it's only one of the perspectives inside of me, while confidence gets me what I want, if I'm careful to consider others in my path. Opposite perspectives can either fight, or play off of the polarity and groove together nicely. Ultimately, the outlook that wants to be *one with everything* insists on seeing the unrecognized perspective in me, and aligns with it. Maybe all perspectives are in each of us, and I just need to fake it—feel as if the perspective expressed by the person before me is fully functional within me, and soon it is.

I'm minding my own business, and the idea arises that I would like a lover to connect with. This seems harmless enough until that lover's gone. Perhaps we had an extremely powerful connection, touching places of raw beauty together. Usually, I hold gratitude in my heart, knowing we'll connect again when the time's right. But, sometimes I feel longing, insecurity, or a desire to know just when we'll meet again. It doesn't matter how much reassurance that there'll be a next time; I can't stop thinking about when or how we'll connect again. Sometimes this obsession can be exciting and fun, so I play that game with myself, but other times I drift into suffering. If the lover is confident and I can't feel that level of confidence within myself then perhaps the opposite, insecure perspective in me is triggered. If I remember that the confident attitude is always in me, then I can harmonize with my lover, knowing we'll meet again, when the time is right. Once I recognize this, I simply fake it until I'm aligned with the reality of the higher perspective. Then I can relax into enjoying the moment, basking in lasting feelings left in my body from the experience, and in the knowledge that everything is in perfect order.

One night Sam asks, "Do you fake orgasms?"

"I can count the number of times I've faked it on one hand," I reply.

"What made you fake it those times?" Sam asks.

"I didn't understand how I'm responsible for my pleasure, even when I'm with another, so I got frustrated when I wasn't feeling an orgasm," I say. "I also didn't know how to speak-up when I felt complete, so I faked being done so he'd finish. I'm not proud of that."

"But you don't stop me, even when I'm taking a long time coming to orgasm," Sam says.

"The times I'm finished with our sexual play before you, I still feel excited for you to have your orgasm. You often hold back so I can orgasm first, so I only have to say, *I want you to orgasm now*, then my body gets extra excited feeling your excitement," I reply.

"When you say that to me, it feels like you're close to orgasm," Sam says.

"I'm usually close, but know I won't go over the edge of orgasmic release. I'm also feeling what you're feeling, and your orgasm feels amazing to me too," I reply. "I've learned how to speak-up when I'm tired, or just complete with our sexual play. I pay attention to my body, and I notice when I'm getting near feeling complete, so I can give you the hints for you to finish." I continue, "If I've been stressed, dehydrated, sleep deprived, worried, or can't masturbate, then it's my responsibility to take care of myself. Sex helps me move through most of it, but my biology is affected, and I may not be able to let go completely all at once."

"It almost sounds like sex is therapeutic," Sam says.

"My ideal is to be clear and centered before we come together sexually, but life isn't always that neatly packaged. When I need healing or revitalizing, sex is one of my top choices, because it's so powerful at moving stuck energy. The great thing about sex is it goes both ways, so I'm benefiting you and helping move your creative energy too," I say with a big smile.

"I enjoy knowing it's a healing session," Sam replies. "We have such a variety of sexual experiences, together we can move mountains."

"That's why I love sharing sex with you," I say. "Your sexual palate is adventurous, and we can dance through any ballroom, mosh pit, stage, street, classroom, even on a cloud."

An example of faking it in the bedroom: Grunts, sighs, mmm aahs, giggles and moans are all part of vocal communication during sex, especially when I'm in subspace, or so deep I don't have my words. Meanings like—that feels good, that feels better, you lost me for a moment (I was so high) but now I'm back. Sometimes, however, I begin faking the faster breathing and louder vocalizing. I'm faking the beginning of an orgasm because it helps my body head toward that peak, and soon I'm actually panting and groaning and mid-orgasm before I know it.

A different example: I was helping a friend who needed my nursing skills. I know it was appreciated because I was thanked and told he was feeling better. Before I left, still in nursing mode, I made a few extra suggestions that were met with a curt frustrated reply. I faked being non-reactive until I was alone in my car. Singing along with a song that reminded me of the remark, I instantly felt sorry for myself. In other situations, defensiveness or anger might be my reaction, but because I was in such a giving space the opposite was triggered. Instead of fighting, or realizing it wasn't about me, I retreated into a victim perspective. Because I had time away from the situation, it was easier to realize this was an emotional response. Instead of wallowing in the mud of self-pity, I considered how hurtful it must be when *I'm* in a grumpy mood, or frustrated, and take it out on others. Faking being non-reactive to someone else's pain gave me enough space to paint a healthier picture in my mind. I shifted and was instantly grateful for the experience.

Last example: I'm alone, my monthly cycle is coming, and the hormones are making my emotions soupy. I feel uncomfortable in my body. I notice that thoughts are constantly flowing, and with them come a myriad of emotions. Suddenly, a downward spiral ensues—the thought of not wanting to miss out on anything, closely followed by, no one has called me yet today. The thoughts continue downward, I slept alone again last night which is instantly interpreted as, I'm not wanted.

Tears come before I blink twice. It's so easy to identify fully with these emotions when the body is weak; I have a hard time identifying with the opposite in those moments. This is when I *fake it*. I step in with the thought that I'm also invincible. Exaggerating the pain of my menses I think—I can thrive all alone, even when feeling as if I've been stabbed in the belly and left to bleed for three days. I then eat healthy foods to balance my brain chemistry, exercise to ground my new perspective into my body, and get some good sleep. Soon I'm strong and attractive. Having felt the opposing emotions fully, I can feel all of them in a blissful state. I could choose to suffer, but I prefer bliss.

And even all this is just a perspective. This concept can go in any direction. If you think you can't do something, or you aren't good enough, you may convince yourself and others and soon feel truncated. Downward spirals gain momentum just like creating what we want builds in the other direction. The best way to catch negativity and turn it around is to utilize the gifts scattered all over the globe. We are all here to help each other. When I want a friend, all I need to do is pick up my phone and give to someone else. Be kind to a stranger, smile, or spread the love in some little way. When I do a few nice things for others I learn how to be a better friend. When I don't have the bandwidth to listen to another's troubles, I listen to nature. Listen, listen, listen, and observe the answers in the trees, waves, sunset, alley cats, butterflies, and the breeze.

People come into my life to help me learn compassion for others and myself. They show me how to embrace my unloved aspects, and make it easier to love more people. If I hate it when Sam is aloof, then Mary accuses me of being detached, I may judge myself for being what I hate. The positive side is that withdrawing is part of having healthy boundaries, so I embrace the detached part of myself and vow to use it with discernment. This strengthens my compassion for reserved people. The more I see of myself, the more I'm able to help others view themselves from different angles, and understand the value of each side. Fake it big, reach for the stars. Try faking being enlightened, a good friend, or an attentive masterful lover.

EXPLORATION #22

What were your initial thoughts on *fake it 'til you make it?*

_____

_____

_____

Transparency and truth are two of my highest values. Faking isn't meant to be falsifying, but rather pretending or acting as a tool to practice something until it becomes true. Not faking a smile, but acting the way I want to be in order to shift my state of mind.

What is your homework on the topic of *faking?*

_____

_____

_____

Examples:

Fake enjoying washing the dishes.

Fake being a good listener and then repeat back what you heard them say.

Fake having compassion for the bad driver ahead of you.

Fake having fun with this and come up with a creative homework exercise.

Chapter 23

Smiling on the Inside

"Love yourself first and everything else falls into line. You really have to love yourself to get anything done in this world." — Lucille Ball

Before age six, with only one TV channel, I didn't know of many stars. There was *Sonny and Cher, I Love Lucy, The Carol Burnett Show, Green Acres, Hee Haw, Daniel Boone,* and *The Ed Sullivan Show*. Visiting Mom's hometown we met my very first Movie Star. While my sister and I traced handprints in the sidewalk, our parents chatted and laughed with Lucille Ball in front of Grauman's Chinese Theatre in Hollywood. I had only seen her in the old black and white reruns and this actress came to life right before my eyes. To my delight, Lucy's hair and heart-shaped lips were bright red, and her eyes sparkled blue as she stooped down to say hello to my sister and me. My little eyes were opened, and Lucy's imaginative way of turning disasters into comedy inspired my developing mind.

One of my favorite sayings is *smiling on the inside, where it really counts*. Just saying it aloud makes my face crack a smile, and share my inner joy with others. One way I attain joy is by finding answers—letting go of thoughts I held as truth, and sit with a question long enough to see that the answer's right there. Question: Why is a penis called a cock? Every morning at sunrise, my grandmother's rooster got up, and woke-up everyone around. Answer: The cock is the first thing up every morning.

I see myself through new eyes when I look into a lake or a dark window, a slender mirror or a curved metal surface. I can also appear very different (even on the same day) in the same mirror with a shift in my state of mind. Family, friends, and community are all unique reflections that teach me about compassion and depth. I'm grateful to those who exposed outdated beliefs, they allow for the next generations to avoid these now-obvious pitfalls. Unresolved childhood trauma, or a repeated self-destructive thought can be more obscure. Freedom is letting go of sadness from the past and worries of the future, and being joyfully present in reality.

Self-absorbed in an upsetting thought, I catch myself in record time. Eventually, I'm aware of events that trigger those thoughts, before they start. Recognizing the trigger is advantageous for disrupting a pattern. Like a startling slamming noise automatically triggers fear, causing me to grab a baseball bat, even if it's just the wind blowing the door. When paying attention, I can hear the wind before it slams the door, and I'm not alarmed.

If life isn't going my way, I need to self-reflect and take responsibility to shift my attitude. When there's a subtle feeling of fear hanging over me, it's like the dirt cloud that follows Linus Van Pelt (Charlie Brown's best friend in the comic strip Peanuts). It feels as if my life will remain tragic until it runs out. Besides catching those triggers, I take six steps to shift my snowballing reaction to life.

Step #1. Create a Ceremony: Release what doesn't serve me any longer, and set a positive intention going forward. There's no wrong way to create a meaningful personal ceremony. Example: Set a glass of water in the sun (supercharge and purify.) Take a shower and dress in clean clothes (rinse away the past, and start fresh.) Sit in the shade of a tree (their roots are interconnected like a web, deep into the ground, and branches reach toward heaven.) Drink the glass of water (intentionally take the vitalized water into your body.) We only have from this moment forward, so start (with a clean slate) now.

Step #2. Connect. René is in town with impeccable timing. Touch-deprived, I don't know how my body will react to the reintroduction of sexual connection. As we lay our naked bodies together, I feel loved, respected, and so much gentleness that my body overflows with orgasmic energy. René's hand caresses my back and hair, as I put his warm, soft cock in my mouth. Holding his vulnerable genital skin in my mouth, slowly swallowing I feel it quietly filling me, expanding down my throat. Again I swallow, pull back from his now erect shaft for air, and slide back down. I feel my vagina ache like I haven't felt since my horny college years. Soon I'm riding his pelvis, grinding, undulating, and squeezing his hips with my thighs. Deep inside, he revitalizes desolate areas. With a releasing breath, I'm back in the flow of life-giving energy.

Step #3. Address my brain chemistry. Balanced blood sugar, oxygenating exercise, feed my brain and body the suitable nutrients, and maintain an eight-hour sleep routine. If I start to crave sugar I know it's emergency time, and I need to eat protein and raw fats. No cheating, because I have too much at stake. I find productive ways to move my body, and improve my posture for healthy circulation. Depending on scheduled activities, I choose specific nutrients to prepare my brain and body in advance.

Step #4. Do relationship assessments to find areas that need tidying. This is the broadest category in my life, yet the one with the most vital impact; therefore I must remain attentive like with any spiritual practice to stay unsullied in all my relations.

When I find someone that I'm *crazy about*, unhealthy attachment or obsession may arise, with a potential for suffering. There may be fear or neediness, and questioning if they'll be in my life forever. I strive to be extra vigilant of letting go, and keeping my thoughts (that can run amuck) in check. Catching these thoughts, and checking in with reality I can avoid creating an unwanted outcome. The past is filled with fears of how things didn't work out, or mistakes I've made. The future is unknown, which is scary. Life exists in present time.

I think of the lovers I hold precious in my heart. Drake excites me (teetering on obsession). I let go of the desire to have a peak experience, like the last time we were together, or the first time we met. I reassure myself that last time with Drake I felt connected, and many of my desires were met (beyond my dreams). I'm clear that I don't want to trap, play games, or *make* him spend time with me. I want to communicate what I liked, and that I'm open to more. I like freedom, and I'm grateful for our connection. I don't want to push my will onto the natural flow of what's meant to be. I want to communicate with grace, without selfish perspectives taking charge. I can only take care of me. I don't have control of what another person chooses to suffer over. Free from expectation, it's easier to genuinely connect, and if Drake's also present, then we're in a peak (real) experience again before I know it.

Then there are those that pursue me. Benjamin desires me, a zany reflection of my attractive nature. I'm grateful for new connections, and Benjamin's persistence creates an opportunity for depth. I clearly express my values, intentions, and am transparent that I'm not in search of just one love in my life. His desire for structure brings us together nearly every Thursday for an opportunity to explore the attraction. We have much to learn from the reflection in each other's eyes. I don't feel it at first, but I open myself to being surprised. He is a unique blend of innocence with gift bearing courting, and kinky queer exploration wanting to share all his deviant ideas and know every detail of my erotic adventures. His intrigue is the opposite of jealousy as the details I share are celebrated, and arousing to him.

I examine my relationship with the environment. Home is a nurturing sanctuary—surrounding myself with beauty and nature is a reminder of the Divine. Even in the city, there's nature all around. One of my greatest joys is providing a desirable healing milieu for physical rejuvenation, mental and emotional relaxation, sexual exploration, and freedom of expression. I initiate an early spring-cleaning to keep the energy fresh and flowing.

People have separate bodies and make individual choices, but at a fundamental level, we're all one. In physical reality, our cells are mostly space and energy-moving electrons. I'm not a physicist, but I'm pretty sure space and energy aren't limited by my skin. When paying attention, I can feel the intensity from across the room if someone's angry. I'm aware of the ability to expand and contract my energy field, and control the quality of the energy I'm allowing others to feel. Our energies touching seems more than just a possibility. Sometimes I imagine the world, looking like a huge connected web, or one big organism.

I contemplate this sea of strange, interwoven beings, and think of compassion. When I witness another doing something judged as negative, I choose compassion, see it reflected back in me, own it as part of me, and then I can feel compassion for myself. Having compassion for self-judgment makes it easier to choose right action.

My junior year at University, I had sex over 360 days in a row (dating multiple people). I didn't start the year with an agenda or goal; it wasn't until midway through my senior year that I even thought about it. Studying psychology and human development, I had unknowingly put myself through a *crash course* of healing my unmet needs, from infancy to adulthood. I used the physical touch, and variety of intimate connections, to foster me through these stages. I was also nurturing these lovers through their growth, because sex is mutually beneficial.

Arthur has been a sexual partner, on and off, for more than half of my sexually active life, nearly 15 years. We don't define or constrain our relationship. We've never lived together, and I don't remember a time when we talked everyday. Our connection ebbs and flows, sometimes needing space, but our paths cross again, continuing right where we left off. He calls me Cheri, and I call him Arthur. To the conservative people in our lives, we say we're *friends*, and give more juicy details to close companions, but we haven't put a label on our relationship, and there are no promises.

I would like to call Arthur a *lover*, a feeling word, describing our spicy yumminess, but I'm aware this may denote ownership. Some may hear *my* lover, but I don't own him. He *is* a lover, and I *am* a lover, and sometimes our *loverness* comes together. There's a special attraction between us, and we care deeply, even when we aren't together. Accumulated experiences show our commonalities, and over time our relationship deepens and evolves.

Relating without promises, or strings attached, requires addressing the perspectives inside that want to know answers. When will I see you again? What do we call each other? How do I describe you to my other relations? How long will we be together? These questions put the relationship in a box so it can be understood. The potential problem is, it may want out, get stagnation sickness, or feel caged in. What if our natural state is freedom, and commitment to be together breads an element of sickness in the relationship? What if the promise of *forever* ends, when we're still alive? Perhaps, it isn't *forever until death*, the way I originally thought. Maybe it's forever in depth, or quality of relating, instead of the quantity of time we're together.

Maybe the definition of love is allowance. Unconditionally allowing others to live their lives in whatever way they choose. I honor Arthur's path, and am grateful when our lives align. Sometimes we practice letting go to avoid creating suffering by trying to possess, or keep things status quo. Having an undefined relationship means when we're spending less time together, we don't need to break-up. The relationship *just is*, and our unique dynamic continues to be precious.

I attempt to avoid a messy start with potential future relationships. I can get to know you, with less of an agenda or focus on what *I* want. Sex may be initiated, right up front. I like sex, and it can be a revealing way I get acquainted. Jumping right in the sack doesn't necessarily make the connection more serious or less serious. If there's no sex in the courtship, I hope for some sexy flirting to move our energies, or maybe we can play music together. Making good music together involves flirting. Finding commonalities, attractions, and if we naturally want to spend time together. The areas of our lives that align, and what we have in common unfolds. It's a process learning how we fit into one other's schedules. I can't expect a relationship to be real, if I have unreal expectations.

I want my connections to evolve naturally, not blindly fall in love with a fantasy idea of what I think I want. Do the qualities they possess align with mine? Do their lines of development compliment my strengths and counterbalance my weaknesses? I look for open, honest people who allow my full expression. I want to give freely, feel appreciated, inspire and be inspired by those closest to me. My brain (and body) lights up when I meet someone who's developed in multiple areas that I value—they meet my intellect, care for their physical body, are emotionally mature, and we have similar communication styles. My body melts into their touch because they're able to be present.

I can't expect to find another who holds *all* my same values, and wants all the same things. Most of us have good qualities and bad ones, and it may be unrealistic to find a mate who's my definition of *perfect*. My values evolve, as I learn about myself and who I am in the world. I change my mental concept of perfection to have harmonious connections.

As I get to know you, I discover what turns me on about you, and I consider areas that turn me off. When I was young, I tried to predict compatibility by whether we could live and raise children in the same house. Now, I look at all the qualities because they're a reflection of me. The aspects that turn me off may be a part of me that I'm not allowing. I desire to see *all* of myself, and then choose which qualities I want to act on. I also choose those I want to be closest to and co-create with. When I support you, our energies join, and your creations are as important as mine.

I also want to be a clear reflection for others, providing a safe place to let go of old patterns. Acknowledging unhealthy aspects ensures that it's seen and allowed. Is this enabling destructive behaviors rather than loving? I don't know if there's a right answer to this question. From this perspective, unhealthy behaviors that become patterns are accepted before they can change—I know I can only point it out and accept it, but I can't make the change for another person. There's a feeling that shifts after a damaging aspect has been acknowledged. In this feeling of acceptance there's space, and all can exist together. If the aspect that's receiving attention wants to take over, then it may be the addictive perspective. At this point I can only be helpful if I don't get carried away in my own addictive perspective.

I want to allow all aspects while keeping my attention diligent on choosing life. The reason for exploring the dark is to feel whole, healthy, completely seen, and to understand power. I explore my deepest hidden parts, to know myself, and not be surprised by what can surface under pressure. After these shadows are acknowledged, and my attention is shifted to healthier traits, will abandonment, betrayal, or anger be activated? I employ the part of the psyche that allows the destructive aspects to feel seen while making healthy choices.

I also want to keep my relationships clean with primary partners. I consider myself my primary partner, and live as a whole being, sharing myself with others. Humans aren't stagnant—our energy flows, moves, morphs, and mutates. Relating with others has a musical rhythm. I stay present and aware, to allow the beings in my life to make their choices freely. When they choose to play with me, and I choose to play with them it's an orchestra. If love is what I am then gratitude is what I feel. Maybe allowance is just allowance—giving space to another to be what they choose. Perhaps love is the in-between parts, where my innermost nature is aware of the connection with your being.

When I have more than one primary partner in my closest

circle, we engage in the co-creating of our common goals. The *chosen family* that I lived and worked with for nearly a decade, Jacy, Felina, and Haven shared common walls, ate from the same kitchen, played together, shared finances, relied on one another for brainstorming business decisions, and co-creating our living space. That depth of reflection was profound due to the closeness and constancy. When living with others, we renegotiate our relationship dynamics frequently, to see what's working, and what's not current any longer. It's vital to be conscious, have trust and stay real.

With multiple partners, the potential for keeping harmony during disagreements is improved. We simplify as much as possible, but not more than necessary, and provide a safe space for catching triggers to avoid cascading reactions. Example: If Felina fell out of the boat, perhaps pulling Jacy or Haven overboard with her, there's usually at least one left in the boat, to remain calm and listen to the upset ones. This decreases the time it takes to get everyone back in the vessel, heading in the same direction again.

The close connectedness of my most intimate relationships allows our *family* the insight to discover personal strengths, providing opportunities for development and full expression. If multiple individuals have opposing ideas, it takes humility to present my thoughts, then listen to all the other ideas before unanimously deciding which one is the most right, or the highest choice. Actively encouraging each individual, having everyone's best interest at heart, and being open to each other's needs, keeps the relationships evolving. When choices are made to transition, or not spend physical time together, the connection doesn't just stop. Our relations are consciously chosen, and we explore continuity without monotony.

In my ideal world, all *primary partners* share sexuality together, without the titles of secondary, tertiary, and without ownership. Our sexual connections would be a natural part of the energy flow and creative connection. Sexuality in an intimate relationship can increase the depth of reflection, speed of growth, and healing. Each individual in the primary dynamic is encouraged to be responsible and engage in the co-creating of common goals. Impeccable communication, with regular check-ins, and clearing misunderstandings is vital. To minimize unhealthy relating patterns in a group, ensure everyone feels heard and all needs are expressed.

No beginning, with a *promise* to commit to be together forever, and no *end*. You can't *breakup* if you aren't *going steady* in the first place. If a desire for structure arises, there's an abundance of ways to respond. Perhaps scheduling *date nights*, or a movie next Thursday night, dance class on Sunday morning, working more structured hours during the week, or doing a hard cardio workout on Tuesday and Thursday afternoons. Then allow the people who join in these activities to be fluid with their timing because their need for structure may differ. I'm clear with my intention to connect, and am happy to support their choice of what they want to do. Sometimes I spend time alone, and need exactly that.

There are many times when I'm focused on learning in one area, or attracted to someone's expertise in an area. In these cases, we may have a very narrow scope in common, but our relationship can still deepen. Dennis and I have no concern about when we'll be together next, but it's easy to be in the natural flow, with excitement when we meet again. My enthusiasm can be intense, so rather than obsess over what I want a relationship to develop into, I use that energy to accomplish other things in my life, i.e. adding credentials after my name, playing a sport, creating art or music, or making money.

As a hyperactive college student, it was difficult to connect deeply unless I was in the ecstasy of sex hormones flooding my system. I had fear around finding the right partner, keeping a good reputation, getting high grades, and working enough hours to keep me afloat. As I started to understand myself, and relax around all these fears, I learned to slow down, to connect in more ways with others. I began to experience real intimate interactions, even if it was just for a moment. I developed depth in my sharing, listening, and feeling another's experience, without agendas of my own getting in the way of a true exchange. These connections go beyond what our bodies are doing. These connections never go away. I may choose not to spend time physically with a particular person, but what has been shared, and what has been learned from them is integrated into me. I'm more aware of who I am from my interaction with each person, and have a greater understanding of the whole, which I am one with.

The concept of being one with everything is a security that's always with me. Choosing not to depend on another for a sense of stability, allows me to trust that I'll always be connected with others. I'll have lovers to give my caring attention to, no matter where I am in my life, or in the world. This freedom is also part of my inspiration, to create a healthy home, open to those I choose. The kinesthetic part of my brain desires physical touch, even though it can sense from across the room and feel without touch. Sexuality speeds up the exchange of energy, and is one of my favorite ways to deepen intimate relationships.

There's a natural flow to connecting with others. If I'm patient and consider the pros and cons, the highest choice that benefits everyone involved will become obvious. If I try to make a solution happen, whether tangling, or untangling with another, it'll feel forced, and will push answers further away. I'm reminded of a lecture titled *The Four Languages of Human Communication* by Richard Greene. Each of us aligns with different parts of the brain, and everyone listens and communicates with a unique combination, depending on how their brain works.

I express myself, to the best of my ability, so that others will have a better chance of understanding. Storytelling is one of my favorite communication styles. There's also analytical detailed research, and scientifically accurate data to enhance credibility. Another communication type is visual, including facial expressions and body language. Lastly, sharing a passion, or feeling connected with the energetic flow, along with the transfer of information through touch. When all these areas are synced up, clarity comes easier. I remind myself to relax around communicating, both in the expression and in the listening, so my brain can fully engage, and I don't get stuck in one mode.

I consider my desire to be in control. I break down the components, in order to unhook from the primal emotional conditioning. I feel pleasure when beloveds freely choose to share themselves with me. Sometimes I want to connect, and the timing doesn't align. I may cycle through an emotional response, but my intention is to quickly return to gratitude, recognizing that they felt safe enough with me, to take care of their own needs. Control and attachment are closely related, and one of the best ways I've found to release attachment to things being the way I want them is to focus on gratitude for the way things are. Looking back, and being grateful for what was, can help break the impractical obsession with how I think the future should be. The more relaxed I can be in the present, the easier it is to be happy.

Happiness comes from being at peace with what is. I just need to feel it, along with all feelings that are always present. When I'm free of the need to control or attach, pure delight arises when a beloved chooses another. I'm able to feel *their* pleasure in my body, as it's enjoyed through another's body.

Step #5. Comedic relief (to shift my reactions). I'm happier when I don't take myself too seriously. Like Lucille Ball, and other inspirational leaders of my time, I've integrated a sense of humor and a compass pointing due north toward the silver lining. I tend to assimilate experiences, learning from most, regardless if it's gaining momentum for success or unpacking hysterical layers of mire for my next song, story or joke. I wanted to be a movie star when I was a teenager. I loved singing and making people laugh. However, in the religion I was raised we weren't allowed to work on the *Sabbath* unless it was absolutely necessary, like saving lives. I liked breaking the rules, but I didn't want to get in too much trouble, so I became a nurse. I had two reasons, I could work whenever I wanted to, and I wanted to learn these skills so I could be a good mom someday like my own mother. Boom.

Step #6. Celebrate my wins. I feel like a new person after letting go of suffering and I find the perfect opportunity to celebrate. This night, at an intimate sex party, I feel ecstatic and want to connect with multiple lovers in the room. I allow myself to *be* where I'm needed, and a powerful experience of compersion unfolds.

Two of my dear long-term lovers are across the room on the couch. Katie's head is in her primary partner's lap giving him oral pleasure, while one of my new lovers is indulging her with his adept hands. A smile emerges as I recall Casey's confident hands inside me, and I become instantly wet, watching Katie's undulating body arching with ecstatic waves. A little to the left, Skyler's shibari rope skills come to life as he ties his baby-mama to Benjamin. I gasp as Skyler tightens a knot and pulls the two closer. I feel their sensations heighten, giving this artful scene added beauty, as they surrender into bliss. Out of the corner of my eye I see my newest lover, Sam, with his face buried in Autumn's juicy pussy.

Kneeling at the feet of an injured soldier, caressing gently, I allow all my sensations to course through my hands into his healing body. My pleasure mounts as I hear Autumn moaning with delight. I know Sam's tongue has the lightest sensitivity, and understands the roadmap of a woman's pleasure. I also know Autumn's body is extremely responsive, and together their electric energy is contagious. Feeling these lovers experiencing pleasure, my heart fills with rapturous joy.

Having only one body doesn't limit the number of experiences I can savor at the same time. I send a blessing to the blissed-out soldier, grinning in his big chair, and crawl toward Katie as she sits in her post-orgasm glow. I've had my mouth on her beloved many times, so I don't hesitate to ask, "May I kiss your sweet lips?"

Katie turns to me and says, "I would like that very much." We kiss, and giggle about our shared experience with Casey's skilled hands. Then I make my way to the sink for mouthwash because not everyone in the room wants to swap unknown fluids. I continue around the room, acknowledging the shared delights of the evening.

I notice my effortless desire to let go of control. I don't want to manipulate a beloved into choosing me over someone, or something else, and I don't want to be controlled. When I remember how I want to be treated, it's easier to know how to treat those closest to me. This blissful sex party is an example of ease in relating with multiple loves.

Other times may not be as graceful, but I remember the basics, and that it's possible to strive toward ease every time. To create safety, I remain calm, try not to make their choice *wrong* because it's different than my desire, and I commit to not punishing them later for that choice. If I have a reaction, I remind myself that what I say to others will be amplified, and may need cleaning up later. Therefore, if I must express myself, I want to be grounded first. If triggering thoughts are swarming or I feel angry, then I take a break. I'm creating my life as I go. I want to create harmony, transparency, mutual understanding, right action, safety, joy, and room to grow. I may need a pee break, to sit alone for a moment and reflect, or a few days to sort my jumbled reactions. I write it, speak into a recorder and replay it, or talk with a trained listener to get the turmoil out of my head.

When I'm clear, and can express my reaction intelligently then I request a time to talk that works for everyone involved. I'm rested, fed, and in a quiet place before I express my inner process. I don't blame them for my feelings of rejection, or any emotional reaction. This sounds controlled, but I've said too many things in an angry, unclear state that can't be taken back. Unloading my angry upset on the one I care about doesn't usually create closeness; however, when I express my process without blame, to another who can listen without guilt, it can create transparent intimacy.

Smiling on the inside is essential for sharing it with

others. The future is hard to predict, but I can shift my attitude, consciously choose my present actions, and I won't regret sharing my inner smile.

EXPLORATION #23

What are your thoughts on authenticity?

_____

_____

_____

I experience authenticity as who I am at my core. My sexual authenticity is the most inner part of that core. I was born from a sexual act, and my animal instinct to connect is a natural drive that propels me. The more I release sexual shame, the more authentic I become.

What is your homework on the topic of authenticity?

_____

_____

_____

Examples:

Write what being genuine, sincere, authentic and real means to you.

Ask five friends if they see any areas in your life that seem inauthentic.

Invite three friends to join you for an adventure to discover what each of you authentically enjoy doing.

Prepare a dinner for a partner, or family, with all the things you truly enjoy.

Chapter 24

No Way To Lose In Love

"Still crazy after all these years." — Paul Simon

It's a warm San Diego afternoon. Mixed emotions in an auditorium filled with people provoked by the morning events. It's the birthday of Marshall Rosenberg, author of *Nonviolent Communication*. He has chosen to teach us instead of sailing on the Bay, or fishing in the Rockies, or snorkeling in Tahiti. He could celebrate his 70th anywhere, but here he is, in front of ungrateful people who are complaining that the group exercises are unclear, and the techniques are too difficult. He's more patient than I. When an audience member is loud enough about an issue, he has them go up on stage, showing how to de-escalate a potentially fraught situation, through first allowing the upset person's anger to be heard.

By 3PM I feel my blood sugar dipping. I want to strangle the next person who puts up their hand. Then it happens. I realize my frustration is more about my own terribly violent communication, and I sense a deep compassion, bubbling up from my sickened stomach, for my endemic ignorance. I melt into self-forgiveness. I feel my compassion oozing through the room until it reaches the strong, rugged presenter on stage. All at once I experience a direct energetic connection with him, and feel the transmission of his sacrifice. My hand shoots up. In this sea of people, many with their hands raised, he immediately calls on me. I'm so full of humbled gratitude I can hardly speak. I know I need to project my quivering voice so he can hear me up there on the stage across this packed room. I take a deep breath and say, "I'm so grateful you're spending your birthday with us, teaching how to communicate and heal our lives."

"Moments like this make it all worthwhile," Marshall says.

Later it sinks in and his words change my life. It isn't about being famous, publishing books, or teaching hundreds of people; what matters is to have genuinely touched another person's life. Even if just one person is affected by a well-lived life, that spark will ignite others, and live on. One shared moment can remind another of their inner bliss, furthering the momentum toward peace on this place we call home. Compassion drifts through this connected web of human consciousness. My hope is that I continue to find forgiveness for myself, and for frustrated people in the auditoriums of the future.

A path can't be taught, only chosen. I learn through experience, paying attention to detail using all my senses. Obsessing about a potential destination is a distraction from taking the immediate step toward the goal. This moment is the only place life and bliss can be experienced.

I've been asked if I knew when, and how I found my path. Is it a continuation of a past incarnation, or inherited from an ancestor? If I try to *find* my personal path, I feel lost. I'm always exactly where I need to be. Questioning my purpose, experimenting with likes and dislikes, saying yes to opportunities, following through, changing my mind, acknowledging mistakes, and celebrating accomplishments are all part of my path.

Relationships are my teachers. I don't remember when I knew my life path would include loving, but I do remember at age four, asking my mother when we'd get to heaven so we could love everybody. I also remember my first crush, and flirting at the age of two. These vivid memories remind me of my beginner's mind—there's always more to learn. I may never know everything about love and relationships.

The key to progressing is to do what's directly in front of me, with a commitment to do my best. Happiness comes when I contribute to others in a positive way. Some choices lead to stagnation (nice for a little break), but the most fun lies in progressing toward harmony, joy, and empathy. Once my mind is at peace I want to explore new frontiers again. Is this why our planet never reaches peace? Does the human brain always want more?

Because of my work in health consulting, people ask me for help in all areas of life. The physical, mental, emotional, and spiritual parts of a person are all connected and one area can affect the whole; more than that every person is also part of nature. They also ask me about open relating, and how to practice transparent communication.

Shortly after Bill Clinton's extramarital peccadillo was exposed, at the turn of the 21st century, I observed an explosion of people wanting the hidden truths of their own sexual orientation and lifestyle choices to be out in the open. Most Presidents before Clinton had clandestine love affairs, but the closest to bringing out the truth was JFK with Marilyn Monroe (which occurred during the time I was conceived.) These presidential examples reflect the direction relationships are evolving— toward transparency. What used to be secretive and private, is now televised and scandalous, but at least it's visible to anyone with access to the media. I don't condone these men's sneaky behaviors, and this may not be the best example of embracing sexuality, but from a big picture perspective, society shone a light on a taboo topic, hashing it out instead of keeping it in a dark closet. Mankind is by no means sexually liberated yet. Both Clinton and Monica Lewinsky were publically drug through the mud. Clinton was impeached for lying, and Lewinsky was shamed for being the *other woman*. However, it was an example of exposing genuine human behavior. There are a few more steps before society becomes honest and shame-free about sexual activities. Each human must do their part to examine their own personal shame of our sexual core.

Henry David Thoreau said that *all good things are wild and free*. He wasn't only referring to nature and animals. Due to my love of the outdoors, I learned initially from my adventurous relationships with animals, trees, water, sunlight, and boulders. My family got our first horse when I was four. Redwing loved kids, and had a gentle spirit. Riding free in the corral close to the house, we'd sometimes run without the restraint of a bridle, bit, or saddle. Redwing was responsible, and cared for my sister and me. One day I fell to the ground; she skidded to a stop, with her hooves sliding just under my back. One more step and she would have trampled my little body. I looked up at her big, soft nose right in my face. She nudged me to make sure I was alright. Now that's connection. Being wild and free helped me learn responsibility, happiness, and a desire to connect honestly with others.

Later I wrote: *To ride a wild horse is dangerous without connection and communication, but to ride a horse with a broken spirit is void of adventure.* The cultural ideal to only have sexual relations with one person (forever) generates taboos and forces most to lie about their natural and vital attractions to others. Ancient religious dogma, attempting to sanction man and *his* wife, doesn't make sense now that we've evolved past the idea of a man owning his woman. I want be honest about the depth of connections I share, and my desire to love everyone. Redwing was my first, but I've ridden many.

With all the inquiries from clients, I was repeating myself, and finding less time to go into the necessary depth of conversation. The questions were universal regardless of their country of origin, age, class, or religious background. And their questions came in emails, over smartphones, and rained down from social media, I was overwhelmed. It became time to open the discussion in an in depth format that could be referenced again.

I spent hours on the phone with Brigham, and shared a few hugs with him and his wife when they were in town. They weren't clients, but acquaintances seeking my willing ear and advise. Jill's openly polyamorous, and he's struggling with conservative ideals. Brigham's the only person I've ever met, (over the age of 25) who's lived a truly monogamous lifestyle. His wife's the only person he's ever had sex with.

I knew the importance of not telling him what to do, so my advice was about helping him stay current with his needs as he examined old beliefs, and to communicate with Jill. I also answered his questions about polyamory and how I justified loving more than one person since I was also from a conservative background. Because both Brigham and Jill have a deep capacity for love, they were able to remain with each other through sorting out their past and figuring out what works for them in the present. They eventually had an uncoupling ceremony, which was a community celebration. The polyamorous community supported both Brigham and Jill, who remained friends through this process. Now, six years later, they still love each other and frequently spend time together.

The highest value that Brigham, Jill and I have in common is that every person has their own path and each path is valid. There is deep gratitude for the areas in common, as well as the parts that need the space to fly free. Listening and sharing my experience empowered Brigham and Jill to make their own decisions.

Brigham wrote: *Cheri, I love you. I love the patience you employ as I struggle with questions and confusion in my life. I love the way you gently help me pick up the shattered pieces of my mind and realize why they no longer fit, rather than try to put them back together. I love the sparkle in your eye, the confidence in your step, the acceptance in your smile. I can be whoever I am, be different each time we meet, and nothing's ever wrong. Wrong isn't even possible.*

Notes of gratitude like this bring me hope.

Scott, a former lover's roommate who'd moved to Spain, writes to me with girl trouble, the same questions I'd heard before. Rather than getting into his story, (just insert your relationship conflict here) I'll share the responses I sent back to him.

I agree it's hurtful to threaten to leave when angry. If leaving is the best next step, discuss it when neither of you are triggered or angry; perhaps with a third party present. In my experience, I've made a boundary not to use leaving as a threat because it's painful to hear, and ultimately we all want to be truthful so the subconscious wants to make what we say the truth. Eventually one of you will leave to remain in integrity with what's said. It sounds like you've had a successful time with her, and whether the relationship continues in the same dynamic can be determined with a few deep breaths, self-reflection, and clear communication.

Look at the quality of time together, lessons learned, connection, love shared; many things make relationships successful. Does she support your dreams? Do you respect who she is? Does she make good decisions? Does the good outweigh the bad? Renegotiate together frequently to determine what works, and what doesn't work. Trying to get all your needs met by one person is often an illusion. We're from different backgrounds and families, so it's illogical to think two people always have the same desires. My relationships feel more relaxed and natural when we have friends, family, and other lovers in our lives, if we agree on how it works.

Often the qualities that attract us to a person are unique and unfamiliar, so remember that next time fear and uncertainty whacks you, and you want to run to the familiar and safe. If you recognize that it's fear, and it's temporary, then you'll be less likely to ditch the entire relationship. Wait, calm down, and face the fears with her before making irrational, regrettable or possibly irreversible decisions.

What's said today influences the choices each partner makes in the future. Being honest may look upsetting, but the outcome is worth it. Our desires change. Like surfing, sometimes you're on top of the wave, and sometimes you're underwater. When it comes back around, if you're still there you may catch the ride of your life.

I close the correspondence suggesting they seek a third person to help them both feel heard, so they can get through the scary parts and back to enjoying their relationship.

Penny, a woman at a crossroads in her life, asks, "How do you determine who you're in a relationship with?

I answer, "What if a relationship is simply who I'm relating with? I try not to make relationship mean any more than what it actually is. It's difficult sometimes to determine what's real because the brain's constantly filling in unknown aspects of relating, to make everything fit into what's known from past experiences. I try to keep it simple, and catch myself when I second-guess the other person, or when I have an idea of how I want the other to fit into my life."

"Do you mean you're *in a relationship* with everyone you relate to?" Penny asks.

"I am enjoying relating with you, and the longer we gaze into each other's eyes, the more relaxed and happy I feel, and the deeper our connection," I reply with a smile. "With business partners, we relate in a way to get along and make good decisions. I relate with family members, and they're always in my heart as part of my blood. Then there are the ones I call friends, and some of them I relate with sexually." I continue, "Some are attractive to the point of obsession, which can be fun if I don't take it too seriously, or try to make that person fit into a box. If I try to cage a free spirit they start to suffocate. If one wants to be caged, they become uninteresting because the cage is stifling. If I'm the only person they're interacting with, they won't bring much to the relationship. When someone's equally obsessed with me, then I want to go for the ride, remembering that everything changes, and hopefully comes around again. If we stimulate creativity and abundance in the world, then that relationship is worth it."

I try to love deeply while maintaining healthy detachment. When I become attached, I feel the pain of self-abandonment. Then I remember I have the capacity to love more than one at the same time, so I can have self-awareness and connection with the one I was attaching to. I learned about non-attachment early on my path. I viewed the following events as unfortunate, but they kept me from being *spoiled* or getting complacent.

My first girlfriend, at age six, was a *preacher's kid* named Laura. My sister had always been the social one. As the oldest sibling, I was terrified with separation anxiety when I had to go *alone* to kindergarten. The difference with little Laura was she and I seemed to actually be connecting on our own. Just as we were becoming friends, her dad got a new church, in a new town; my new best friend moved away. I never saw Laura again. Honestly, I don't remember thinking of her again until later in life, when I observed that many of my closest friends were named Laura.

This was about the same time our parents divorced, and Mother took my sisters and me 300 miles away from not only our home, but also our budding friendships. I remember visiting Dad, at my *other home* the following summer, and some of these kids were still there, just as we'd left them. This pattern of my sister attracting friends for the both of us (I was painfully shy) was shattered my freshman year in high school when we transferred to a new school. I went from 13 kids in my 8th grade, to an overwhelming 103 in my freshman class. Meanwhile, my sister spent her 8th grade year learning how to socialize with a bigger class. By the time my little sister was a freshman, she was the most popular girl in school, while I remained scared and weird. I eventually made friends, on my own, in all the different cliques, but I didn't *fit in* to any one group.

I also learned about attachment through my relationships with animals. Duchess was the runt of the litter, but had grown into a large lovable *Lassie* dog. She'd made the transition with us to California, and was a great comfort when I missed my home. One night Mom came into my room, and said, "Duchess has been hit (killed) by a car."

I didn't cry, or show any emotion. Not because I couldn't, but I had cried good and hard for much larger things, and it hadn't changed anything. All I could think of was how I heard the Mustang racing down our street, and the eerie screech. I didn't blame the driver; he wasn't out to kill. I had no idea that paradoxically, one day I would both share that thrill of speed, yet also strive to drive responsibly. That fast car never raced down our street again, but it was one night too late for my little world.

Then there was Butch, a little bay colt, born in our backyard on a chilly February evening just before my 9th birthday. I fell in love. He responded so playfully to my affection, running to me whenever he heard my voice. One day he let me put a small halter on his soft whiskered muzzle and pull it up over his attentive ears. I taught him how to lunge, change directions, stop, backup, and his gates (walk, trot, canter, and gallop,) all before he was big enough to carry a saddle. Butch was a brilliant, well bred Arabian, and went for a good price to his new owners. Sure, I wished he was my very own to keep, but that money went to providing a good home for us, and feeding our other horses that I could ride and play with anytime. Butch wouldn't have been born into our family if we hadn't paid top dollar to breed his handsome mother with a champion stallion. It was terribly sad the day Butch was loaded up in the strange horse trailer, but the mares had delivered again, and there were other foals awaiting my attention.

By the time I went away to college, my cousins were getting married, and our summer adventures together were changing forever. They endearingly called me *crazy*, because I fearlessly pushed up against taboos. The crushes on my cousins, and their friends, would never develop into anything more than summer flings. Graduating from college I lost many lovers, and began to acknowledge that non-attachment was a choice.

And, that choice would allow others to make one without my interference with their chosen path.

I sold my rare 1972 Datsun 240z to a young mother-to-be. Crying, I watched the faded red racer disappear down the dusty dirt road, having no idea that soon I'd be driving my first convertible muscle car. I felt the sadness, and made space in my garage for what's next. In all these examples I had to choose whether to suffer or let go of attachment in my life.

I attempt to stay connected to everything I love, and avoid everything I hate. It's unreasonable to think I can have *everything* I want with only one body, yet (the seeming opposite) I'm connected to everything. Being connected with everything means I can't avoid what I hate; it's part of my intrinsic reality. Attachment to being connected and wanting to avoid are both troublesome. We live in a universe with both daylight and darkness. I experience pain when I insist on attachment and control. I want to make relationships fit into my known world. When that doesn't pan out, I experience loss as painful. These natural cycles, and what other humans choose to do, are out of my scope of control. Having a physical body is a gift, a tool, a vehicle for learning, and part of the big picture. I want to use it wisely. Supporting others in what they do best, is a rewarding way to accomplish more than I can with only one body.

Acknowledging my choice to suffer, I have a good cry, knowing there are multiple perspectives present to shine a light. I bring the perspective to the front that reminds me to choose a *deep connection* with people, animals, cars, or all that makes my life full of adventure. Non-attachment has become a way of life, so I can choose to embrace profound connection in my life, and feel it as new each time.

Intimate partners are reflections of the most inner parts of myself. It can be an impulsive reaction to hold on to those deep connections. I might mistakenly project the need to be seen or accepted onto a lover who sees my darkest parts yet still loves me. This isn't dissimilar to projecting frustration or anger onto someone. Projecting anger at another is often unrecognized self-anger. If I project the need for acceptance onto another, it's unrecognized self-acceptance. Nobody's responsible for reassuring me, but when someone freely chooses to love me, simply because they're filled from the inside and want to express it, I smile.

I selfishly write these pages to find others who flirt freely, encourage them to express their *crazy* views, and help alleviate suffering around the *perceived pain* of Love. It's brave to venture out in Love—an amazing and vital part of life. More bliss and less suffering is an internal job, but once I make the choice it influences my close beloveds and echoes joy to those within their reach. There's no way to lose in love.

EXPLORATION #24

What are your thoughts on health?

_____

_____

_____

I experience health from a holistic approach. The physical, mental, emotional, and spiritual parts of a person are all connected and one area affects the whole. How a person relates to nature, communicates with others, and functions in the world is all part of health.

What is your homework on the topic of health?

_____

_____

_____

Examples:

Ask three people, that you consider physically fit, to race you for one mile.

Find an intelligence test online. Ask three people that you consider smart to take this test with you.

Ask three people that you have a relationship with (ie. family, partner, friend) to discuss with you something they don't like about you.

Do a three-day vision quest in nature. Make sure two people know exactly where you will be. Take a phone for an emergency call only.

Chapter 25

Harmony, It Just Sounds Better

"He who lives in harmony with himself lives in harmony with the universe."
— Marcus Aurelius

I nicknamed my baby brother Marcus Aurelius, mostly because I liked the ring to it. The significance wasn't obvious, as he didn't have ambitions to rule an empire. Born into a blended family—his mother has two children, whom my father adopted, and I have two sisters born to another mother. When he was born, his mother had a large tumor in the womb with him, and it was a miracle he survived this toxic twin. His birth was a uniting experience for our growing family. Marcus was a happy baby with four big sisters playing mommy, and a big brother to keep him on his toes. Harmony came with the new little life, and thirty-something years later his presence continues to exude peace and virtue.

Today I spent a few choice hours in traffic court. I knew it would be a magical experience from the moment I got the court date of 11-1-11 at 8AM assigned to me. My ticketing CHP officer showed up to make sure I didn't get the *Collect $200 get out of jail free card.*

I sit close to the front, in an aisle seat, ready to be called before the judge. In comes a peculiar woman. I notice my anxious mind about to judge her, but stop to appreciate her positive attitude. She's not outwardly attractive, but she emits a sparkle from the inside that shines out through her smile. She walks around conversing with a line of officers sitting on the other side of the courtroom. I hear her say, "You make me blush," to a man dressed in full police uniform, as she walks to the next, speaking briefly to each one. I soon realize she must be an attorney representing a number of cases. Her personable attitude is shared with each person as she continues to greet the clerk, bailiff, and judge, before sitting down directly in front of me.

I feel intimidated by the judge's position, but as I look closer, she has a thoughtful face with warm eyes. All the cases before me change their plea to guilty, if the officer's present, with the exception of the man directly behind me. His thick Irish brogue insists, "I didn't run that stop sign," and under his breath says, "That angry little cop isn't my father."

Finally, I hear my name. As I stand, the judge asks, "Do you want to change your plea to guilty, or have a trial?" Adding, "You can speak privately with your ticketing officer before giving an answer."

I remain calm with a pleasant attitude while talking outside the courtroom with the officer. He politely answers all my questions about his evidence, and shares everything he'd say if we went to trial. Soon we realize we're at a stalemate. I came this far, and need to give one last attempt at saving my driving record for my commercial license.

As we sit back down, the amiable attorney turns around and whispers, "Did you ask him for a non-moving violation?" She encourages me to go back and ask him.

I do, and he agrees.

The judge calls the helpful woman to go over her cases, and she speaks up, "I think they've resolved their case if you want to take them first."

By this time we're the only three people left in the audience. So the Judge calls my officer and me up to the stand. I don't have to say anything because the officer asks her if she'll change my speeding ticket to a non-moving violation. The judge looks down at my nearly perfect driving record and agrees. I thank each of them and happily pay the $235 fine. It's a win-win-win, and everyone's smiling. The officer does his job, the court gets their money, and my chauffeur license is safe. (In case I ever need a second job, or get the opportunity to drive more than nine children to Disneyland.)

I'm grateful for creating my reality. There were many chances to mess it up—buying into the negativity of those around me, reacting to the cop's firm accusations, cowering in front of the judge, or focusing on the unfavorable aspects of the lawyer, and sending unfriendly energy toward her. Any one of those choices could have changed the outcome of my day in court. I feel blessed that my outer world reflects the bliss and peace I feel on the inside. I'm able to observe the perspectives in me that want a voice, and only allow the ones that are in the highest harmony to prevail. I'm far from perfect, but it's great when I have a good day!

Years before this traffic court date, a group of students enter into a shared intention, of sitting in the womb of Mother Earth. While inflicting extreme hardship on my physical body, I open my consciousness to the collective experiences, far beyond myself, and the immediate circle of humans in this sweat lodge.

At first, my hands dig into the dirt, searching for cool relief from the fire-pit of hot rocks, only inches from my bent knees. Survival is at the forefront until the shaman speaks, and I realize we're all in this together. My head bows and I inhale. Slowing down to the still point, I allow myself to notice one intention—connecting to the earth below me. I have a strong sense of what bonds humans. There are many emotions, but when starting from nothing, the first common feeling I notice is the pain. I sink into the earth, and into the depths of human misery beyond what I think I can bear. Then it transmutes into bliss, and I realize if I feel something completely it becomes pleasurable, even if that something is heart-breaking pain.

If I'm quiet, I can still feel an aching agony, emanating from the people of our planet. I'm grateful for the tangible awareness of this global connection, but breaking the hold of suffering, and taking control of my expression, is fundamental for creating personal (and global) happiness.

Interconnected, we each create our own reality. I used to dislike the way the word tolerance was used to describe accepting differences in people. It seemed harsh, but now I get it; we don't have to agree with others. All of our singular differences are what make the whole of *God*, and if we look deep enough, individual people aren't that different. I appreciate others for their original, and valid, ways of reaching their bliss.

In silence, I drive down that long, heart-wrenching road, away from an overwhelmingly *perfect* lover's bed. Tears are no strangers to this stretch of the road, as I release energetically sticky expectation and attachment. The difference today, is that I'm leaving after a less than pleasant goodbye. Before I left, Drake shared how women, including girlfriends, ex-wife, and his own mother have disappointed, upset, and betrayed him. As I sympathize, my mind wants to understand how we can have relationships with *anyone*, when there's so much distrust and pain in our hearts. I want to know what to say to comfort and relieve. I want to love him, and allow him to choose how much he wants to suffer. There's also a part of me, wanting to ease his suffering, and mine in this moment.

Because the majority of our weekend was sexy and fun, I had an extra dose of feeling connected. Oxytocin, the bonding hormone, isn't just related to breastfeeding and imprinting. It's released during genital or nipple stimulation, or any pleasurable interaction as simple as a hug. This release can initiate a deep primal nesting instinct, along with a strong desire that can feel like a need to attach or bond. After infant needs are met, human connections are still vital as an adult.

Reality gets foggy under the influence of the oxytocin hormone induced feelings. I'm learning to differentiate between logic and the conditioned thoughts of what I was told I *should* do with desires. The *Misery Dilemma*, as I call it, is when the perceived options are to choose between abstinence or engaging in the natural act of sexual connection, which can be used to supercharge our creative life-giving energy, but it's dumbed down to an act that feels shameful or indulgent. I observe clingy feelings stimulated by my released hormones and remember that I was already whole and complete before engaging in the sexual act. With this clarity, I freely enjoy this supercharged sexual energy, and direct it to strengthen intentions in my life, and in the lives of my sex partners. Healthy bonds are what I strive for.

If I'm responsible for my feelings of attachment, I'm also responsible for my broken-heartedness. Sitting comfortably in the driver's seat, holding the steering wheel with both hands, I let go of thoughts (that trigger feelings) of wanting to own, control, or manipulate the one I engage with sexually. I'm free, and want my partners to be free. I can give deeply of myself, and know that what I want for another is for them to be free, connected, and blissful.

When I redirect this powerful hormonal energy, I create a nest for art, music, ideas, mentorship, and healing. I direct the feeling to attach to the present moment. Then do the same in the next moment, and the next. This focus allows me to respond to my body and mind, and then I can share what I've learned with others. I attach to where I put my focus, and that attachment helps me be fully present. In this practice, I observe that the nature of this physical world is change.

What once gave me a miserable feeling is now a tool for leading me back to bliss; I remember we're all connected. The masculine and the feminine within my own being are making love; I'm completely at peace. Which gives me the space to remember the extent of the dualistic war that used to rage inside of my own skin, and I recall what Drake had said about the unsettled feelings between so many men and women in the world.

"The 70's ruined women. The modern woman has a sense of entitlement, without the appreciation and common kindness toward men. Most women demand, complain, and don't appreciate what they've got," Drake had said before I left. "Women used to have it easy when they could stay home and have children, while their man provided for the family. Many men have become disinterested in relationships," he said.

He raved on, with some valid points. Then he ended by prophesying, "The human race is heading for extinction!"

As I drive, I feel deeply into the separation because that's what the female nature does. Grounded and safe, my masculine side holds space (for her) to go even deeper into the pain of this separation.

There in my car, tears spill onto my cheeks. As a woman, I begin to deeply sense the pain of my male counterpart. My silence is broken with faint words, repeating in my head at first—*For all the times I've hurt you: I'm sorry, please forgive me, I love you.* This ancient forgiveness practice, resurrected from a workshop, began to morph and evolve.

From a deep murky place in the collective psyche, arose a whisper on my lips, "On behalf of all women," my voice deepened, slowed, and there was a pronounced clarity, "On behalf of the Goddess herself, I want to apologize to all men; to God himself. For all the times I've hurt you: I'm sorry, please forgive me, I love you. For all the times I didn't respect you: I'm sorry, please forgive me, I love you. For all the times I lied to you: I'm sorry, please forgive me, I love you. For all the times I tried to manipulate you: I'm sorry, please forgive me, I love you. For all the times I was selfish: I'm sorry, please forgive me, I love you. For all the times I was needy and clingy: I'm sorry, please forgive me, I love you." Intensely immersing into the anguish, I declare, "For all the times I was greedy: I'm sorry, please forgive me, I love you. For all the times I allowed my tongue to be used by the perspective that just wants to fight: I'm sorry, please forgive me, I love you. For all the times I doubted myself and wasn't strong for you: I'm sorry, please forgive me, I love you. For all the times I wasn't with you when you needed me: I'm sorry, please forgive me, I love you."

Suddenly, I feel as if Drake is sitting right next to me in the passenger seat. I continue speaking, "All the women who came before me are the culmination of who I am at this time, and influence how you relate to me now. My only wish is that I learn to create harmony," and I break; it's a lot to hold. Comedic relief interrupts me with the thought; harmony, it just sounds better. I begin singing Bono's lyrics, *"I can't live, with or without you."*

That's when I feel the core of the misery dilemma. I want it, but it's bad. How many times have I felt that dilemma? Silence comes over me again as I sense my body releasing the pain, and observe as my mind continues to unwind the weekend's events. Then it happens. As I release the pain, I let go of past shame and guilt, and thoughts of undeserving.

Feeling a liberated relief, I know something profound is happening. At first, I want to remember every word, so I can share it with Drake, and somehow heal his pain. But as it sinks in, I realize I'm the one who needs to open my heart. I need to allow all of him, and compassionately listen to him. I'm opening myself, to allow all of his pain, disappointment, frustration, rage, and hurt to be heard, allowing all of it to flow and be acknowledged. I need to expand my capacity to feel his pain, and comprehend all the injustice that has been done to his pure, innocent, undeserving heart. How can humans inflict so much violence on one another?

In my deep contemplative silence, the answers begin to emerge. I glimpse into the vast understanding of how the human psyche is evolving. Becoming self-aware is a process. I see the importance of the roles men and women play as sounding boards for each other. Allowing the pain of our ancestors to finally be heard, and released, so that gratitude can enter our hearts. I don't know much about forgiveness; I just see this as the process of humans finding their voices. Often we don't know what to do with all the *shit* that builds up in the collective psyche, so it gets flung, hitting the ones closest. We're learning how to clean it up, and harder yet, how not to fling it on the next one.

As my car pulls into the garage, I sit for a moment in silence. A song pops into my head again, and I smile. Wondering, how much pain is witnessed through the expression of songs? Reminding us that we're not alone, and furthering the quest for greater knowledge. I send my dear lover a text: *Made it home. Safely.*

EXPLORATION #25

What are your thoughts on forgiveness?

_____

_____

_____

I experience forgiveness as a powerful way to stay clear and present with others and myself. When I fail at something it's vital that I look at what I've learned and move toward success. When I disagree with another person or they fail to live up to their highest potential I do the same—find the lesson with a kind heart and then let it go. When it's hard to forgive someone, the answer is found in our own shadow.

What is your homework on the topic of forgiveness?

_____

_____

_____

Examples:

Think of someone you are upset with and why. Say, I hate it when (name of person) does this thing. Then imagine them sitting next to you and say, I hate it when you do (this thing). Then say, I hate it when I do the same thing. Bring the lesson home by seeing how you are similar. Are you upset at that part of yourself and are you capable of doing the same thing that you're angry about?

If that first exercise example is hard for you to do then look up "The Work" of Byron Katie and Ken Wilber's 3-2-1 process. Or contact me for some personal coaching.

Write the words, *for all the times I've hurt you: I'm sorry, please forgive me, I love you.* Write it again and exchange the words *hurt you* for *lied to you*. Then write it again and keep getting more specific.

Forgive the person and yourself, and then write a song about your experience.

Chapter 26

The Ultimate Connection

"Peace doesn't require two people; it requires only one. It has to be you.
The problem begins and ends there. — Byron Katie

TTNT, The Thursday Night Thing, is the monthly event at a museum across from Union Station where we're always entertained, in one way or another. Buckling up my thigh high boots, I'm feeling optimistic as Lola reads the news article about the evening performances and art exhibits. Girl's night out, and we're dressed as if we've got a part in the show. I'm in a fetish mood. Tonight's the perfect night to act out my fantasy of being tall enough to see over crowds, because of my (now 6'2") stature, and the numbers expected to attend tonight's event. Heads turn when we arrive, something I usually don't notice, but from this vantage point, I'm seeing the world anew, not knowing what to expect becomes part of the excitement. After walking through the photography exhibit with introspection, we round the corner like the inner opening of a labyrinth, just in time to see a woman lowering from the 30-foot ceiling. She's dancing mid-air, balanced on silk ribbons. Suddenly she drops another 10 feet, caught by her left foot, pirouetting like an upside-down ballerina. Gasps from the gathering crowd, we applaud after catching our breath.

Across the room, amongst the sculptures and oil paintings, is a live Kinbaku (Shibari) art demonstration. Three elaborately tattooed, exquisite bodies are bound in compromising positions with precisely knotted ropes. "What a scene!" Meagan mouths with a hushed tone.

Speechless, Lola and I nod. We witness as the figures are contorted into stunning shapes with the skill of the artist cinching down on one side of the ropes, then knotting, and stretching. My breath quickens as the skilled hand grasps the central knot, bonding all three together, and yanks them to attention. I turn to see Meagan and Lola, wide-eyed and about ready to salute.

We head upstairs to the balcony wine bar for a look around, and perhaps a sip. The band, in the courtyard below, is about to begin. Before investigating the rest of the exhibits, we take advantage of our bird's eye view. After sharing a glass of wine, the alluring music sounds danceable. We meander back down the narrow staircase to ground level, in front of the stage, to inspire the musicians.

We're just warming up, but it's getting chilly out, so the lead musician announces their final song. After thanking the players for the great beat to move to, we head back in for more action. The stairs prove to be a fun place for eye contact with someone, or to brush in passing. "Lots of smiles on the banister," I say, winking at Lola and Meagan.

"It's great exercise in heels," Lola scoffs.

Emotionally unprepared for the next exhibit, sandwiched between the ground floor and rooftop, we move toward a straggly line of people exiting through a dimly lit hallway. A handwritten sign points us in the direction of a large open room. As we enter, directly to our left are a few unglamorous items hanging on the walls; each spotted with the low glow of a reading light. Upon closer examination, with my nose right up under the light, I ascertain that it's photographs and news articles about World War II atrocities. As I follow the string of brutalities along the wall, I listen as one of the clusters of people scattered around the room discuss the circus acrobats downstairs, and another talk about the band that was playing earlier.

Near the center of the room, there's a pulpit-height box with a dial and a graph. The dial has a zero center point with positive numbers to the right, and negative ones on the left. There's a description of the experiment on the graph under the dial. The left goes toward peace, and the right goes toward war. The instructions explain to turn the dial if you want to experiment with war.

It took awhile for the significance of the whole thing to come together. I turn the dial to the right and back to the left. It's subtle, but the music seems to get slightly louder when the dial moves toward the right. Again, I turn the dial to the right; this time more keenly aware of the minute changes in the room. All the lights in the room brightened, making it much easier to see the photos, and read the articles from a further distance. Again I listen to a group a people, this time discussing some of the horrors that the Japanese committed before the bombing of Pearl Harbor. Another group talks of political reasons for creating the United Nations, while another discusses the pitfalls of the current administration. The agitation rises so I turn the dial back to the left.

Then, over the tops of the heads in the room, my attention is drawn to three towering men standing near the door. They must be taller than me, I surmise. So wrapped up in this exhibit, I haven't noticed them conversing, and looking quite attractive. Have my girls seen them? Not likely, they're still reading the disturbing articles on the walls.

While my eyes are diverted during this moment of distraction, someone turns the dial all the way over to the *war* marker. The room becomes chaotic, voices talking over the music, and there's more movement. The alarming thing is the tone of the conversation going from soft and jovial, to short harsh words. I reach over and turn the dial back down. The room begins to mellow, but then the knob is turned to the far right again. This time I try a new approach. Facing the one who cranked it up, I inquire, "Do you know what this exhibit's about?"

He shrugs, shakes his head no, and turns away. I quickly move the dial to the left. He seems fascinated to see what war is like, but with the noise, it's difficult to communicate about it. Soon the crowd begins to calm down, responding to the gradually dimming lights and softening music.

Meagan and Lola spot the *tall ones*, and head toward me to regroup. Soon we're deep in conversation with the lovely giants about what we've discovered. Someone turns the dial to one side, then the other, before the pseudoscientist leaves it in the middle. We continue chatting, and giggling like teenagers. Every few minutes when the chaos kicks in, making it very difficult to continue our conversation, I reach my stealthy arm through the bodies to tone it down. We determine that I'm acting as the peacekeeper, distinguishing from peacemaker, because I *silently* keep the peace, without drawing attention to the act of minimizing the chaotic stimulation in the environment. I'm not fighting to make anyone be peaceful.

I've another motive for keeping the lights dim, and volume down, as we're trying to interact. It's hard to flirt while yelling. As they tell me their disparate lines of work, I wonder how it is that an engineer, lawyer, and computer technician came to be such fast friends. We're equally diverse: Meagan's a doctor, Lola's a teacher, and I'm a psychiatric registered nurse turned holistic-artist-entrepreneur. Group dynamics have always fascinated me, and this unexpected lot is finding multiple avenues to explore.

Out from behind the wall a mystery man emerges, walking with authority straight toward the centerpiece. I overhear him speaking to other observers, and realize it's the artist. Did he witness me single-handedly calming the entire room, from a roaring river to a bubbling brook of intimate conversations?

My excitement isn't contained as I share my detailed observations with him, and ask questions about his exhibit. His demeanor lights up as we continue. "No one else has understood this piece to these depths," he declares.

Smiling as we go into greater detail, I disappear into his eyes. For a few moments the rest of the room disappears with a pleasurable ease. Suddenly, I realize I can't hear his words. Is the volume too loud again? Perhaps it's a stroke? Did I stop listening? In that moment, as I put my attention on my ears, they catch up; as if my brain rewinds, and replays it fast-forward. I haven't missed anything he's communicating, none of it! His eyes, his heart, his hands, his inflections, and the way he wants to listen to my thoughts. So much is conveyed beyond words.

I want to tell you about the crazy sex in the janitor's closet, or how we fall deeply in love, but it's not like that. Our love went deep and wide in those few moments, without even touching our physical bodies together. We didn't even exchange names. It's simply a perfect connection, perfect in the comprehensiveness and wholeness. As we finish speaking, I notice his face for the first time. I don't see much about his life, his age, or if he's handsome. What's obvious is that his smile is as big as mine. Each has acknowledged and been acknowledged, each has seen and been seen.

As for the three lofty observers, Megan and Lola are still chatting with them and exploring details of their dynamic. Before parting, we all exchange numbers, and eventually become friends. We build bonfires on the beach, go on a weekend water rafting adventure together, celebrate birthdays, and yes, we dive deep into crazy fun sex!

EXPLORATION #26

What are your thoughts on attachment?

_____

_____

_____

I experience attachment and connection as opposite ends of the continuum of the same thing. Attachment is being with another person when I'm ungrounded and needy. Connection is when I am whole and choose to be with another person. Part of true connection is to hold it loosely in my hands, and let it come and go as it wishes.

What is your homework on the topic of attachment?

_____

_____

_____

Examples:

Write your basic needs and desires. Then check off which of those needs are already met, which ones you can meet on your own, and which ones can be met by multiple sources.

Ask ten people to join you at a park with a monkey gym. Together design a mini Ropes course to create trust and teamwork exercises with the equipment you have.

List three ways you like to connect. Interview four people; ask them examples of when they feel connected.

Invite a small group to a gift exchange party. Pick numbers and when it's your turn choose either a wrapped gift from the center, or one that has already been unwrapped by one of the people in the group who went before you. How does it feel when a gift you like gets taken from you?

Chapter 27

The Swedish Interview

"May your choices reflect your hopes, not your fears." — Nelson Mandela

I'll relax and let my truth flow. But what if that flow is just what's on the surface, or what's up for me right now? I'm always doing the best I can. If asked the same questions again in a year, I may answer differently. This is a conversation starter to stimulate deeper contemplation of these inquiries. I'll encourage her to talk with others to get a broader perspective on these topics. This interview spans over a three-month period during Maja's stay with me in a shared polyamorous home. From her room, she sends me a question via email as it comes to her in the middle of the night, but mostly we talk face to face.

It's an early spring morning in Southern California, daffodils still brilliant, and the irises are beginning to unfurl. Maja has settled in after her long flight from Sweden, and is ready to begin the interview process. She's an experienced journalist, but never has she gone on a work assignment with such a personal agenda. "My answers may be unfamiliar to you. The brain tries to make things fit neatly into already established beliefs, and may try to simplify them into familiar categories," I say before we begin.

"Give me an example," says Maja, tilting her head.

"You might believe polyamory is the opposite of monogamy; therefore you must be one or the other. This simply isn't the case; there are boundless lifestyle options: celibacy, polygamy, harem, pimp, prostitute, arrangements, secret affairs, BDSM contracts, swingers, and all variations of love," I say.

"So, it's possible to deeply love and have relationships with multiple people, while choosing to have sex with only one other person," Maja says.

"Exactly, it's good to think outside the box, and keep the mind flexible," I reply. "I appreciate your willingness to explore options of relating, and your sincere desire to improve relationships."

Sitting naked on the grass, she soaks in the warm sun as we begin our dialogue.

Maja (M.) Why choose a polyamorous lifestyle?

Cheri (C.) I love deeply, forever. I want it all, spiritual and sexual connection, freedom, honesty, peace, and responsibility.

M. Do you ever feel like you're missing out on something by not being in a monogamous relationship?

C. I have a full life and a variety of lovers that keep my sex life from getting boring. Yes, when I'm not in a primary relationship there are times when I miss having someone in my bed, but I can always call someone. I have so many people in my life. I don't think I'm missing out on anything. I have travel companions, and it doesn't have to be the same person every time. It doesn't matter if I'm in a monogamous relationship, open, or celibate, I must choose happiness and the kind of life I want to live. I also have alone time, and when you live with someone you don't always get that so, I have the best of both worlds.

M. Where's the stability without marriage?

C. My socially conditioned thoughts say, I can only get

stability, exclusivity, and happiness if I force my will on one person for the rest of my life, or surrender to another person's will. When I sit with those options, it feels like a trap. My stability comes from knowing myself, and from trusting the lovers in my life who intimately know and appreciate me. The depth of exclusivity I experience in one moment of looking into another's eyes is more rewarding than a lifetime of owning or being owned by another. Happiness is endless when it's freely chosen and I'm beyond happy when I choose life.

M. What's positive about open relationships?

C. This lifestyle's about living in the present moment with mindfulness, choice, and honesty. I like creating safety within my relationships by being honest about my other lovers. My biggest reward is, knowing the ones I'm relating with are freely choosing to relate with me.

M. How important is sexuality in relationships?

C. I love sex! It's a fun way to connect, and an amazing tool for moving energy. Creating energy flow is vital for life, but there are many ways to accomplish that. It's possible to live a fulfilled life without sex; however, my personal preference is to rate sex as highly important.

M. Could you live a polyamorous life without sex?

C. Not all of my relationships are sexual. I have many platonic Loves in my life. On a few occasions, I didn't engage in sexual connection for many months.

M. Is there a way to find profound communication without the sexual encounter?

C. Like what we're experiencing right now? When we're dissecting intimacy and gazing into each other's eyes, I can't imagine being any closer to you. I feel deep love for this communication, the topic, your receptivity, and for you. Correction; I can imagine being closer to you, but this is profound.

M. Is there a danger of staying superficial, whilst jumping from one partner to another?

C. I don't love one partner less when I'm with another. Connection isn't superficial, even for only one night can be profound. Whether with one or many, there's much to learn from each person. My relationships continue to deepen in truth, freedom, healing, letting go, or creating peace on earth together.

M. Do you see an aspect of fleeing in not committing to one?

C. If I want to escape responsibility, and play with a stranger, it can be messy. I'm accountable for what I create with another, and I want to keep my energy clear. When I'm fully present with another, not fleeing, it's much more rewarding. Escaping is what the movies are for.

M. Is it possible for you to deepen with the one?

C. To me finding the one is a myth, it sounds good, but which one? Rather, I deepen with each one.

M. Would monogamy be of interest to you?

C. Monogamy sounds delicious with almost every new lover I encounter, for the first few hours. I used to fantasize about a life happily-ever-after, in a castle on a hill away from everyone else. I haven't experienced it in reality to be something that turns out as projected. I'm a social creature, with a variety of interests, and connections. I may go years only having sex with one person, but I love many.

M. Is the individual just part of a greater scheme, where we're all one?

C. Each individual connection reflects a unique part of the self. As I see these alienated parts reflected back, I recognize and allow them to mend. Once an aspect of self is healed, it becomes infinitely easier for others to do the same. We work together as a collective in this way to evolve as humans.

M. Is it possible to stay connected with one partner whilst being with others?

C. Absolutely. I feel deeply, and love deeply with more than one at a time. I haven't closed my heart; in fact, I'm happier and more open when in multiple connections. This expansion is more inclusive, not exclusive. I love deep and wide. It hurts when I feel disconnected, or my heart closes, and everything slows to a halt like a broken cog in a wheel. This feeling of disconnect is my responsibility to clear. Connection is an internal experience, not an enmeshment with one partner.

M. What happens when you leave one partner for the next?

C. It isn't necessary to leave one for the next when I love more than one person. Each connection is unique and valuable. It has to do with more love, deeper connections, loving more completely with the individuals in my life.

M. What makes you return to some partners and not others?

C. Preferences I guess. Some partners don't return to me. Sometimes it takes time to process challenges, so we take a break. Sometimes, there simply isn't much to learn from a connection. If a connection is mostly about helping the other person through something, or if it's all about me, it tends to burn out. My favorite kind of partnership is where we are mutually benefiting, and are both excited to be relating. I find it best when we share values and goals, and have complementary skills we can apply toward a common vision that contributes to the greater good. When another doesn't resonate with my frequency any longer it becomes clear, and we choose to spend less time together. When I resonate more with another, we choose to spend more time together. It's as natural as all of nature, the ebb and flow of tides, waxing and waning of the goddess moon, seasons, colors, wildlife, and my wild life.

M. When you're not with a partner, where does the connection go?

C. It always just is. Even when we are apart forever, that connection will always be. Like my relationship with nature, always connected, one living breathing organism.

M. How do you label your partners and who are they to

you?

C. I mostly call partners by their names, rather than a label that's bound to change. It's human nature to be curious about who's sleeping with whom. Perhaps, when being transparent, I could share the last time we connected sexually when I'm introducing someone. Each partner is a unique, intimate part of my life.

M. It seems less secure than having the title of husband/ wife, boyfriend/girlfriend. Is it ever frightening to leave?

C. It's more frightening if my sense of security is tied to another. Outward security is an illusion. A bus could hit anyone, at any time. There's no true security in a title. They could change their will & testament right before getting hit by that bus, or have a prenuptial. Entitlement or ownership is a game; play it only if both parties are well informed and willing participants, and you're into that kind of thing. I prefer the security of having my feet planted on the ground below me. My security comes from knowing I'm already connected and I am love. The more I connect with myself and learn how to connect with others, the more chances of having multiple secure lifelong relationships. Marriage can be a false sense of security, and can suppress or cause stagnation if relying on that piece of paper. When I develop my ability to listen, provide for, and connect with others, I notice less fear. Coming from this place of security makes me a progressively better friend and lover, forever.

M. Does one person mean more to you than others?

C. I appreciate each for their unique gifts, and the way our connection reflects back parts of me. When I'm judging a part of myself, I may turn that outward and judge another person. If I haven't allowed that part of myself, I may crave a connection that reflects the elusive part of me. I want to learn about the whole—all perspectives, the parts I like and don't like. Maybe I favor people in my life similar to liking some parts of myself better than others. I hope to eventually like all of me, and everyone.

M. Is that okay?

C. Who's the judge? Life is what it is. What's happening is exactly what has to happen in order to have realizations, and turn the amazing next page in life!

M. Why would you choose to marry one, but not the other?

C. I would not choose to marry. This seems to be an outdated paradigm. In conventional marriage, there's ownership, control, a bit of killing one another, and a lack of freedom. I prefer deep spiritual and sexual connection AND freedom. If I choose to explore this world with one, it's a process to find my freedom within that marriage, and allow my beloved to experience a deep bonded connection along with freedom.

M. I know you're Poly, but do you have a primary partner?

C. I'm my primary partner. Being Poly means I love many, including myself. There are many definitions of Polyamory; I'm pretty literal. Under every label is a deeper explanation. I don't like labels, but it's just an opening line to express my relations. Each of my partners/lovers/intimate friends/relationships is fluid; I play different roles, at different times, with each one. Sometimes I spend more time with one, or travel with specific ones, or cohabit with one or more. I also co-create, invest, make money, do business with other partners. I love falling in love, and I allow my masculine and feminine within me to flirt, crush on, and fall in love often, with each other and with another.

M. Is there a longing to stay with one, to explore further?

C. An intimate connection doesn't have to only be about the future. It's in the moment, not comparing the one before me to a relationship in the past, or make it mean marriage, children, living together, or anything other than what is real right now. I explore deeper with only a handful of lovers because there's only so much time. The number of close connections fluctuates. Some lovers are on a different timeline, and I may only see them occasionally, but each time is a deeper experience, learning more, seeing more, and feeling deeper.

M. What happens if you get stuck with one?

C. Ideally, we're both able to stay present to move through the stickiness. Attachment to one person, feeling, or experience requires a constant process of letting go, to stay present and blissful. If we're both in the present, then we're probably not stuck.

M. Is it a sign that you've encountered where you're stuck within yourself?

C. You got it! And, this is where moving sexual energy comes in handy. The sexual energy is the seat of creativity. Allowing my expanding sexual awareness up my spine, it helps move hidden blocks in my body, and psyche. Avoiding, or going around stuck areas, is asking for more suffering. It's often difficult, in any relationship, to move toward a block. I go toward the stuck energy, sit in a state of allowance, ask what's needed, and then do what's necessary to move through it. Remembering that on the other side of the hard spot there's more freedom, ease, and creative flow for everyone involved. When a lover reflects a stuck spot back to me, I like using our creative sexual energy to move through it together.

M. Is it best to resolve with a person you want to leave, or just move on to the next?

C. It's just as important to look at the things that are repulsive, or make me want to leave, as it is to look at what makes me feel attracted to an individual. I do my best to support people in their process. I also want to resolve conflict in the present relationship, or it will surface again. I prefer to deal with it, and reach a mutual understanding on issues, as soon as possible. I don't want to strand a lover in a stuck place; I care for their evolution as much as my own.

M. I keep coming back to the moving on. Are you sharing your energy/letting it flow?

C. Because we now have the means to easily communicate all over the world, I have deep connections with people in many different villages. There's a natural flow, and choices that affect where I share my energy. I continually practice letting go of attachment, in order to be clear and present. I'm not moving on from a person, just from the attachment to that person. I strive to be fully present, and detach from what my old conditioning says I want. When I'm in right relation with the past and future, and in a peaceful way in the present, then I'm in the flow with the one before me.

M. How do you deal with longing for someone?

C. Longing feels a lot like suffering. As soon as I get done feeling sorry for myself, I slow down and breathe. I then go into the feeling to experience it, and allow it to move. When I identify with the perspective in the psyche that longs, the object of the longing fascinates me. Usually, it's a person, just one person as if the longing needs to choose one thing to long about. When I get over longing for one person, the part of me that longs will find something else to long for, like ice cream. The key to not suffering over the longing is, notice the longing is always there, but so is the satisfied, satiated, and all the perspectives that when felt simultaneously become bliss.

M. Just hearing this makes me feel more relaxed and at peace. I'm starting to see what you're meaning. It seems like a constant state of a mild meditation.

C. Observing the calm within the chaos, being present with my relations, and remembering I am Love.

M. How do you deal with jealousy?

C. Similar to how I deal with longing. The difference is, jealousy usually involves other people. The emotions of jealousy are stuck. I breathe deep to expand my body, and allow the feelings to move. Then I feel jealousy pass through, without getting stuck in suffering. The hiccup comes when there's a great deal of judgment, taboo, or conditioning around what triggered the jealousy. Identify all the individual emotions tangled up in the conglomerate of emotion we call jealousy. Feeling left out, not good enough, rejection, betrayal, anger, disappointment, frustration, fear of a repeat from the past, fear of failure or loneliness in the future, etc. I chunk out the overwhelming emotions we call jealousy. Next, I remind myself to release the judgments as being good or bad. The trigger and the reaction are already in the past. Finally, I move toward it. If it's involving a partner, I physically get closer or initiate communication with them. I move toward it, instead of retreating or shutting down with the paralyzing fear of getting stuck in overwhelming suffering. I let go by communicating gratitude, even before I can feel the release.

M. How do I face what I feel strongly about? Acceptance and an open mind are tough to get to.

C. My process has gotten easier, and quicker with practice. I've been stuck in jealousy when my heart hurt so badly I felt I might die, and I cried myself to sleep many nights in a row. Recently when I felt jealousy, I went to the bathroom and cried for about 30 seconds as I released all the landslide of emotion, then I walked right back in and expressed a positive response. The feeling dissipated so quickly my heart hurt for less than 5 seconds. The key is making the choice to practice getting back to love and allowance every time, creating positive examples that develop neural pathways in my brain to continue making it easier.

M. I hate jealousy and haven't been caught in it for a long time. I may be tiptoeing around the emotions that provoke it, and missing out on other stuff in the process. I'm choosing to stay with the fear instead, which seems less shameful to ask for help with. Any advice?

C. Hate, tiptoeing, and fear, are all pointing toward being stuck. Choosing to shutdown, or not confront an emotion, makes all emotion more muffled. To truly feel deeply, I must feel all of it, the good, the bad, and the ugly. Life gets better and better as I clear old stuck beliefs, and free myself to feel everything more vividly.

M. What if I can't handle the emotions, and hurt somebody, or do nasty things? It happened before, and I don't want to go there again.

C. Freedom within a relationship isn't for everyone.

There's a protector perspective inside each of us, that won't allow more than we can handle. Overwhelm is emotion spilling out past our comfort zone, beyond the familiar. I breathe deep, and acknowledge it's an opportunity to expand my capacity to feel. We don't really want to hurt others, and it can hurt our reputation, they might fight back, get revenge, or it can backfire when we don't treat others with respect. Fear is a stuck emotion. Choose to move through the illusion of being stuck, to find expansion, opening, and love.

M. Will you give more details on how you handle jealousy and attachment?

C. I used to freeze up, and get nauseous if I felt jealous. Now it's just another emotion that lets me know I'm alive. One Saturday night I felt it. Not with my partner Jacy, at home with his lover Felina, but at a party with Bobby, playing with a new friend. I don't want to identify as a hypocrite, so I love others the way I want to be loved. I don't want to be controlled, possessed, or manipulated, so I don't do that to others. To shift, out of the feeling of overwhelming jealousy, I breathe and I ask for assurance. I don't ask Bobby, and interrupt their flow. I ask Harper to hold my hand and walk me toward Bobby and Clara. If I'm going to participate with them, I need my energy to sync with theirs and be part of the flow. There's no need to speak of what's going on inside my head because that brings the drama out into my external world. The act of moving toward the perceived object causing me pain was enough to immediately dissipate 70 percent of my angst. I bend down and ask, "Can we join you?"

Harper and I are greeted with smiles, laughter and nodding heads. Together Bobby and Clara say, "Yes, please."

Kisses and touches flood my brain with oxytocin and serotonin, the feel-good hormones. Instantly my body remembers, there's an abundance of love in this world to experience. It's better to risk a beloved choosing to spend time with another than try to hold on. Insecurity and the feeling of lack aren't magnetic or attractive, but releasing the smothering control allows everyone involved, the space to appreciate freedom. I like being a free agent (unless I choose submission.) It feels better knowing the other is freely choosing me, without guilt, manipulation or obligation.

M. I appreciate your honesty; I'd have problems watching my boyfriend do what yours did. I don't let my wild passion carry me away anymore; I'm afraid of the consequences of my jealousy and anger. This limits me from flowing free. How can I find balance?

C. Yes, I hear your dilemma. Bobby and I talked about the party ahead of time. We made an agreement to go home together, even if there were other connections made; it was about more love. It was Bobby's first experience where a girlfriend allowed him to play with another honestly, without sneaking or lying. He was grateful that I held that space for him; the weeks following were extra hot and juicy for us. The few minutes of slowing down, feeling through the jealousy, and going toward my fear, without retreating or listening to my thoughts, was worth it. Had I been overcome with the jealous thoughts, and reacted, I would've missed out on a fun party, and the increased intimacy with Bobby. Remaining centered is nearly impossible. How quickly I get back to my center and joy, now that's life.

M. What's the secret to maintaining relationships? Sometimes I have so much anger I just want to leave.

C. Relating with another takes work. When two or more are in repeated close proximity, wisdom is exchanged. Relationship growth is like Ping-Pong. When one learns something, growth is close behind, followed by change. I catch myself assuming that I know why the other is reacting, but change is challenging because it's unknown. It can trigger a core animal instinct, releasing fear hormones to fight, or get away. The secret is, if I'm the one growing then it's my turn to practice compassion, and completely accept them right where they are. I must stop myself from wanting them to change with me, and love them for who they are. From that place of allowance, I can then nurture their growth like a loving parent. They're likely thinking the same thing when it's their turn to grow, wanting me to change, and thinking I won't.

M. Is polyamorous living the ultimate solution for all people?

C. No. For me, I don't want to look for the one and only then shut down once that's achieved. I think many people love more than they're willing to admit. Polyamory is being honest about all the attractions. Practicing honesty improves the ability to relate with others, which generates peace and aids in the relationship evolution, so we won't need a revolution. Adding new people to existing relationships brings hope and growth opportunities. One relationship style isn't right for everyone, but sharing viable relationship options is helpful and gives people a choice.

M. Do polyamorous people become lovers with each attraction?

C. Everyone's choice of how deep they go with each individual is unique.

M. It sounds freeing to explore other attractions, but what do I do if my partner does the same?

C. It all starts with wanting to be free. Live in the present so each connection can be real, not compared to a past trauma or attached to future fears. What if I'm not the one-and-only to the one I want to own? I let go of trying to fit into another person's idea of me. Freedom's letting go of attachment, resentment, hatred, and fear; it's choosing baby steps toward loving everyone. When I release the chains off those I control, we both can experience freedom. My partners and I connect with open hearts, and flirt just because it's fun.

M. What about transparency? Do you keep a sacred room within yourself, for only you? Or do you choose to share it all with those closest to you?

C. Growing up I learned to withhold to avoid criticism and punishment, so choosing transparency is my cutting edge for growth in relationships. I have fears of not being liked, or my partner getting upset and leaving me. It feels amazing to be seen and accepted by others, but transparency can be met with resistance. Withholding blocks the energy flow but if I communicate my truth clearly, and reach understanding to avoid misinterpretations, then everyone feels safer and more harmonious.

I'm mindful to develop patterns of choosing the perspectives that move toward my goals, not my fears, like the example with Bobby and Clara. If I hadn't moved toward them, I may have voiced my fears instead, but I considered the consequence of letting fear have the driver's seat. All the perspectives, including fear and jealousy are lurking, but courage and strength are also always present.

It's not popular to be transparent, and sometimes it's easier to sneak around to avoid confrontation or being called a slut if dating more than one person. Feelings of second best or not good enough run rampant in our psyches already, so it just seems better to be truthful. If we share our truth, and allow those around us to take responsibility for how they receive that truth, then we have an honest platform to relate from and make our choices.

M. What do you mean by transparency is your cutting edge?

C. Because I came from a family with secrets, showing people who I am didn't come naturally. I began to see how secrets affect physical health, and how mental and emotional health develops around them. Societal conditioning also creates shame and fear of being in truth. I'm grateful for my family, and the era of human evolution I was born into because by revealing the truth in my lineage, I found a lifestyle based on transparency. My biggest challenge and greatest joy is going down this (nearly forsaken) path of creating intimacy with transparency. Fear of transparency is an illusion and truth is ultimately the path of less chaos. Living by example, I want to create a safe place to help others speak their truth too. Going toward fear, while speaking my truth, rather than focusing on fearful thoughts, is the first step. It's easy for communication to get sloppy with the most intimate people in my life. I don't want to withhold, or assume, or say hurtful things with anyone, especially them. I choose to be honest—transparent.

M. Do you keep a little, sacred room inside for only you, or do you share it all with those closest to you?

C. My sacred space is full of *God*—everything and everyone. The ones closest to me get as much as I can give. I struggle with verbal self-expression. I was painfully shy as a child, and couldn't even speak on the phone, or make friends. I made a conscious choice to shut down even further at age 14, after a traumatic pregnancy experience. Asking people in high school if they thought I was weird. That's just weird! I've worked on opening up, becoming friends with my weird perspective, and now enjoy sharing the intimate truths of my soul.

M. How did you get to this place of being able to share yourself?

C. Practice. My journey includes inner searching, connecting with hundreds of people, and listening to their intimate reflections. I made a choice to be free, and transparent connections are at the center of freedom.

M. Any last words, for this interview, on Polyamory?

C. This isn't the path for those who want to avoid challenges or change. The relationship with myself is where I start. Addressing the frustration with myself teaches me patience with others. Learning through relationships keeps me from becoming stagnant, no matter if I'm with six partners or only one. Attempting to love everyone is radical. I've opened my heart so much that I felt God and the devil fucking inside it. Closing down is a mudslide; when I feel myself slipping I remember that locking up is as much of a choice as opening. Bliss becomes more profound with every choice to feel all of it. If I'm going to love many, I want to feel each one in their troubles and ecstasy. I want to live and love big.

Maja still has six weeks left of her California summer vacation. Yesterday she and I returned home from a road trip through the Southwest. We attended my family reunion in Utah then drove down the Vegas strip via the Grand Canyon. She had only seen these places on television. Back in San Diego, sitting at the kitchen table on this mid-July night, Jean joins us for a cup of chamomile before bed. "You seem distracted this evening Cheri," Jean says as she pours tea in her cup. Jacy and Felina are in bed already.

"I thought it was just the post adventure letdown, but I am feeling preoccupied," I say.

"Tell us about it," Maja says.

"Are you both available to listen to my venting?" I ask.

"Yes, thank you for asking," Jean replies.

"I've never witnessed anyone asking permission to rant before. I'm all ears," Maja says.

"Perhaps it's the heat," I begin, "I'm hearing from many lovers, confessing how they're suffering from feelings of attachment."

"I know that one," Maja says with a nervous laugh.

"One of the blessings of having so many lovers is the support from all sides when I need it, but the downside is when many are in a bad place at the same time, my heart feels heavy," I say.

"It might help to share some of the burden with us," Jean says.

"Thanks for listening mindfully. This is so you can understand my pool of emotions, and not to gossip. I'll tell you only what I'd share if they were sitting around the table with us," I say.

"I understand. I feel safer just knowing you're so responsible with your friendships," Maja says.

Jean nods, and I dive in. "There's an email from Fritz, with his five children, feeling an empty nest as his youngest is starting college in the fall. I got a text from Harper, who's a secret lover of another. He wants to practice transparency in all his relationships, yet this lover has him feeling second-rate because she hasn't told her friends about him. He can't just give her the boot. The hardest is, one of Drake's lovers was recently diagnosed with end stage cancer, and he wants to make the most of their time left together. I want to spend a minute on this one because death's profound and the heaviest," I say, taking a sip of the calming herb.

"What an intense karmic connection to help another pass from this existence, as we know it," Jean says.

"Hard to imagine how he can stay present with her," Maja says.

"That's an insightful question for any relationship. Having no expectation of what the relationship might look like in the future, and letting go of any shit from the past, in order to be truly present. Jean, I appreciate you initiating this to help me be more present," I say.

"Sure. How's Autumn doing with her new lover?" Jean asks, as she looks down at her near empty cup.

"Who wants more?" Maja asks, as she tips the teapot into her cup.

"Autumn's excited but worried about how long it'll last. She wants to keep it fresh for as long as possible. Can we just be here now! The one that took the cake was a phone call from Katie. She was so upset because her new obsession hadn't called in two days, that her mind was playing tricks on her emotions. The kicker is that she has a date scheduled with him tomorrow! She and I got a good belly laugh over that," I say, laughing. "Thanks, I feel lighter already."

"Kinda like a mother hen, who realizes she doesn't need to smother her babies, just love all of them," Jean says.

"Ya, it sure feels better when I let go of my own

attachments, and allow my lovers to go through their struggles their way while I love them," I say.

Ancient cell memory and conditioning from the past, add to the suffering we create. Happily-ever-after is a fucked delusion, and deep down we want to be free. Our bodies seem to have a mind of their own, and can run away with the emotions without warning. Pop songs and stories of what romance should be, add to the suffering, where we choose to wallow. You can cry yourself to sleep, somehow getting a strange pleasure from feeling sorrow. This addictive melancholy gets so much attention one can easily get stuck. I choose to allow, acknowledge, and include all emotions, without attaching to any one emotion, rather than reinforce suffering in my life and those around me. I'm not saying that crying's bad—It's a great shortcut to moving and releasing energy, but so is laughter.

A few weeks after Maja returned home, I received a long letter asking me about her personal monogamous relationship dilemma of possibly exploring polyamory. I never know what to say when someone asks me my opinion on their life.

I wrote back: Stay present, keep your heart open, listen to each other, be gentle and kind, and your answers will reveal themselves as you go.

I like hearing what's real. We live in a world shaped by a monogamous (loving one person at a time) construct. When I don't have a primary partner all I want to do is look for one, but when I have one all I want is my freedom. Therein lies the rub— if I'm looking outside myself for happiness it becomes elusive. I look internally at the relationship dance inside, between my masculine and feminine aspects, and honor my wholeness. Then it's essential to have relations with others—the deeper I go with a beloved, the deeper the reflection of my soul. It's good to resolve relationship conflicts before considering adding more people to your family, or inner circle. Unresolved issues resurface again, until fully seen.

My disillusionment with the monogamous paradigm is

the string of broken hearts left behind when relationships fall out of right relation and aren't transitioned with respect and kindness. I think of my relationships like my Audi—regular maintenance is a given, but I also drive with care and go the extra mile to keep her clean, polished, garaged and filled with premium gas. Relationships work best when maintained and cared for. Even when transitioning out of lovership or untangling a marriage.

The land where I have my home is my responsibility. If I don't personally do the gardening I must pay the maintenance fees, otherwise the fire department may give me a ticket for the tall weeds, not to mention the benefits of getting my hands in the dirt, and being surrounded by beautiful plants. The people closest to me are my responsibility and they will also nurture me. I look at the hundreds of relationships in my life, and I'm filled with gratitude for each of them. That's a big statement, and I don't say it recklessly. It doesn't matter if I lived with a Beloved for five years, or eye gazed with another for five seconds, I value the connection and the exchange of energy. Each unique one reflects back a piece of the big picture. It's not necessary to have hundreds of relationships to understand myself, but being myself is key to inner happiness. Getting to know my desires, my strengths, choosing confidence and transparency are all things that help me express my true self.

Variety is the spice of life, and flirting is the spark. Flirt with life, allow the inner masculine and feminine to flirt, flirt with a lover, flirt with other responsible adults, let the inner spark out, and flirt with open eyes because the adventure has ignited.

EXPLORATION #27

What are your thoughts on jealousy?

_____

_____

_____

I experience jealousy as an overwhelming bundle of reactions that must be chunked out and honestly identified in order to resolve each thought and ease the physical pain. I notice that all the emotions are present, including the positive ones, and then what I want is clear and what I'm not getting becomes a choice.

What is your homework on the topic of jealousy?

_____

_____

_____

Examples:

Remember a time you felt jealous. Make a list of all the separate emotions present in that moment—negative and positive.

Find a partner, and alternate saying individual emotions that you are feeling right now. Partner one says "sad," both breathe, then partner two says "silly," both breathe, repeat with different emotions.

Place a treat of your choice in front of you. List what you want. How many things do you have right now? How realistic is your list? What would it take to get everything you want? Are you willing to experience half of the treat now, and the other half after you accomplish something else you want from your list?

Practice relaxing your thoughts and not reacting to a thought that triggers jealousy. Make a different choice. Go toward the perceived cause of your reactions, and ask to join them. Imagine they say yes with open arms!

Chapter 28

Oneness

"Home is where the heart is." — Pliny the Elder

Sometime after my 40th birthday, I lost the ability to guess someone's age accurately. It used to be one of my prized party tricks. It didn't matter if they were close to my grandfather's age, or much younger than me; once I was able to glance at a woman's breasts and announce, "She's 25 years old!" I no longer look at age in the same way. I stopped viewing men as potential fathers for my unborn children. I no longer felt like I was wading into a mating pool when I went to social events.

Friends don't pay attention to the age of my girlfriends. Meagan is 20 years older than me, Shawna and Ruth are 10 years my senior, while Autumn, Katie, and Mary are much younger. There's more taboo associated with the men in my life. Franco is 16 years older, but he is so very youthful that we're often mistaken for siblings. When asked, he says yes, before planting a passionate kiss on my lips! Kris, Henry, and Skyler are a dozen years older, but I haven't been teased about dating my Daddy. Timmy is nearly 20 years younger, and the term cougar has become all the buzz. I'm told it means an older woman who seeks sexual relationships with a much younger man. Strange, my first twenty-something boyfriend was when I was 14, and I've dated guys in their twenties every since. When did I get so old? How am I the older woman all of a sudden?

The day comes when Timmy surprises me by driving me home to meet his parents. His mother's making spicy chili for a cook-off, and is thrilled to have fresh tasters in her kitchen. She and I flirt a bit, and laugh at the idea of fitting into normal. His dad's sitting at the kitchen table reading about a car show and housing prices. He doesn't seem to mind that I'm nearly his age and dating their son. What's age anyway? This is when I decide to one-up my mocking friends.

The next day I proudly declare myself a Jaguar, a term I coined, clarifying that I'm older than my boyfriend's mother. No longer a Cougar, I'm now officially a Jaguar.

When did I cross that invisible line? Or had I? At age 30, dating another 30 year old it hit me that it's all about connection. When there's attraction between people, whether group synergy, or between two people, the desire to explore that connection is a driving force. Connection doesn't always lead to sharing sexually. Feeling connected to everything meets the basic need— being part of something. When I'm aware of an intimate moment it doesn't matter if I'm holding a crying infant, or gazing into the clouded eyes of a senile senior; elation is present for me.

I smile with my eyes, and volumes can be exchanged with just a glance. I used to avert my eyes due to the perplexity around permission to relate with only a select few. In my twenties, a *spiritual* man actually told me that I shouldn't look into men's eyes. He was, however, unable to adequately explain why. If I'd better understood the concept of responsibility, and applied that wisdom to his words, I may have realized that he meant to say, *he doesn't know what to do with the feelings he gets when he looks into my eyes.* Letting go of how relating is *supposed* to look is a blessing, freeing the possibility to see desire, and the ways I overlap with the people. No matter what our differences, it's a survival instinct to connect with the same species. When I feel free, I can joyfully share my smile with anyone who's available without the fear of unhealthy attachment.

Attachment is a primal survival response to fearful thoughts of insecurity, undeserving, self-loathing, scarcity, not enough love, etc. The belief that I need a primary partner leads inevitably to the thought that my needs aren't being met. The initial attachment to a mother's breast is a pleasurable reward, and it's a fact that without touch and nourishment an infant would die. However, this instinct isn't as essential after an infant grows teeth to chew its own food, learns to walk away from danger, and develops a bit of street smarts. Sometimes adults revert back to that desire to attach when threatened or feeling weak.

It's still fundamental to feel connected and exchange energy with other living things. Alignment with the same species is advantageous for learning and evolving the human psyche. It's also helpful to connect with nature. When I mature, and my infant needs are met, this urge transforms into a responsible desire to connect and interact, using sex for soothing as I reset my sympathetic nervous system from past stressors.

The lovers in my personal circle ebb and flow with my life based on their personal rhythms, but this doesn't take away from me. It can feel like being robbed if I'm married to the idea of a relationship staying consistent, or if I want another to continue to stay close beyond their desire. Who I am can't be added to, or taken from by anyone or anything outside of myself. It's too easy to desire a certain type of connection, only to experience that relationship as stagnant. If you and I have similar life intentions then we can start each day fresh, and make a conscious choice to be together. Getting that connection is not a destination; but being a constantly evolving lover of life is a commodity for like-minded lovers.

I want the people in my life to have connections with many people too. I don't get feelings of specialness from anything outside of myself, just like I don't look for love outside of me because love already exists inside. I am love; I'm already special. I bring my special unique love to the party, sharing it with all the lovers in my life. Whole fulfilled beings don't need much, and can choose to share abundantly with other whole beings.

I recognize I'm growing up, and breaking old patterns of infantile fear. Learning to see beyond the caveman era, when primal instincts were only used for surviving. We've evolved beyond where a man owns a woman, and fights for her because he may not get another. The objective to populate the earth, breeding for the survival of the human species, has been surpassed. The new frontier is the human relationship evolution. How can our species become more feeling, awakened, and intelligent?

Part of the collective human psyche is still afraid, while another part thrives; yet, we continue to push past the edges of survival into unchartered territory. When I venture into an unknown realm, there's a level of discomfort accompanied by the thought that I need support, which may seem like a need for attachment.

I acknowledge the steps taken by those who came before me. Their work helps me see my patterns, so I can choose new behaviors to adapt and thrive in this modern world. The challenge is admitting to myself where I'm blindly following what feels safe, and seeing where I need to evolve so I can contribute positively to the next phase of human development. I'm patient with myself, and have compassion for my past choices, and for others. Compassion may be all there is, a channeled guru said years ago. I don't remember anything else I heard at that ashram, but this seems to be an important contemplation.

When I let go of the suffering around attachment, it becomes connection. As I step into self-responsibility, no longer waiting for a savior, I step into a new view of relating with others. I see how having a community, who are also looking at the world through fresh eyes, is a supportive luxury giving me a purpose for looking deeper into how we relate together. As I connect with a wider variety of humans, I see how I no longer need to control, attach to, fight over, or manipulate the ones I want to be close with. Allowing those around me to have free choice affords me space to develop my talents and contribute to my community. I seek to be in right relation with all of the people in my life. Remembering if someone I desire, chooses to be closer to another person, it doesn't have to create suffering in my life. I can be at peace, knowing that I'm always exactly where I need to be.

There are times when I withdraw in order to contemplate deeply, and other times I dive into the deep end of a group of intimate lovers. When looking for a dating pool, sometimes I feel that I can't find my kind—thinking I don't fit in with the people around me. This disconnect is a choice, but when I'm caught-up in suffering, I don't see that I'm choosing it.

Disconnecting from a group can give me distance in order to see discrepancies, and avoid following the mob mentality. Each individual in any group contributes to the energetic makeup of that particular gathering. I feel the emotions and fears of those closest to me, and it's important to remain clear so that I can differentiate between their thoughts and emotions and mine.

One day, at a get-together with close friends, I experience a feeling of scarcity. My observation is that everyone in the room is pairing up into primary partners. To compound my angst, three of the newly coupled are my preexisting intimate lovers. Another new flirt appears to be heading toward deepening his connection with Mary. It's tempting to let old victim thoughts take over—like something is being taken away from me, or losing a competition because someone other than me is chosen. Then a deeper, more current pain surfaces.

I think of the societal taboo of dating more than one person, and how I've hidden love connections from social scrutiny in the past, being discreet to avoid causing a lover the embarrassment of polyamorous dating. Feelings of unworthiness surface—like not good enough to be seen as an equal visible partner. Seeing all the paired couples reminds me of the norm that was taught to me as the only option when I was young. I'm trying to move beyond that belief because there are other valid relationship options. As other members begin to talk into the circle, I realize I'm not the only one feeling this exclusivity energy. One single person gets up to go to the bathroom, while another is sitting a few inches back from the rest in the circle appearing disconnected. I really want to leave, even though another part of me wants to keep trying to connect.

Identifying these limiting thoughts helps me unwind. I reflect for a moment on the bigger reality that I have plenty of people in my life available for connecting, willing to hold my hand in public, or 3-way kiss. I remind myself of the brave ones who take me home to their parents, and introduce me to friends at their company picnic. I tell myself to stop wanting a certain level of connection from this group of paired people, in this moment. I smile at the thought that next time we meet, I can introduce new lovers to the group and mix up the odds. I remind myself that every day each of us makes new choices, and that next time I participate in an event there'll be a different combination of people, making a whole new group dynamic.

One by one people step into the center to share what is up for them right now. I choose not to discuss these thoughts out loud with the group, because spoken thoughts become more powerful. I don't want others to view me as judgmental, and think this is who I am, or rather, *all* that I am. I stay seated because I choose to speak what I want to manifest in my life, and right now my thinking is shitty.

Sharing my internal discussions can be helpful when brainstorming ideas, or with the intention of sharing intimacy so another doesn't think they're the only one with those thoughts. Speaking negative thoughts, with the intention of letting them go, is helpful *only* when the ones listening can fully release all the thoughts and interpretations with me. It takes emotional maturity to listen to another's internal banter and completely let it go. If I speak in the circle, and they think all the torment I spew out of my head is what I want to be, then I've created a bigger mess to untangle.

Even my complaining bitchy perspective wants to be loved and allowed. I'm not able to rally my trusting perspective and speak it out loud. Am I capable of completely allowing and hearing every part of the human psyche, even the perspectives judged inside my head right now? Maybe, because I've been so loved by those outside of me, I've learned to hear and allow a wide range of thoughts. I just want to give voice to the thoughts that'll make the next moment more pleasurable. If I'm feeling all of it, isn't that enough? Does *everyone* need to feel *everything*, in everyone? That's the key to transparency in a relationship, but do I want to be that open to misinterpretation in a group? Does accepting myself create an environment for others to accept their own multidimensional, beautiful, twisted psyches, too?

I want to allow all of me, and get back to a place of accepting others in the room. Suddenly, it's clear—each person in the room has agreed to the level of attachment they want to participate in with another. It seems so elementary, but I was stuck in judgment. My friends are choosing to connect with one person more than another, and I am choosing to connect with many. We can change our minds as often as we want, and I may choose differently tomorrow.

To stay current, and compatible with another, I constantly renegotiate the chosen agreements. At any given time each of us is agreeing to own, control or manipulate another, and we're willingly choosing the level of ownership, control, and manipulation we accept from another. This can apply whether in a marriage, friendship, or dating. Negotiation simply looks different in every relationship dynamic. I remind myself that I want partners who are open to negotiate agreements, and are willing to have healthy attachments.

With my needy thoughts dispelled, the suffering no longer creates fear or judgment, and even the group appears less needy. I feel my body relax around my delusion of disconnect from those around me. Like a warm flood of joy, I let the abundance that's all around me enter my thoughts and penetrate my soul.

There's space for more love in this world, and in this room. I don't need to be afraid. Connection is a fundamental component of the human experience, and therefore an important choice.

Now I feel my vulnerability with this group, and it's easier to assess why I was engulfed in judgment and hesitation. I realize there's a specific person in the group that has betrayed my trust. Rather than drag the entire group through the mud I will make a date with her to clear, so I can move though my stuck judgments. Feeling present, I walk in the circle and say, "I'm different than the majority of polyamorous people here. I know I live alone right now, but I don't align with the term solo polyamory. I've experienced many different living situations, including living with just one other person in an open relationship, and living in a house full of lovers. Sometimes I forget my desire to accept you in your journeys, and I feel excluded. I try building a *protective* wall of judgment, but that's not what I want. I catch my cynical mind running away with thoughts of lack, as if there's not enough love." I look around the circle, and notice the concentrated attention. "I feel acceptance radiating from many of you in this circle. I allow myself to let the light shine on my shadowy judgments peering through the fog. As soon as I see that I'm caught in negativity, it's easier to remember that I want to love deeply. There's room for more love everywhere I go. Thanks for reminding me to align with humanity's emanating brilliance," I say, and sit down with a glowing smile.

I may not choose to date in what I call the old paradigm, or in the same way dating's typically viewed. I tend to mix it up by dating groups, couples, or an individual. When on a date, I let the new encounter know it's an experiment. I show up as a whole person, learning new ways to communicate, connect, flirt, and practice non-attachment. I want to discover how I can contribute to those who are making a difference in the world, without detracting from my purpose. I celebrate the connections where our intentions align, and working together is mutually beneficial. We find where we harmonize and continue negotiating to keep our unique connection dynamic. I'm not looking for my other half, but it's vital for me to find other whole beings with which to create and explore this amazing world.

As far as modern cyber dating goes, I'm still in a learning curve, figuring out how to interpret short, choppy, emoticon inserted, Freudian auto-spell miss-corrected slips, and oh-I-pushed-send-too-soon embarrassments. I find it challenging to know which perspective is typing when I receive a message. There's no way to hear the tone, and I can't see their facial expressions or postural clues. The intellect can switch so quickly between perspectives, making it hard to follow without using the senses to observe the changes. I do my best not to react to written communication, or take things personal. If triggered by a written text, Facebook post, tweet, messenger, hangout, chat, email, etc., I re-read. I practice seeing how many different interpretations I can come up with, until I remember it's not about me. I attempt a response to clarify their need or request. Often I simply pick up the phone, speaking directly so we can attempt to stay on the same wavelength while we chat. At least our voices and ears can connect.

Even as one who loves to write, I suck at cyber dating. Void of physical context, it's forcing me to verbally communicate clearer, or shall I say, choose my written words more accurately in order to be clear with my communication. So, here it is for those of you who're like me, and scan the last pages before deciding to read a book, LOL. I prefer personal, face-to-face, body-to-body, eye-to-eye, and yes, sex-to-sex communication. :~) Recognizing the significance of human connection, I ask:

What if you and I sit before one another each day?

What if we dream together every night?

What if we play chess, or music brilliantly together?

What if we hold each other as the sacred beloved in our hearts?

What if our perceived differences—in the dented pickups or rain-spotted convertibles—don't matter?

What if each threesome is worthy of being called a first?

What if we connect purely, whether we're 50 or 21, whether it's new love, or old?

Can I be aware of my energy, whether I radiate blissful love, or use it as a cloche?

Can I give and receive unconditionally?

Can I stay present, honest and real?

Can I feel like I'm in the right place, on the right path, and with the right people?

Can I remember to choose the highest perspective?

Can I stay in right relation?

Can I take responsibility for my overwhelming emotions, jealousy, and triggers?

Can I make clear requests, and respect another person's no?

If I cry tears of sorrow and joy, will I stay present, and allow all that I am?

When anger, hatred, old wounds, or unknown fears are present, can I stay completely present in love for a moment, or a lifetime?

You and I are one, forever, whether we connect for a moment with a glance, or with every separate cell wanting to blend together and create next generations. That urge to pass who I've become on to future generations was the inception of the smile on my face. From the moment I first experienced the power of sex and the ability to co-create life, I was hooked. I cried three times today because I'm close to giving birth, and that's frightening. I didn't create a baby from my flesh, but I have humbled myself to the point where I can allow others to see my inner workings. Just like a new mom, I hope to inspire greatness in someone with the ambition to save the world. Mastering responsible sexual freedom in the relationship evolution is just the beginning.

We land in Maui, sample the sweetest pineapple ever tasted, and make our way along the coast to a secluded nude beach. It's hidden from the main beach, but paradise is found as we climb over a huge fallen tree. The pristine, untrodden white sand invites us in. Kicking off a week of indulging our senses, transcendent coconut oil massage parties, and diving into the surrender of group sex with lovers and their enchantingly strange-to-me lovers. The penetrating sun is intoxicating. Lying on our bed of sand next to me is my gorgeous friend Gwynn, with her silky golden hair glistening. Next to Gwynn is the bronzed skin, hazel-eyed Santiago, her husband, laughing at our jokes. Raising my arms toward the sun, I call out, "Take me to your master!"

Bliss radiates from my being; there's no place I'd rather be in this moment. Held by Mama Earth, my naked body's fully seen and entered by Father Sky. My arms rest back down on the soft, warm sand, and that now-familiar feeling settles—I am home.

EXPLORATION #28

What are your thoughts on Polyamory?

_____

_____

_____

I experience Polyamory as the desire and ability to ultimately love everyone. When it comes to sexual partners, there is transparent honesty and communication with everyone involved. There is a kindness of heart that does not shame people for their differences and allows the shame that is held inside most people to be expressed and released.

What is your homework on the topic of Polyamory?

_____

_____

_____

Examples:

Count how many people you love. Call three of those people and tell them how you feel.

Sit before a loved one and tell them about a time you were not as honest as you could have been.

Ask a lover how they experience shame. Then ask how you can make it safe for them to explore that shame in order to accept it and let the charge around it go. Perhaps touching their belly and telling them that they are strong and healthy.

Make a list of all the people you are attracted to. Invite three of them to discuss what Polyamory means to them.

Glossary:

Amrita — Sanskrit word for immortality, and is referred to as nectar. In modern Tantra Amrita is female ejaculate fluid excreted from the Skene's glands in the vagina.

BDSM — Bondage/Discipline Sadism/Masochism — The play between dominance and submission.

Burning Man — A yearly festival at a temporary city in Nevada since 1990 with over 60,000 participants.

Bandwidth — Mental capacity that decreases with stress levels.

Chakras — An energy center or gateway in the body. There are seven along the spine that correlate with the major glands in the body, as well as in the palms of the hands and base of the feet.

Compersion — An empathetic state of happiness and joy experienced when another individual experiences happiness and joy.

Downward spiral — A situation that continues to decrease or worsen.

Eco-sexual — Nature lover, sun worshiper, tree hugger, stargazer, and skinny dipper are all examples.

Energetic orgasm — When the peak of sexual excitement is felt throughout the body like an electric current, with or without discharge.

Expansion — Evolutionary process of growth and opening the mind, body and soul.

Kama Sutra — An ancient Indian Sanskrit text on sexuality, eroticism, emotional fulfillment, and a manual of sexual positions.

Kriya — A spontaneous body movement related to awakened sexual energy flow.

Lingam — A phallic symbol of divine generative energy.

Merlin — A legendary druid, wizard of magic, and father of King Author with shapeshifting abilities.

Polyamory — Engaging in multiple sexual, emotional and energetic relationships with the consent of everyone involved.

Puja — The Sanskrit word for worship.

Shadow work — Revealing the unconscious aspect, or dark side, of the personality. Based on the work of Carl Jung.

Shakti — A Sanskrit word for divine energy, personified as a female deity.

Shiva — One of the Hindu trinity, the destroyer deity, and father of Ganesh.

Subspace — A term used in the kinky BDSM community to describe the state a submissive can enter as a result of being dominated.

Tantra — A pre 7th century magical text of Hindu or Buddhist mantras, meditation, yoga, and ritual.

Tantrika — Sanskrit word meaning: Relating to Tantra. Often used to describe one who practices the temple arts of Tantra.

The playa — The alkali clay earth in the dry desert lakebed basin of northern Nevada where the Burning Man festival occurs.

Yab-Yum — A seated partner yoga or Kama Sutra position, symbolizing sacred union, where one person (usually a man) sits cross-legged and the other one (usually a woman) sits on top facing him with legs wrapped around his back.

Yoni — The Sanskrit word for the female divine procreative energy, counterpart to the male lingam.

For more information on health coaching, comprehensive lab testing, and integrative medicine, please reference
www.NurseCheri.com
to request a free copy of my e-booklet "Top Ten Health Deal Breakers" describing the most critical areas to focus on for optimal health.

Look for

Smile Tarot

Tarot / Oracle Cards

Intuitive guidance cards inspired by *The Smile on My Face,* written by Cheri Reeder with illustrations by Cutter Hays.

To use as Oracle cards: If you want some insight on a situation, ask a question, then pick a card. Read the back of the card for inspiration about your answer.

To use as Tarot cards: Think of a question. Next pick one or more cards, according to the Tarot spread of choice. Study the illustrations on the front of the card as well as the quote on the back side of the card for insights.

Special note: There are 52 cards plus 4 Fools and 4 suits, so feel free to use this deck as playing cards.

SmileTarot.com

Time

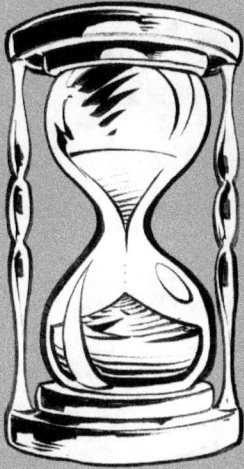

King of Cups

Emotion   Water

A relative concept
measured as the planet
orbits the sun, yet
uniquely experienced
by everyone. How is
time influencing your
actions today?

Reeder.press

www.ingramcontent.com/pod-product-compliance
Lightning Source LLC
Chambersburg PA
CBHW051947270326
41929CB00015B/2566